Creative Hands-On Science Cards & Activities

by
Jerry DeBruin

illustrated by Liz Fox

Cover by Jeff Van Kanegan

Copyright © Good Apple, Inc., 1990

ISBN No. 0-86653-538-1

Printing No. 98765

Good Apple, Inc.
1204 Buchanan St., Box 299
Carthage, IL 62321-0299

Special Thanks

*The author thanks Mrs. Ruth Flaskamp, fifth grade teacher at Stranahan Elementary School, Sylvania, Ohio, for permission to field-test this book with youngsters.

*The author thanks his university students who field-tested this book with youngsters. The author thanks the students for their suggestions, thoughtful ideas and comments.

*The author thanks Mrs. Tina Hughes, secretary, who typed the original version of this book before it was sent to the publisher.

*The author thanks Mr. Thomas Gibbs, B.S. Ed., M.Ed., J.D., retired teacher, counselor, naval officer and locomotive engineer for his kind contributions, suggestions and assistance in making this book the best book that it could be.

*The author thanks Mrs. Elaine Scott and Mr. Jim Corcoran for their contributions to this book.

*The author thanks the following fifth grade youngsters who field-tested the activities in this book. Their names and some of their comments about the book follow: Jeff Carr, Dimitria Gantzos, Dawnetta Hayes, Krista Hines, Jenny Jepson, Alicia Kuchinic, Ashley Lindsley, Ryan Mann, Melanie Many, Brian Markin, Mike Miller, Amy Papio, Kara Rodriguez, Steve Shenefield, Don Stormer, Scott Taylor, Courtney Tonoff, Amy Vrooman, Sara Waggoner, and Brian Wisniewski.

Youngsters' Comments:
> It (the book) was challenging and I like challenges. . .I like being able to do research. . .
> I liked having a book of my own. . .I enjoy these kinds of things and I'm good at them. . .
> I like being able to work together in a group and doing it with friends. . .It was fun, educational
> and taught me something. . .I thought it was fun because it helped you start to learn
> about how to agree with each other. . .If I could give the book a higher rating than 10,
> I would.

THANKS

for your comments

TO: Jerry DeBruin
P.O. Box 7143 RC
Toledo, Ohio 43615

FROM: _____
_____
_____

Comments:
_____
_____
_____
_____
_____

GA1150

Dedication

This book is dedicated to purchasers and subsequent users of nearly one-half million copies of my books. It is hoped that you and those you touch will continue to enjoy and learn from the experiences found in these books. This book is also dedicated to the over 10,000 teachers and parents who have attended my classes, workshops and in-service sessions. A special welcome is also extended to all newcomers who chose to participate in these growth experiences. To all of you, from all walks of life, this book is dedicated to you.

Focus Here

GA1150

Table of Contents

Introduction:
A Note to Teachers and Parents

Dear Friends,

Thank you for the many kind comments about my previous twenty books—Touching & Teaching Metrics Series; *Cardboard Carpentry; Creative, Hands-On Science Experiences;* the Young Scientists Explore Series, Intermediate; *Scientists Around the World; Look to the Sky* and *School Yard-Backyard Cycles of Science*—all published by Good Apple, Inc., from 1977 to 1989.

This book, *Creative Hands-On Science Cards & Activities,* is written as a result of your comments, and suggestions, comments that suggested a need for child-centered, hands-on science process cards and activities which could be duplicated for students' use.

Creative Hands-On Science Cards & Activities is written for people of all ages and for those in any occupation. Classroom teachers, administrators, youth leaders, camp guides and parents will find it useful. The book focuses on *science process* activity cards and the use of common, everyday materials, which can be obtained free or purchased rather inexpensively, or found around the home, school or in the community. Major emphasis is placed on starter cards and activities, designed to prompt children to ask "why" or "what would happen if" type questions about science events.

In an ever-changing society, there is a growing need for youngsters to become actively involved in problem-solving science using *science process* skills with application of the knowledge gained in school directly to the home setting. *Creative Hands-On Science Cards & Activities* meets this need with its unique contents.

Creative Hands-On Science Cards & Activities is grounded in and supports current research findings in science education. Convenient, ready-to-use teacher and student cards, materials and activities support these findings in at least eight ways. First, the cards and activities are "hands-on" and reinforce the notion that people learn science best by becoming involved in concrete experiences, rather than by mere rote memorization of abstract, trivial and unrelated facts. Second, concepts mastered when doing the cards and activities are appropriate for the developmental level of elementary, middle, and junior high school students. All youngsters, teachers and parents who choose to become involved will find the cards and activities challenging and useful. Third, the cards and activities help teachers, youngsters and parents reach the #1 goal of education which is to stimulate people to *think*, then take action. In addition, the cards and activities feature an extensive utilization of higher order thinking and *process* skills. Memorization of irrelevant facts, at the knowledge level only, is kept to a minimum. Fourth, cards and activities help teachers and parents involve youngsters in experiences that will enable youngsters to master concepts well beyond those found in the standard curriculum in commercially available textbook series. Fifth, the cards and activities feature the integration of science with other academic disciplines. By participating in the cards and activities, youngsters, teachers, and parents experience an interdisciplinary, integrated view of science with an emphasis on learning holistic science. Sixth, the cards and activities enable youngsters to apply knowledge gained in school directly to their home settings. Seventh, *Creative Hands-On Science Cards & Activities* is child-centered. To accomplish this goal, the cards and activities feature individual and small group work. Lastly, *Creative Hands-On Science Cards & Activities* provides necessary background information in the form of teacher tips and specific content information on the teacher guide pages. Thus, it is hoped that teachers, youngsters, and parents will benefit by the renewed emphasis on content and methodology found throughout the book.

My hope is that the contents of *Creative Hands-On Science Cards & Activities* will touch many minds, hearts and hands and that much personal growth will be experienced by all who use the book. Keep in touch. Let me know how you are doing. It is always good to hear from you. Until then, best wishes for your continued growth as a scientist and as a complete human being.

Sincerely,

Jerry DeBruin

Jerry DeBruin

GA1150

Overview: How to Use This Book

The pages in *Creative Hands-On Science Cards & Activities* are designed to be copied for student use. Any copy machine will do. Press "light" if a duplicating machine is used. The major focus of the book is on interdisciplinary *science process* cards and activity sheets as illustrated on page viii. Copy the cards. Have youngsters cut apart the cards, mount them on single-layered cardboard and store them in the appropriately labeled box made from the pattern on page ix. Youngsters can display individual cards by using the cardboard display stand pattern (page x), store them in small plastic or shoe boxes (page xi) or insert them in plastic pocket sheets (page xii), the latter purchased from dealers of sports cards.

Creative Hands-On Science Cards & Activities features forty-four Learning Activity Packets (LAPS) with accompanying Student Activity Pages (SAPS). Each of nineteen major sections, introduced by an individual seated at a display screen, features a major *science process* skill. These can be color-coded and used as dividers to highlight each science process skill found in the book. Contained in each LAP is a teacher guide page that identifies the science process skill, describes the purpose of the activity and outlines teaching tips, answers and extending sources. In addition to the teacher guide page, cards and activity pages are included in each LAP. Wild cards are interspersed throughout the text. Cards lend themselves well to the playing of such games as Euchre, Clue, Treasure Hunt, Old Maid, Memory, Concentration and various trivia games.

It is recommended that the cards and activities be used over an entire year with special LAPS being introduced on special occasions such as LAP 18, Black Scientists and Inventors, being used in February, Black History Month. At least one LAP can be done per week per school year with emphasis placed on individual and small group work. Extend the study into the summer by presenting each youngster with a Student Diploma for Summer Science (LAP 44) along with a completed copy of the Student Report Card found on pages 321 and 322. Enjoy your LAPS and SAPS.

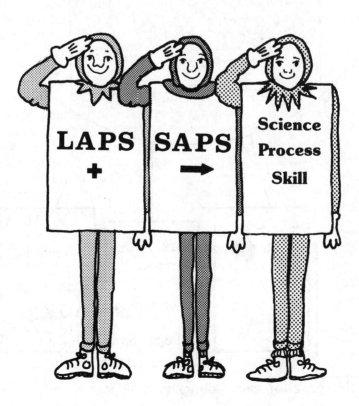

LAPS + SAPS → Science Process Skill

The Processes of Science

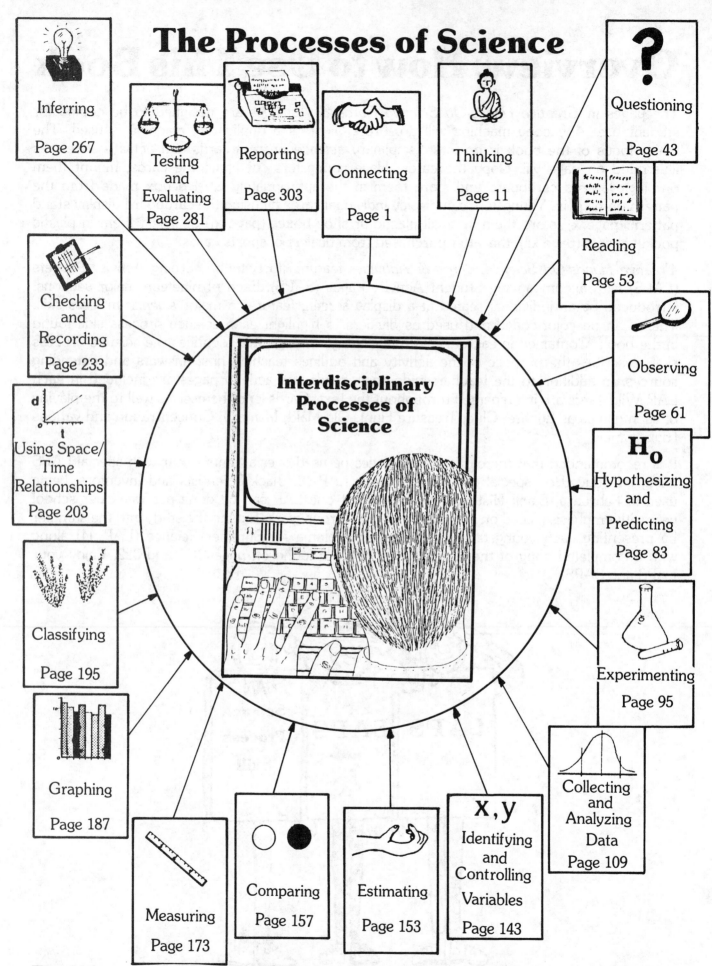

Inferring
Page 267

Testing and Evaluating
Page 281

Reporting
Page 303

Connecting
Page 1

Thinking
Page 11

Questioning
Page 43

Reading
Page 53

Checking and Recording
Page 233

Observing
Page 61

Using Space/Time Relationships
Page 203

H_o
Hypothesizing and Predicting
Page 83

Classifying
Page 195

Experimenting
Page 95

Graphing
Page 187

Collecting and Analyzing Data
Page 109

Measuring
Page 173

Comparing
Page 157

Estimating
Page 153

x, y
Identifying and Controlling Variables
Page 143

Interdisciplinary Processes of Science

Tip: Make a copy of this page for each youngster and post a copy in the classroom for all to see.

GA1150

Cardholders of Science:
The Cardboard Box Pattern

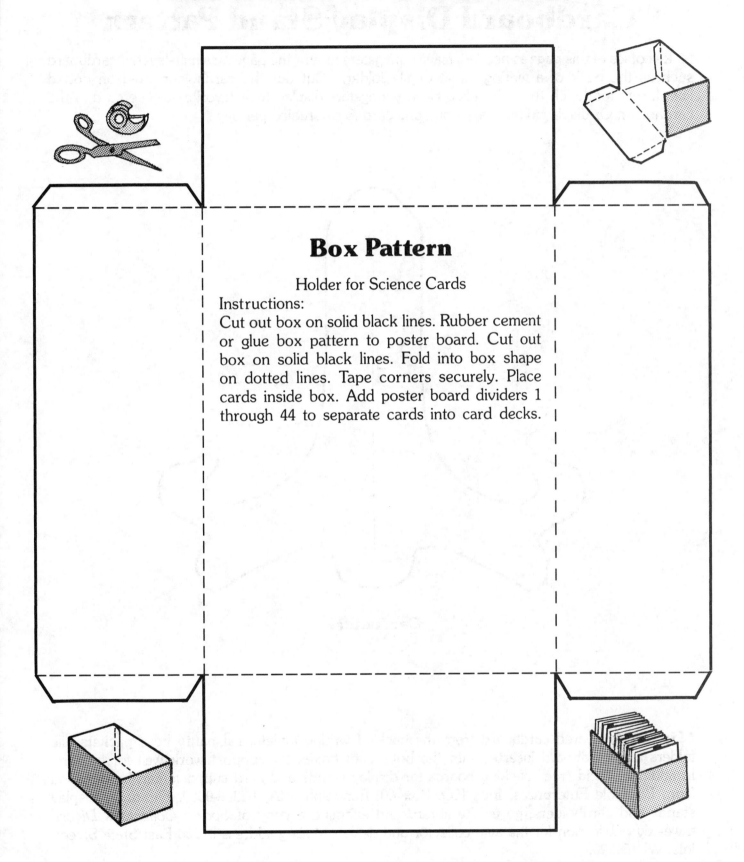

Box Pattern

Holder for Science Cards

Instructions:

Cut out box on solid black lines. Rubber cement or glue box pattern to poster board. Cut out box on solid black lines. Fold into box shape on dotted lines. Tape corners securely. Place cards inside box. Add poster board dividers 1 through 44 to separate cards into card decks.

GA1150

Cardholders of Science:
Cardboard Display Stand Pattern

Make copies of this page as needed. Have youngsters mount the page on single-layered cardboard such as the back of a writing tablet or file folder.* Cut out the cardholder. Fold on dotted line. Insert toothpick through holes. Have youngsters display their favorite science card in the cardholder. Or display in the classroom, one card to be studied per day.

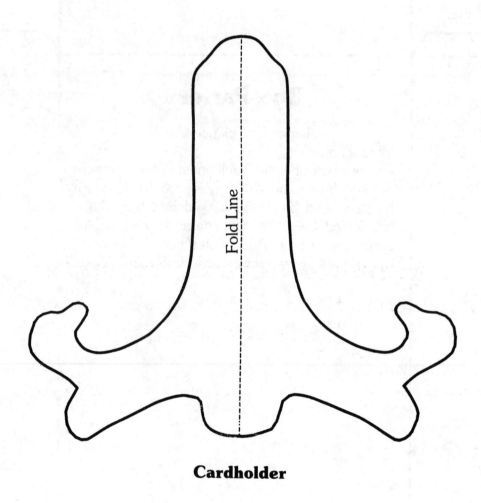

Fold Line

Cardholder

*Tip: Single-layered cardboard from the back of writing tablets, flat panty hose packets, file folders and cardboard inserted into the bottom of boxes for support work well for holders. In addition, "acid free" backing boards for display stands and card supports can be obtained from Bill Cole Enterprises, Inc., P.O. Box 60, Randolph, MA 02368-0060. For other display stands and cardholders, go to the library and examine a copy of *Sports Collector's Digest*, a weekly publication for the avid collector and dealer. Mailing address is 700 East State Street, Iola, WI 54990.

Cardholders of Science: Plastic Boxes

In addition to the cardholder box made from the pattern on page ix, various plastic boxes can be used to store cards found in this book. One such box is shown below and is used to store sports cards such as baseball cards. Boxes such as these may be obtained from dealers of sports cards.

Some of these include:

1. Durta Enterprises
   Dept. D-68
   235 S. Lindberg
   Griffith, IN   46319

2. Rothman Plastics
   4 Brussels Street
   Worcester, MA   01610

3. Down Jennings
   Dept. C
   2120 Metro Circle
   Huntsville, AL   35801

4. Cardboard Gold
   3410 West MacArthur Blvd.
   Suite F
   Santa Ana, CA   92704

5. Sports Design Products
   23851 Ryan Road
   Warren, MI   48091

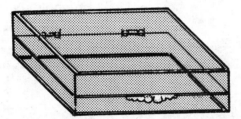

Cardholders of Science: Cardboard Shoe Boxes and "Acid Free" Storage Boxes

Youngsters' shoe boxes may also be used to store the cards found in this book. Shoe boxes may be obtained from your local shoe stores. Also, cardboard boxes used to store various sports cards such as baseball cards are excellent storage devices. These "acid free" storage boxes can be obtained from:

Bill Cole Enterprises, Inc.
P.O. Box 60
Randolph, MA   02368-0060

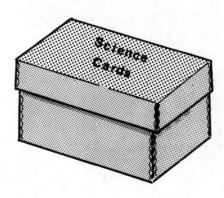

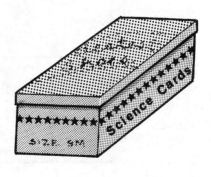

GA1150

Cardholders of Science: Plastic Sheets with Pockets

Plastic sheets called "card displays" feature individual pockets in which cards can be inserted. These are particularly useful for the display of cards such as those of "Famous Scientists" found on pages 125-134 along with "Cycles" on pages 159-165 and "Spring Seedlings" pages 168-171. This makes an attractive display of the youngsters' favorite cards which can later be stored in an album. Plastic thirty-card displays such as these may be obtained from dealers of sports cards. Some of these, in addition to those found on page xi, include:

1. Baseball Card World
   P.O. Box 970
   Anderson, IN   46015

2. New York Card Co.
   159 W. Sanford Blvd.
   Mt. Vernon, NY   10550

3. Ball Four Cards
   Box 19696
   West Allis, WI   53219

4. Hobby Supplies
   P.O. Box 596
   Freehold, NJ   07728

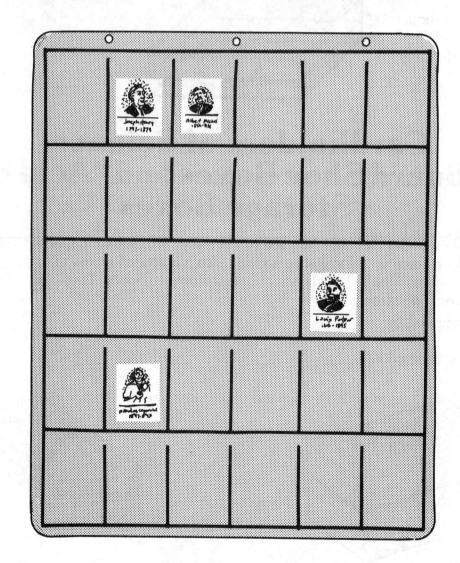

Science Process Skill 1: Connecting

Learning Activity Packet 1:
Send Greeting Cards to Scientists (p. 2)

Learning Activity Packet 2:
Postcard Science (p. 7)

1

GA1150

Teacher/Parent Page

Learning Activity Packet 1: Send Greeting Cards to Scientists

Science Process Skill 1: Connecting

Purpose: To establish communication links with famous scientists and to identify their contributions to science

Teaching Tips: This activity gives you and your youngsters an opportunity to write and extend greetings to four suggested scientists. It is possible to write to many others using the sample greeting cards. Make copies of the greeting cards, one per class or one per student. Fold in fourths on dotted lines. Print pertinent information about yourself and class in appropriate spaces. Insert into standard long envelope. Add proper postage. Using sample addresses below, print name and address on envelope. Be sure to include return address. A self-addressed stamped envelope (SASE) may also be included for a reply from the scientist; perhaps an autograph will be given. Design additional greeting cards to be sent to other scientists on special anniversaries. (See extending source below for pictures of the scientists and their discoveries.)

Special Tip: Be sure to include a self-addressed stamped envelope (SASE) for the return message.

Addresses for sample greeting cards and special occasions include the following:

1. Happy Birthday—January 2, 1920
Isaac Asimov
10 W. 66th Street, Apt. 33A
New York, NY   10023
(Author of over 350 books, biochemist)

2. Happy Anniversary—February 20, 1962
John H. Glenn
Senate Office Building
Washington, D.C.   20510
(First to orbit the earth; presently a U.S. senator)

3. Happy Birthday—May 26, 1951
Sally Ride
400 Maryland Avenue, S.W.
Washington, D.C.   20546
(First U.S. female astronaut in space)

4. Happy Birthday—June 4, 1936
Augustus A. White, III, M.D.
Harvard Medical School
330 Brookline
Boston, MA   02215
(Orthopedic surgeon)

Answers: Completed greeting cards. Hopefully an autograph and message will come in the return mail.

Extending Source: Jerry DeBruin, *Scientists Around the World* (Carthage, IL: Good Apple, Inc., 1987).

GA1150

Send Greeting Cards to Scientists

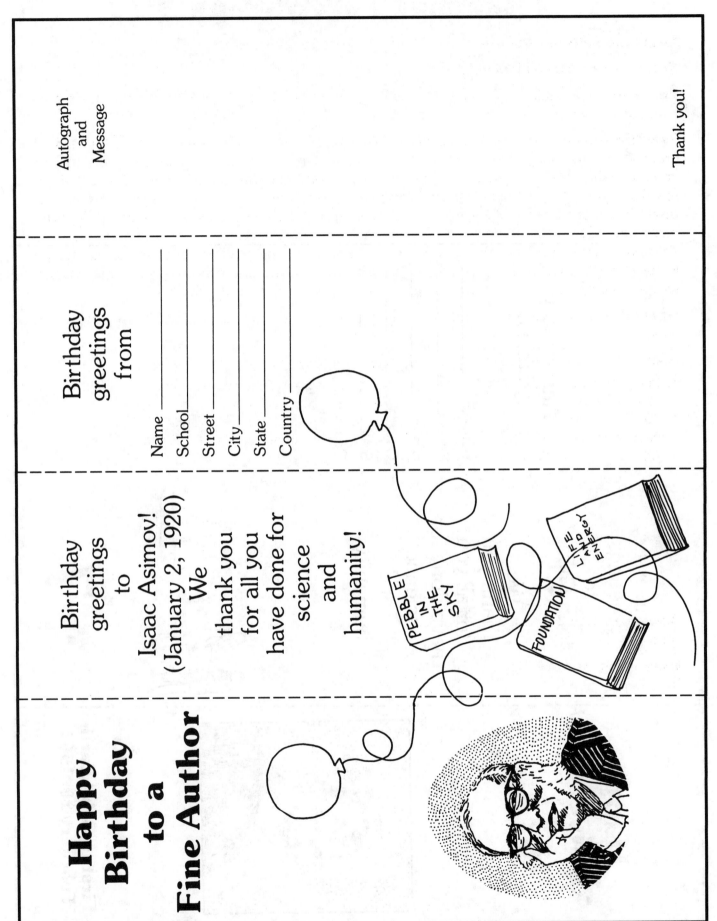

Autograph and Message

Thank you!

Birthday greetings from

Name

School

Street

City

State

Country

Birthday greetings to Isaac Asimov! (January 2, 1920) We thank you for all you have done for science and humanity!

PEBBLE IN THE SKY

FOUNDATION

LIFE AND ENERGY

Happy Birthday to a Fine Author

3

GA1150

Send Greeting Cards to Scientists

Autograph
and
Message

Thank you!

Anniversary
greetings
from

Name

School

Street

City

State

Country

Anniversary
greetings
to
John Glenn!

We
thank you
for all you
have done for
science
and
humanity!

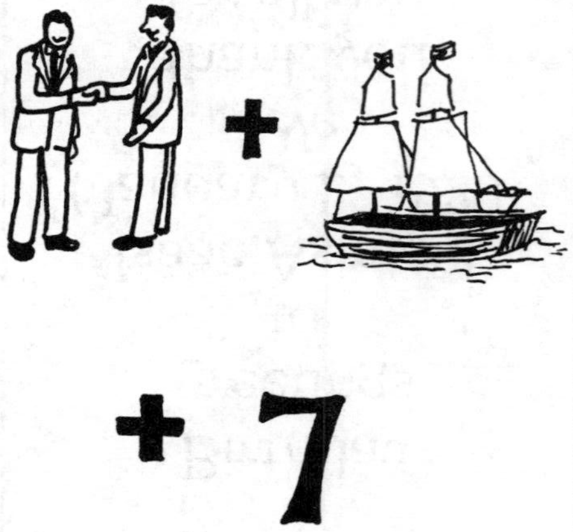

+

+7

Happy Anniversary

**First to Orbit Earth
February 20, 1962**

Send Greeting Cards to Scientists

Autograph
and
Message

Thank you!

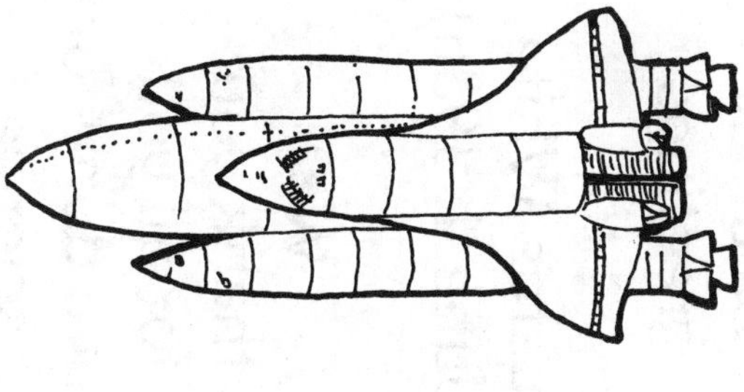

Birthday
greetings
from

Name
School
Street
City
State
Country

Birthday
greetings
to
Sally Ride!
(May 26, 1951)

We
thank you
for all you
have done for
science
and
humanity!

Happy Birthday

Send Greeting Cards to Scientists

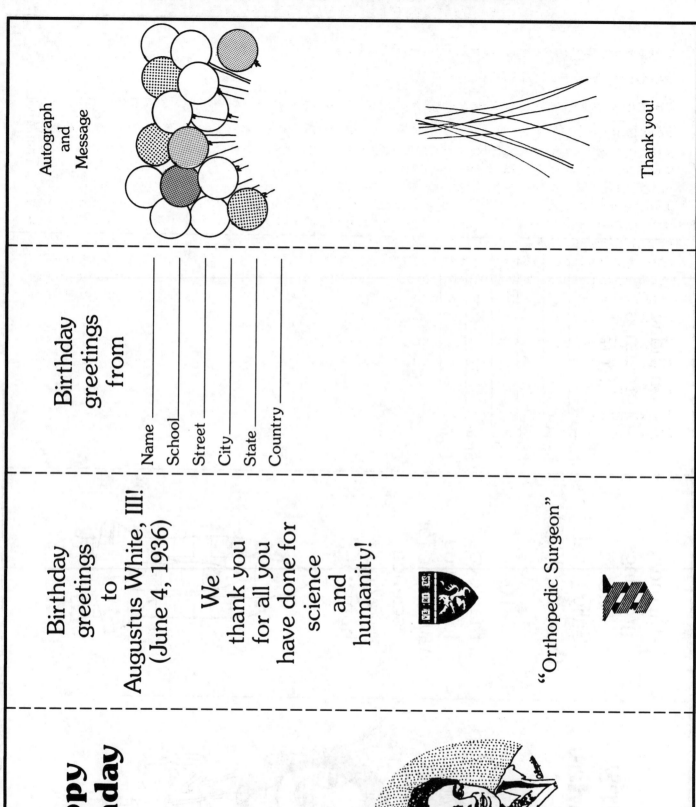

Autograph and Message

Thank you!

Birthday greetings from

Name
School
Street
City
State
Country

Birthday greetings to Augustus White, III! (June 4, 1936)

We thank you for all you have done for science and humanity!

"Orthopedic Surgeon"

Happy Birthday

6

Teacher/Parent Page

Learning Activity Packet 2: Postcard Science

Science Process Skill 1: Connecting

Purpose: To identify postcards as a means of communication between two or more individuals

Teaching Tips: This activity provides an opportunity for youngsters to write and extend greetings to their friends and/or scientists by the use of postcards. Make copies of the postcard pages for the youngsters. Have youngsters cut out the postcards and fold in half. Slide piece of light cardboard between the two halves and glue or tape back to front of postcard. Have youngsters describe the scene on the front of the postcard by writing a short description to their friend and/or scientist on the reverse side. Add address of a friend and/or scientist and return address. Have youngsters exchange postcards in the classroom. Encourage youngsters to design (include postmarks) and give their postcards to friends and family members on special occasions. Discuss how postcards are an effective means of communication between people of all nations. Extend activity further by having youngsters collect postmarks and postage stamps from cards or letters received from pen pal friends.

Special Tip: Youngsters may want to form a postcard collecting club called "The Deltiologists." Have youngsters collect postcards from as many cities in states and foreign countries as possible.

Answers: completed postcards

Extending Source: Michael Levine, *The Address Book: How to Reach Anyone Who Is Anyone* (New York: Putnam Publishing Group, 1988).

GA1150

Postcard Science

GA1150

Postcard Science

From:

To:

Use this space for writing message.

Postcard Science

_____
_____
_____
_____

From:

_____
_____
_____

To:

PLACE
STAMP
HERE

Use this space for writing message.

GA1150

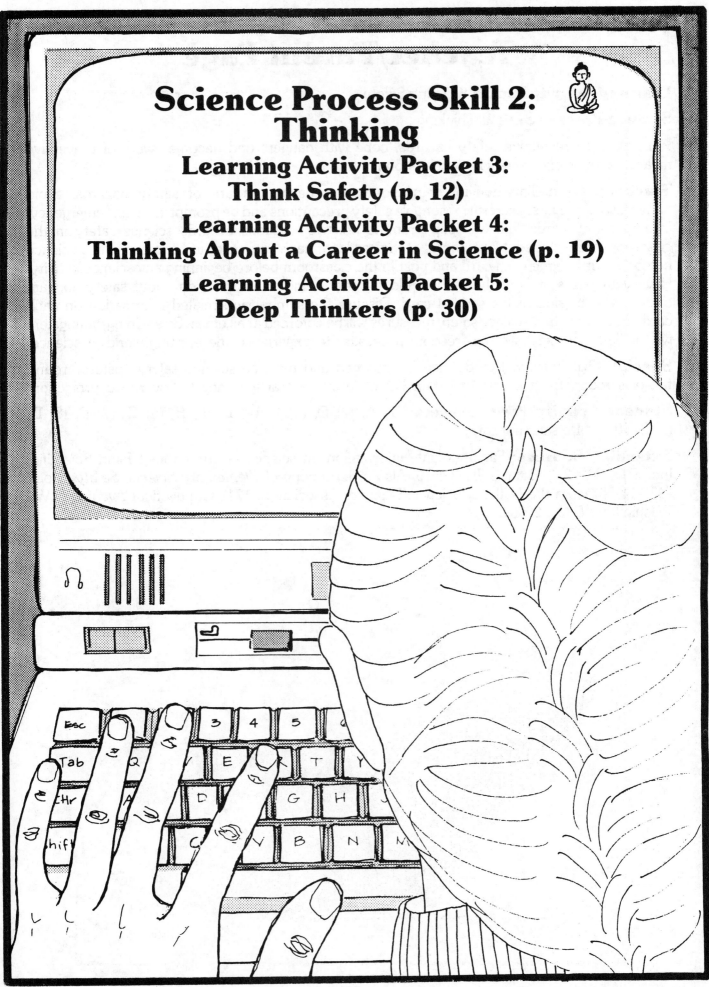

Science Process Skill 2: Thinking

Learning Activity Packet 3:
Think Safety (p. 12)

Learning Activity Packet 4:
Thinking About a Career in Science (p. 19)

Learning Activity Packet 5:
Deep Thinkers (p. 30)

Teacher/Parent Page

Learning Activity Packet 3: Think Safety

Science Process Skill 2: Thinking

Purpose: To recognize safety hazards, cope with dangers and become aware of preventive measures for science safety in the classroom

Teaching Tips: This activity helps youngsters become aware of safety hazards, avoid unnecessary dangers, exercise reasonable safety precautions and be prompt in case of emergency. Twenty safety cards that will help promote positive attitudes towards science safety in the classroom are included. Make copies of the cards for each youngster to be included in a science notebook, or enlarge each card and post in the classroom before beginning any science activity. Have youngsters cut out the cards. Fold on dotted line so information about safety appears on the *reverse* side of the symbol card. Discuss the symbol and related information on each card. Emphasize that science safety measures will be enforced at all times. By so doing, youngsters will be safe and yet have the freedom necessary to experience the exciting world of science.

Special Tip: Individual cards may be enlarged and used as science safety posters around the classroom. Each poster can then be made into a transparency for overhead projection.

Student Activity Page Answers: (1) A, (2) D, (3) D, (4) D, (5) B, (6) C, (7) D, (8) D, (9) C, (10) D. Be safe, not sorry.

Extending Sources: For up-to-date information on science safety, contact Flinn Scientific, Inc., P.O. Box 231, Batavia, IL 60510. Also order a copy of *Elementary Science Safety* (Stock #471-14750) from the National Science Teachers Association, 1742 Connecticut Avenue, N.W., Washington, D.C. 20009.

GA1150

Think Safety Cards

2 Clothing Protection

Clothing Protection
* Wear laboratory smocks in the science class.
* Roll up long sleeves and tie loose clothing at the waist.
* Keep work surfaces clean and neat.

4 Hand Safety

Hand Safety
* Always wear gloves when working with chemicals or animals.
* Use tongs when heating test tubes. DO NOT hold test tubes in your hand while heating them.
* Dissect specimens in dissecting pans—never while holding them in your hand.

1 Eye Safety

Eye Safety
* Wear safety goggles in science class when doing experiments.
* If anything gets into your eyes, tell your teacher immediately.
* Never look directly at the sun, even for short periods of time.
* Contact lens should not be worn when doing science experiments.

3

H Y G I E N E
C A R E I C

Hygienic Care
* Always wash your hands before and after doing science experiments.
* Keep your hands away from your face and mouth in science class.
* Remove all jewelry from your hands before doing science experiments.

GA1150

Think Safety Cards

6

Radiation

Hazard

Radiation Hazard

* When you see this picture on a door, do not enter the room.
* When you see this picture on a piece of science equipment or material, do not use such materials or equipment.
* Ask your teacher about proper protection from the sun's rays.

8

Fire Safety

Fire Safety

* Keep things that might explode away from fire.
* Tie long hair back and roll up long sleeves.
* Never reach across an open flame.
* Know the fire drill procedure and the location of fire exits and fire extinguishers.

5

Poison

Poison

* Tell your teacher if you see things that have this symbol on them.
* Never taste anything in the science classroom. Do not eat or drink from laboratory glassware.
* Do not eat or drink in the laboratory.
* Do not bring chemicals near your eyes or skin.
* Never return unused substances to original containers.

7

Glassware Safety

Glassware Safety

* Check with your teacher before using any glassware. Tell your teacher about any broken, chipped, or cracked glassware; it should not be used.
* Let glassware dry in the air. Do not use toweling to dry glassware. Do not use glassware that is not completely dry.
* Do not pick up broken glass with your bare hands. Sweep the glass up carefully.
* Never force glass tubing into a rubber stopper.
* Place glassware on the table surface, not near the edges of your work surface.

14

GA1150

Think Safety Cards

11 Explosion — Danger

Heating Safety
* Ask your teacher to help you light a Bunsen burner, propane torch or candle.
* Turn off hot plates, Bunsen burners, and other open flames such as candles when not in use.
* Heat approved science containers on a ring stand with a wire gauze between the glass and the flame.
* Heat materials only in approved glassware.
* Turn off gas valves on burners and torches when not in use.

12 Heating Safety

Explosion Danger
* Avoid things that may explode when you jar, heat, expose them to air or put them together.
* Always use safety goggles when working with science materials.
* Never heat materials in a closed container.
* Never risk an explosion by heating rocks or minerals directly.
* Always point the open end of a container away from people.

9 Electrical Safety

Electrical Safety
* Do not use electrical equipment near water or with wet hands.
* Never play with a plug in an electrical outlet.
* Keep electrical cords away from places where someone may trip on them.
* Watch for loose plugs or worn electrical cords.

10 Gas Precaution

Gas Precaution
* Do not smell fumes directly. When told to smell a substance, wave the air toward your nose and smell gently.
* When you and your teacher use a Bunsen burner, torch or candle, wear goggles, gloves, and smock. If the burner does not work, turn the gas completely off.
* Always have adequate ventilation when working with fumes and flames.

GA1150

Think Safety Cards

Corrosive Substances

Corrosive Substances
* Tell your teacher about any materials that might be rusting.
* Tell your teacher about any spilled materials immediately.
* Look for materials that might be weakened by corrosion.

Animal Safety

Animal Safety
* Wear leather or thick gloves when handling laboratory animals, especially rodents.
* When working outside, beware of poisonous or dangerous animals in the area.
* Do not touch or approach wild animals.

Caustic Substances

Caustic Substances
* Tell your teacher about anything that spills.
* If any harmful thing gets on your skin, run cool water over it and tell your teacher.
* Wear a smock to protect your clothing.
* Never add water to acids; always add acids to water.
* Always point the opening of a container away from you and other students.

Water Safety

Water Safety
* When working near water, always work with a partner or adult.
* Do not jump into water whose depth you do not know.
* Always wear a life jacket.
* Do not work near water during stormy weather.

Think Safety Cards

18 — Plant Safety

Plant Safety
* Be aware of poisonous plants that grow in the area.
* Never put your hands near your face and mouth when handling an unknown or poisonous plant.
* Never eat any part of an unknown plant.

20 — Oxidizing Substances

Oxidizing Substances
* Be aware of the processes of combustion, corrosion, and respiration while doing oxidation and reduction (redox) reactions.
* Observe proper safety precautions when adding oxygen to a substance (oxidation) or (loss of electrons) removing oxygen from a substance (reduction) (gaining of electrons).

17 — Humane Treatment

Humane Treatment
* Using gloves, pick up all animals gently. Consider their comfort. Do not poke at them or injure their skin, scales, or body parts.
* Clean cages and tanks regularly. Dispose of wastes properly.
* Make sure animals have food, water, ventilation, and exercise.
* Be sure that you put only animals that get along well together.

19 — Proper Waste Disposal

Proper Waste Disposal
* Clean up your work area after you are finished.
* Follow your teacher's directions on how to get rid of waste materials.
* Place broken glass in a specially designated container.
* Save glass, pop cans, plastic containers and discarded newspapers. Take to recycling center.

GA1150

Student Activity Page: Think Safety

Safety Quiz: Write the letter in the blank at the left that best answers the question on the right. Be safe in your responses.

1. _____ Before doing a science experiment, you should wear (A) safety goggles, (B) contact lenses, (C) shorts, (D) sunglasses.

2. _____ In science class, glass or plastic containers should be used for (A) eating, (B) drinking, (C) storing food, (D) watering plants.

3. _____ In science class, each youngster should (A) know the fire drill procedure, (B) be patient, (C) report all accidents to the teacher, (D) all of the above.

4. _____ When your teacher helps you light a candle, you should (A) tie long hair back, (B) roll up long sleeves, (C) strike match away from you, (D) all of the above.

5. _____ If you have a burn or scratch, you should (A) keep quiet about it, (B) tell your teacher immediately, (C) wait and see if something happens to it, (D) ignore it.

6. _____ You should do only those experiments that (A) seem interesting, (B) could burn, (C) your teacher tells you to do, (D) could melt.

7. _____ When doing a science experiment, you should (A) be patient, (B) follow instructions, (C) think before you act, (D) all of the above.

8. _____ When you want to smell something, you should (A) wave the materials around, (B) take a big sniff, (C) have your friend smell it, (D) waft your hand over the object or container and sniff a little.

9. _____ If you spill something in science class, you should (A) quickly clean it up, (B) get a friend to help you clean it up, (C) tell the teacher immediately and then follow directions, (D) leave the area.

10. _____ When you see something dangerous or hazardous, you should (A) wait and see what happens (B) have your friends look at it with you, (C) leave the room, (D) tell your teacher immediately.

 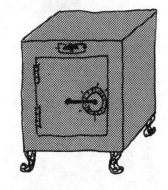  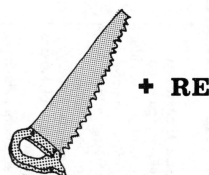 **+ RE**

18

GA1150

Teacher/Parent Page

Learning Activity Packet 4: Thinking About a Career in Science

Science Process Skill 2: Thinking

Purpose: To construct an object that when used will stimulate youngsters' thinking about choosing science as a career

Teaching Tips: This exercise features eighteen cards related to various careers in science. Each card is divided into four parts: career name, symbol, definition and activity. Make copies of the eighteen cards for each youngster or assign as individual tasks. Have youngsters fold each card on the dark lines to make a figure with four sides. Tape edge A to edge B to hold figure together. Tape soda straw inside figure so youngsters can turn the figure easily in their hands. Working in pairs, have youngsters quiz each other. For example, one youngster turns the figure so the symbol for an anatomist (human body) faces another youngster who supplies the term *anatomist* with appropriate definition. Then have youngsters do the "hands-on" activities on side 4. Discuss individual careers in science with youngsters. The eighteen cards can also be laminated and cut into sections. Use sections for classification exercises (biological, physical, earth and space science careers). Emphasize the importance of choosing science as a career.

Special Tip: Some youngsters like to tape soda straws on flat page before taping structure together.

Card Answers: The following answers apply to the careers listed below:

Card 1—Entomologist: Bee

Card 8—Anthropologist: American Negro

Card 10—Astronomer: "W" constellation is Cassiopeia

Card 16—Nurse: 98.6° F (37° C) for a well person; over 98.6° F (37° C) for a person with a fever

Student Activity Page Answers: (1) variable, (2) variable, (3) igneous, sedimentary, metamorphic, (4) variable, (5) pharmacy (prescription), (6) variable, (7) 72, (8) American Negro, (9) variable, (10) Cassiopeia, (11) lift: power or force available for raising; thrust: forward directed force in response to rearward force; drag: something that slows motion; gravity: force that draws all bodies to the center of the earth, (12) variable, (13) skin, (14) pistil; stamen, (15) 2000, (16) 98.6° F, (37° C) well; over 98.6° F (37° C) ill, (17) variable, (18) stars 6 and 7 should be circled.

Extending Source: Jerry DeBruin, *Scientists Around the World* (Carthage, IL: Good Apple, Inc., 1987).

GA1150

Thinking About a Career in Science Cards

Activity	Definition	Symbol	Career	1
Enter the numeral 338 into the display of a calculator. Turn calculator upside down. Name the insect. Then make more names of insects with your calculator. Edge B	A person who studies the science of insects		**Entomologist** Edge A	

Activity	Definition	Symbol	Career	2
Make a chart that shows the hair and eye color of each member of your family. Try to find out if you received your hair and eye color from your mother or father or both. Make a record of your results. Edge B	A person who studies the science of genes and how they determine various characteristics of offspring		**Geneticist** Edge A	

GA1150

Thinking About a Career in Science Cards

Activity	Definition	Symbol	Career 3
Go outside and find ten rocks. Line the rocks up from smallest to largest, then lightest to heaviest. Were the orders the same or different? Then learn at least three other ways that you can classify rocks.	A person who studies the earth, the rocks that make up earth and its changes over time		**Geologist**

Edge B · Edge A

Activity	Definition	Symbol	Career 4
Fill two-liter plastic soda bottle with water. Partially fill medicine dropper with water. Place dropper in bottle. Squeeze sides. Make diver dive to bottom and surface again. Pretend that you are inside the diver. Write a story about what you might see on a trip to the bottom of an ocean.	A person who studies the geography, history, motions, and physical and chemical behaviors of the oceans		**Oceanographer**

Edge B · Edge A

GA1150

Thinking About a Career in Science Cards

Activity	Definition	Symbol	Career	5
Visit a pharmacist at a local pharmacy. Ask the pharmacist what this symbol means to his/her profession. $\mathbf{R_x}$	A person who studies medicines and their effects, and who prepares and dispenses drugs		**Pharmacist**	
Edge B			Edge A	

Activity	Definition	Symbol	Career	6
Place one ice cube on a white piece of construction paper, and another on a black piece. Time how long it takes each cube to melt. From this experiment, determine the color of clothes you would wear in summer and in winter.	A person who studies the states and properties of matter and energy rather than living things and chemical changes		**Physicist**	
Edge B			Edge A	

GA1150

Thinking About a Career in Science Cards

Activity	Definition	Symbol	Career	7
Count the number of times your heart beats in one minute both before and after exercise. Find the difference. Then find out how long it takes for your heart rate to return to what it was before you exercised.	A person who studies what goes on inside living things and how different parts of living things work	Nerve Muscle fiber	**Physiologist**	

Edge B — Edge A

Activity	Definition	Symbol	Career	8
Find out whether this skull is that of (1) American Negro, (2) Australoid, (3) Plains Indian or (4) Caucasoid. 	A person who studies the science of humans and their works		**Anthropologist**	

Edge B — Edge A

23

GA1150

Thinking About a Career in Science Cards

Activity	Definition	Symbol	Career 9
With permission from your teacher or parents, add several drops of vinegar to a teaspoon of baking soda. Make a written record of what you see and hear. Remember, do not taste the mixture of baking soda and vinegar.	A person who studies what things are made of and their reactions to one another		**Chemist**

Edge B — Edge A

Activity	Definition	Symbol	Career 10
With a sharp point on a compass, punch holes like this in the bottom of a discarded 35mm film can. Look through film can at a light. Identify this *W* constellation. She's a real queen.	A person who studies the stars and other bodies in space		**Astronomer**

Edge B — Edge A

24

GA1150

Thinking About a Career in Science Cards

Activity	Definition	Symbol	Career 11
Blow over the top side of a piece of paper held slightly below your mouth. Observe "lift" of paper. Study how this lift helps an airplane to fly. Look up Bernoulli's Principle. Define the words *lift, thrust, drag* and *gravity* and explain how each affects how an airplane flies.	A person who is the pilot of an airplane or other heavier-than-air craft		**Aviator**

Edge B

Edge A

Activity	Definition	Symbol	Career 12
Go outside and make a list of ten living and ten non-living things that are smaller than you. Place an *o* mark next to those things that are good for the environment, an *x* mark for those harmful to the environment.	A person who studies the science of living things		**Biologist**

Edge B

Edge A

25

GA1150

Thinking About a Career in Science Cards

Activity	Definition	Symbol	Career 13
Have a friend lie down face-up on a piece of paper. With a marker, trace around your friend's body on the paper. With your friend's help, draw the major organs found inside the body on the paper. Identify and label each organ.	A person who studies the structure of animals and plants, especially humans		**Anatomist**

Edge B · Edge A

Activity	Definition	Symbol	Career 14
Smell a flower today. Then see if you can observe these parts: sepals anther pistil style ovary ovule petals pollen tube pollen grains stigma stamen	A person who studies the science of plants		**Botanist**

Edge B · Edge A

GA1150

Thinking About a Career in Science Cards

Activity	Definition	Symbol	Career 15
Clip the nutrition information label from a cereal box and attach it to your notebook. Make a record of the percentage of U.S. recommended daily allowances for various vitamins and minerals for your diet. Edge B	A person who studies the planning of, taking in and digestion of food		**Nutritionist** Edge A

Activity	Definition	Symbol	Career 16
Draw a picture of a thermometer that shows the body temperature (^{0}F— ^{0}C) for a well person. Then draw a thermometer that shows the body temperature (^{0}F— ^{0}C) for a person with a fever. Edge B	A person who cares for the sick or wounded under the direction of a physician		**Nurse** Edge A

GA1150

Thinking About a Career in Science Cards

Activity	Definition	Symbol	Career 17
Design a bumper sticker with a message telling others about the rights of your favorite animal.	A person who studies the science that deals with all forms of animal life		**Zoologist**

Edge B

Edge A

Activity	Definition	Symbol	Career 18
Go outside and find the Big Dipper in the sky tonight. Draw a picture of what it looks like. Be sure to include its "pointer stars" and how they would help an astronaut find the North Star.	A person who travels outside the atmosphere of the earth		**Astronaut**

Edge B

Edge A

28

GA1150

Student Activity Page:
Thinking About a Career in Science

Card #   **Activity**

1. List two other words made by numbers in your upside-down calculator.

   a. _____   b. _____

2. Eye color: Dad _____ , Mom _____ , Me _____

3. Rocks can be classified into three groups: a. _____   b. _____   c. _____

4. As an oceanographer, the best line in my story is "_____
   _____."

5. The symbol R_x means _____.

6. Melt time for ice cube on black is _____. Melt time for ice cube on white is _____.
   I wear _____ clothes in summer, _____ clothes in winter.

7. Average heart rate is _____ beats per minute.

8. The skull on card number 8 is that of a (n)_____.

9. Mixture _____ and _____.

10. The constellation punched in the bottom of a film can is _____.

11. Four forces that help airplanes fly are a. _____   b. _____   c. _____
    d. _____.

12. _____ is good for our environment; _____ is bad for our environment.

13. The _____ is the largest organ in the human body.

14. The _____ is the female part of the flower; the _____ is the male part of a
    flower.

15. A child should eat at least _____ calories per day.

16. The body temperature of a well person is _____ ° F, _____ ° C. The body
    temperature of an ill person is _____ ° F, _____ ° C.

17. On a piece of paper, draw a 1-10 scale where 1 is *agree* and 10 is *disagree*. Circle the number
    that best represents your feelings about whether you feel scientists should be allowed to experiment
    on animals to make new discoveries.

18. This is a picture of the Big Dipper. Circle the numbers of the two pointer stars.

                                      1 ★

                                   2 ★

                                   3 ★

                                   4 ★
                               5 ★

                                   6 ★ 7 ★

29   GA1150

Teacher/Parent Page

Learning Activity Packet 5: Deep Thinkers

Science Process Skill 2: Thinking

Purpose: To help youngsters develop skills in problem solving, right brain creative thinking and spatial relations

Teaching Tips: Many school-related activities promote left brain thinking with emphasis on logical and sequenced activities which often leads to rote memorization of scientific facts by youngsters. Deep Thinkers expose youngsters to right brain experiences which coordinate creative right brain thinking with the more logical left brain memory. Looking at situations in different ways permits the right brain to consider numerous possibilities while the left brain logically recalls the phrase or term for the puzzle's solution. Introduce Deep Thinkers on the student activity pages. Help youngsters answer the puzzles. (Debug, Peak Performance.) Then make copies of the eighty Deep Thinker Cards. The verbal picture puzzles can be given to youngsters daily throughout the year on an overhead and/or posted on a bulletin board or used in a Deep Thinker activity center. Youngsters may work individually or in small groups. Encourage family members to participate. Help youngsters solve thinkers creatively as some puzzles have more than one answer. Encourage students to write their own thinker cards to be included in a classroom or library scrapbook or published in a school newspaper or newsletter. When placed in order, the cards tell the life story of a person who looks back over his lifetime.

Special Tip: Enlarge Deep Thinker Cards. Make one card per transparency. Display new card each day. Hold a contest to see who can decipher the eighty cards first.

Card and Student Activity Page Answers: (1) Just Between You and Me; (2) Spoken from the Bottom of My Heart; (3) Looking Back over the Years; (4) One Day at a Time; (5) High Priority on Education; (6) Hands-On Science; (7) Trial by Error; (8) Putting Ideas Down on Paper; (9) Mind over Matter; (10) I Understand; (11) Three Degrees Below Zero; (12) Teaching by Example; (13) Inside Job; (14) Down to Earth; (15) 6:00 a.m.; (16) Top of the Morning; (17) Great Day in the Morning; (18) Eggs over Easy; (19) Hurry Up; (20) Your Heart Isn't in It; (21) Dark Circles Under Eyes; (22) Long Underwear; (23) Nerves on the Edge; (24) Misunderstanding Between Friends; (25) Tenants; (26) Pain in the Neck; (27) In over My Head; (28) Argue over It; (29) One on One; (30) Shut Up; (31) Initial Shock; (32) Head over Heels; (33) Knockdown; (34) Cross-Eyes; (35) Splitting Headache; (36) Countdown; (37) Goose Down; (38) Neon Light; (39) Split Level; (40) Broad Daylight; (41) Going in All Directions; (42) Hill of Beans; (43) Upheaval; (44) It's About Time; (45) Change of Heart; (46) Side by Side; (47) Make Up; (48) Arm in Arm; (49) First Pair; (50) Two Peas in a Pod; (51) Bird in the Hand Is Worth Two in the Bush; (52) Saved in the Nick of Time; (53) Task at Hand; (54) Light on the Subject; (55) Read Between the Lines; (56) Debug; (57) Backwards Glance; (58) Feedback; (59) New Invention; (60) Out of Sight; (61) Thumbs Up; (62) Walking on Cloud Nine; (63) Sailing over the Seven Seas; (64) Floating down the River; (65) Strong Undertow; (66) Two Ships Passing in the Night; (67) Waterfall; (68) Man Overboard; (69) Up the Creek; (70) I'm Underwater; (71) Crossroads; (72) Life Begins at 40; (73) Triple Bypass; (74) Space Program; (75) Dark Ages; (76) Friendly Undertaker; (77) Six Feet Underground; (78) Pie in the Sky; (79) Life After Death; (80) Arch of Triumph

Extending Source: Games Junior, P.O. Box 2083, Harlan, IA 51593-0280.

Deep Thinker Cards

GA1150

Deep Thinker Cards

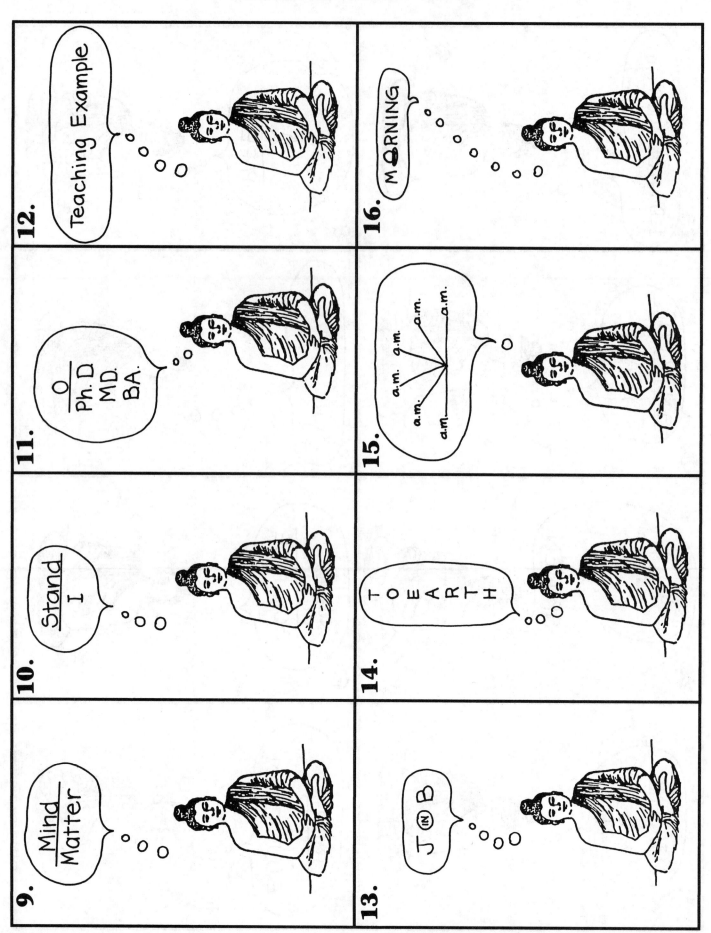

32

GA1150

Deep Thinker Cards

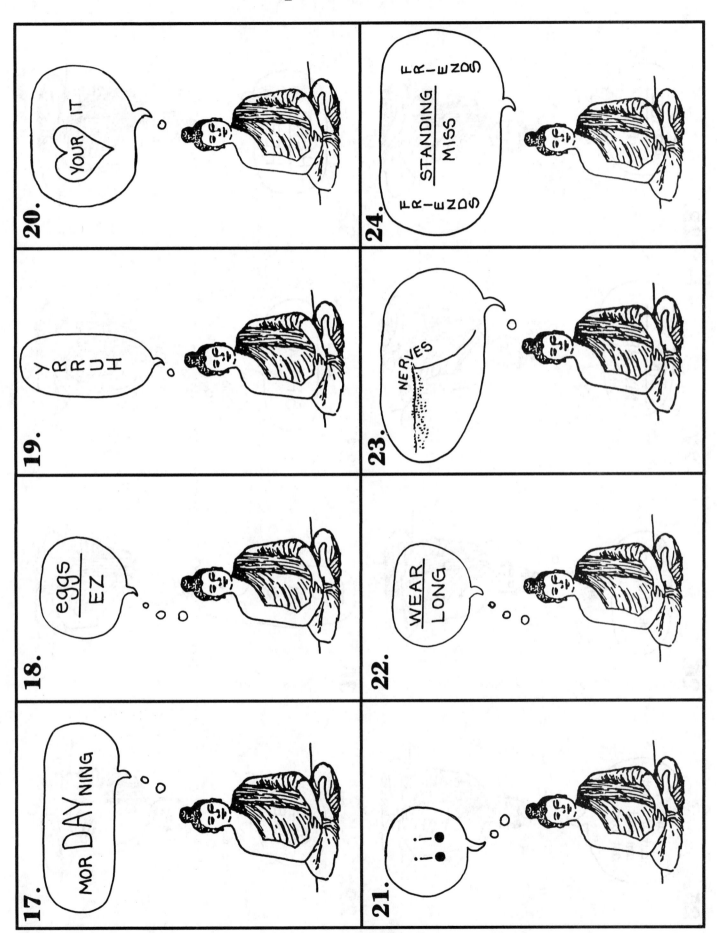

33

Deep Thinker Cards

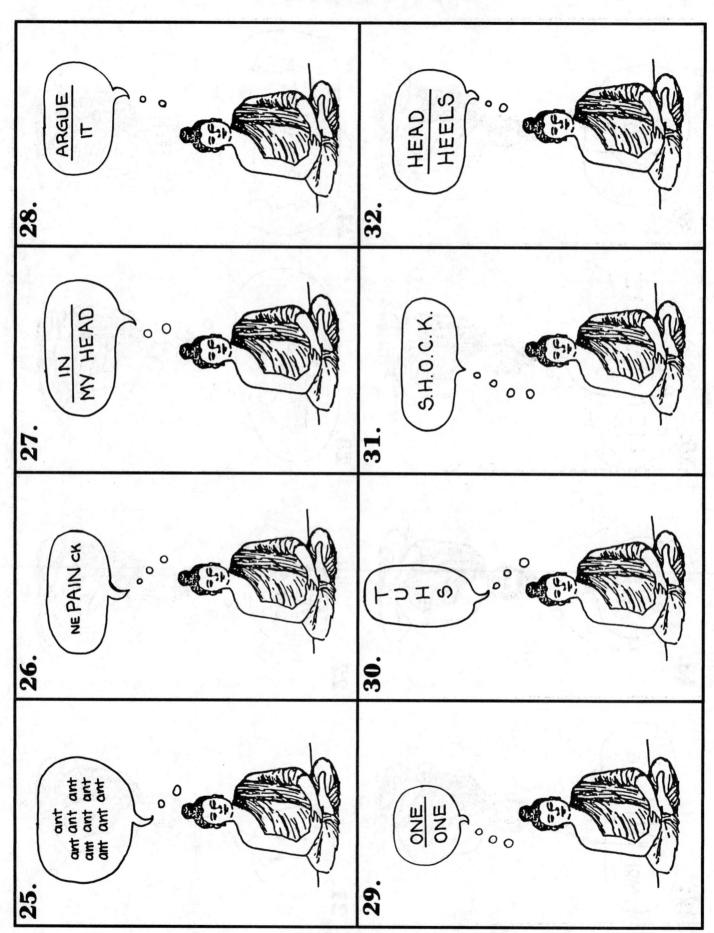

GA1150

Deep Thinker Cards

35

Deep Thinker Cards

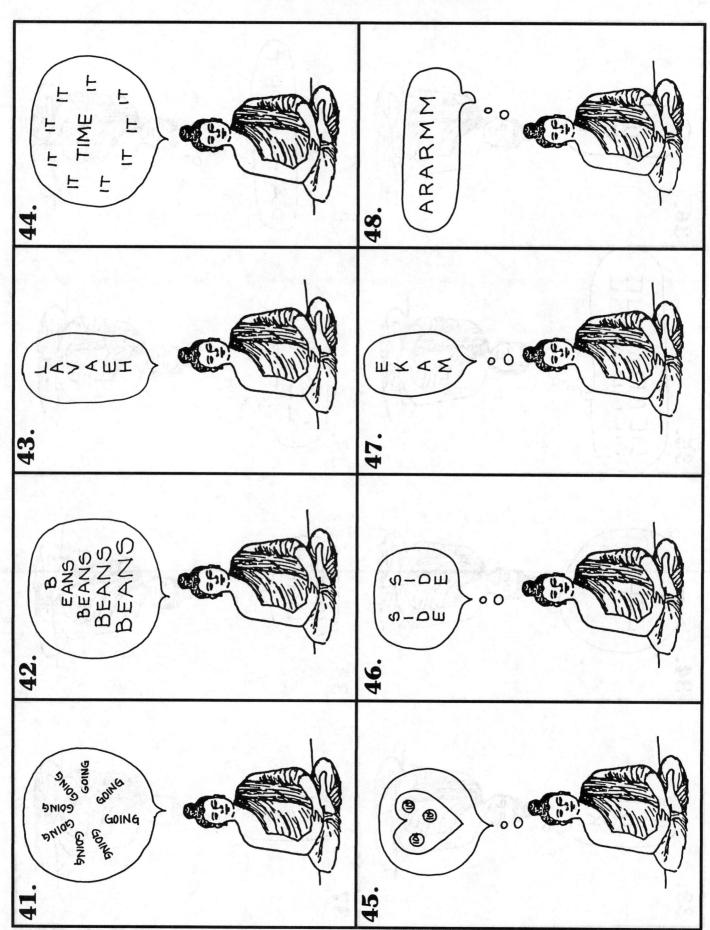

Deep Thinker Cards

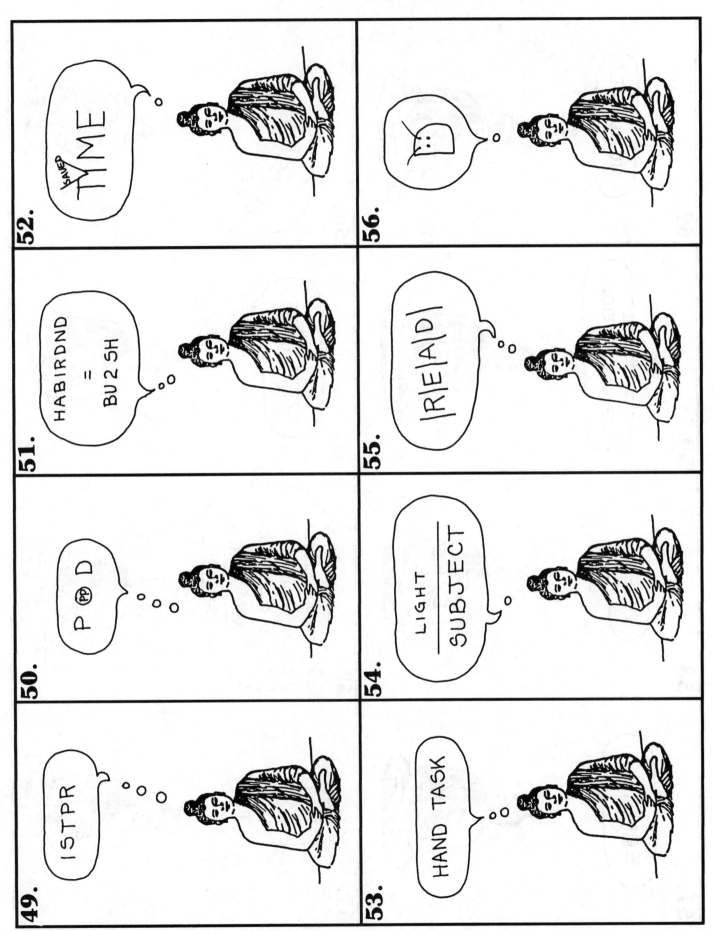

Deep Thinker Cards

Deep Thinker Cards

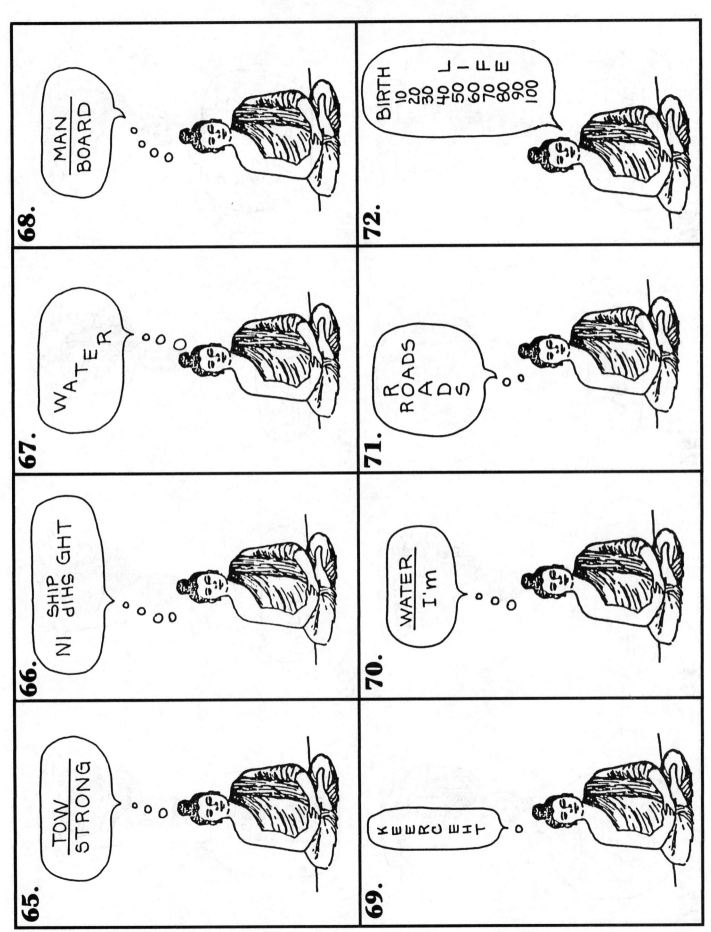

Deep Thinker Cards

GA1150

Student Activity Page:
Deep Thinkers

Your mission is to **D** the eighty Deep Thinkers and write their solutions in the blanks below.

1. _____
2. _____
3. _____
4. _____
5. _____
6. _____
7. _____
8. _____
9. _____
10. _____
11. _____
12. _____
13. _____
14. _____
15. _____
16. _____
17. _____
18. _____

19. _____
20. _____
21. _____
22. _____
23. _____
24. _____
25. _____
26. _____
27. _____
28. _____
29. _____
30. _____
31. _____
32. _____
33. _____
34. _____
35. _____
36. _____

Student Activity Page: Deep Thinkers

37. _____
38. _____
39. _____
40. _____
41. _____
42. _____
43. _____
44. _____
45. _____
46. _____
47. _____
48. _____
49. _____
50. _____
51. _____
52. _____
53. _____
54. _____
55. _____
56. _____
57. _____
58. _____

59. _____
60. _____
61. _____
62. _____
63. _____
64. _____
65. _____
66. _____
67. _____
68. _____
69. _____
70. _____
71. _____
72. _____
73. _____
74. _____
75. _____
76. _____
77. _____
78. _____
79. _____
80. _____

If you identify this thinker, you will know your performance. Fill in the blanks. Congratulations!

My performance was a

_____

performance.

GA1150

Science Process Skill 3:
Questioning
Learning Activity Packet 6:
Scientific Trivia (p. 44)

Teacher/Parent Page

Learning Activity Packet 6: Scientific Trivia

Science Process Skill 3: Questioning

Purpose: To develop youngsters' questioning skills by having them ask each other about basic scientific words and phenomena. A "hands-on" activity in which youngsters apply the scientific phenomenon to their everyday lives is included after each trivia question is answered.

Teaching Tips: On the following pages are twelve sets (two cards per set) of scientific trivia cards. Make copies of each set of cards. Have youngsters cut out the cards on the solid black line. Fold each card in half on dotted line. Insert piece of cardboard (back of writing tablets or poster board) between the pages of each set (see insert). Tape edges shut. Laminate sets or cover with clear Con-Tact paper as some of the hands-on activities require the placement of liquids on the cards. (Cards can also be inserted in small plastic bags before placing liquids on the cards.) Have youngsters ask each other scientific trivia questions. Then have youngsters do the "hands-on" activities on each card. Answers to trivia questions are found at the bottom of the card on the *reverse* side. With a paper towel, wipe off all activity cards after use. Cards can then be stored safely for further use.

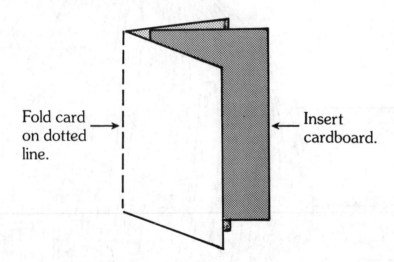

Fold card on dotted line. → | ← Insert cardboard.

Special Tip: Cards Q and R: There is a difference between primary pigment colors for paint (red, blue, yellow) and for light (blue, red, green).

Card and Student Activity Page Answers: A = 75%; B = 50%; C = stethoscope; D = lungs; E = hydrogen, oxygen; F = oxygen, (1) hydrogen, (2) oxygen (3) hydrogen; G = moon; H = sun; I = compass; J = barometer; K = North Star; L = Little Dipper; M = graphite; N = fingerprints; O = core; P = lava; Q = blue, red, yellow; R = blue, red, green; S = 206; T = ear; U = salt; V = salt; W = pupil; X = eyeglasses/contact lenses

Super Scientific Trivia Wild Card Answers: (1) you, (2) large African antelope; (3) orangutan; (4) far side of the moon; (5) Greenwich Meridian, 0⁰ longitude, Greenwich, England; (6) a three-dimensional image made by light; (7) Zero degrees Kelvin temperature is measured in Kelvins in science; therefore absolute zero is zero Kelvin or OK. (8) 5 billion years

Extending Source: Professor Quizzle's Quiz Wizard Trivia Science by RAMCO Games, Inc. Stock No. 403, 1984.

Scientific Trivia Cards

A What percent of the earth is covered by water?

(Record your answer on the student activity page and in the blank on Card B.)

Activity for B: Draw a line on the earth below that shows the amount of sunlight the earth receives at any given time. Then shade in the part *not* lit up by the sun.

Answer for Card B: _____

B At any given time, what percent of the earth is being lighted by the sun?

(Record your answer on the student activity page and in the blank on Card A.)

Activity for A: Put a penny on the picture below. Using an eyedropper, find out how many drops of regular tap water you can fit on the heads and tails side of the penny.

Head   Tail

Answer for Card A: _____

C What instrument does a doctor use to listen to your heart?

(Record your answer on the student activity page and on Card D.)

Activity for D: Breathe normally. On the lung below, record the number of times you breathe in one minute.

Answer for Card D: _____

D Where are alveoli found?

(Record your answer on the student activity page and on Card C.)

Activity for C: Feel your pulse. On the heart below, record the number of times your heart beats in one minute.

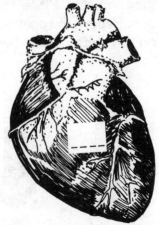

Answer for Card C: _____

     GA1150

Scientific Trivia Cards

E What two gases make up water?

(Record your answer on the student activity page and on Card F.)

Activity for F: Number the electrons in the oxygen atom below. Color each electron yellow.

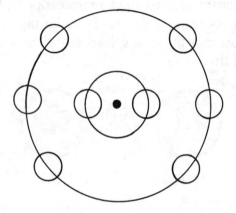

Answer for Card F: _____

F Name the gas, made by plants, that we breathe. This gas is necessary for life.

(Record your answer on the student activity page and on Card E.)

Activity for E: In the circles below, write the letters of the atoms that make up water.

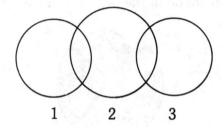

Answer for Card E: _____

G Name the satellite that revolves around the earth.

(Record your answer on the student activity page and on Card H.)

Activity for H: Read the temperature on a thermometer. Place thermometer in the sun. Record the change in temperature on the thermometer below.

Before   After

Answer for Card H: _____

H What is the name for a giant ball of hot gases at the center of our solar system that gives off energy?

(Record your answer on the student activity page and on Card G.)

Activity for G: Below are eight phases of the moon. With a pencil, shade in the part of each moon that is *not* lit by the sun.

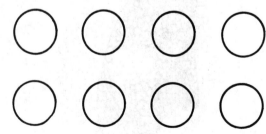

Answer for Card G: _____

GA1150

Scientific Trivia Cards

I What magnetic instrument is used to find directions?

(Record your answer on the student activity page and on Card J.)

Activity for J: Draw in the hands on the barometer below to show the current barometric pressure.

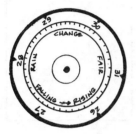

Answer for Card J: _____

J What instrument measures air pressure?

(Record your answer on the student activity page and on Card I.)

Activity for I: Name the four cardinal and four intercardinal points on a compass. Identify a compass rose. Then find north by using a compass.

Answer for Card I: _____

K Polaris is another name for what star?

(Record your answer on the student activity page and on Card L.)

Activity for L: On a clear evening, locate the Big Dipper. Draw an imaginary line through the pointer stars to the North Star in the sky.

Answer for Card L: _____

L The North Star is located in what constellation?

(Record your answer on the student activity page and on Card K.)

Activity for K: In the picture below, circle the North Star.

(pointer stars)

Answer for Card K: _____

GA1150

Scientific Trivia Cards

M What mineral is found in pencil lead?

(Record your answer on the student activity page and on Card N.)

Activity for N: Place finger on pencil rubbing. Press finger here to make fingerprint.

Answer for Card N: _____

N What are patterns of lines on your fingers called?

(Record your answer on the student activity page and on Card M.)

Activity for M: Rub side of pencil back and forth here to make pencil rubbing.

Answer for Card M: _____

O Name the center of the earth.

(Record your answer on the student activity page and on Card P.)

Activity for P: Make a volcano. Fill a can half full of liquid soap. Add red food coloring and baking soda. Slowly add vinegar. Observe results.

Answer for Card P: _____

P What is molten hot rock called as it comes out of a volcano?

(Record your answer on the student activity page and on Card O.)

Activity for O: Cut an apple in half. Compare to Earth. Identify the core, mantle (pulp) and crust (peeling).

Answer for Card O: _____

GA1150

Scientific Trivia Cards

Q Name the three primary pigment colors.

(Record your answer on the student activity page and on Card R.)

Activity for R: Cover a small piece of blue cellophane paper with a small piece of red cellophane paper. Hold up to light. Name the new color.

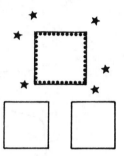

Answer for Card R: _____

R Name the three primary light colors.

(Record your answer on the student activity page and on Card Q.)

Activity for Q: In the circle below, mix one drop of red and one drop of blue food coloring. Name the new color.

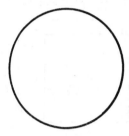

Answer for Card Q: _____

S How many bones are there in the human body?

(Record your answer on the student activity page and on Card T.)

Activity for T: Determine whether dogs or humans are capable of hearing higher pitched sounds. Then find out how a dog whistle works.

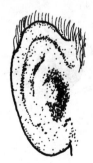

Answer for Card T: _____

T Where are the hammer, anvil and stirrup?

(Record your answer on the student activity page and on Card S.)

Activity for S: Make a sketch of your femur here.

Answer for Card S: _____

GA1150

Scientific Trivia Cards

U What is put on icy sidewalks in winter to melt ice?

(Record your answer on the student activity page and on Card V.)

Activity for V: Using the Periodic Table of Elements, write the chemical symbols for salt on this salt crystal.

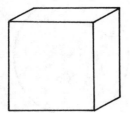

Answer for Card V: _____

V What is the common name for sodium chloride?

(Record your answer on the student activity page and on Card V.)

Activity for U: Obtain two equal-sized ice cubes. Put salt on one. Find out which one melts faster.

Answer for Card U: _____

W What is the hole in the middle of the iris in your eye called?

(Record your answer on the student activity page and on Card X.)

Activity for X: Find out the difference between nearsightedness and farsightedness. Tell whether concave or convex lenses are used to correct these vision problems.

Concave   Convex

Answer for Card X: _____

X What do people wear to help them see better?

(Record your answer on the student activity page and on Card W.)

Activity for W: Look at the size of your pupil in a mirror. After being in a dark room for five minutes, look again. How does light affect pupil size?

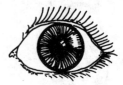

Anwer for Card W: _____

GA1050

Student Activity Page: Scientific Trivia

Card	Answer
A	_____
B	_____
C	_____
D	_____
E	_____
F	_____
G	_____
H	_____
I	_____
J	_____
K	_____
L	_____
M	_____
N	_____
O	_____
P	_____
Q	_____
R	_____
S	_____
T	_____
U	_____
V	_____
W	_____
X	_____

GA1150

Super Scientific Trivia Wild Cards

1

Who is Homo sapiens?

2

What's a gnu?

3

What animal's name means "wild man"?

4

Where is the loneliest place to which a person can travel?

5

Where does east meet west and west meet east?

6

What is a hologram?

7

What does *OK* mean in science?

8

How long will the sun continue to shine and keep us living?

Science Process Skill 4:
Reading
Learning Activity Packet 7:
PSST: The Word Is *Science* (p. 54)

Teacher/Parent Page

Learning Activity Packet 7: PSST: The Word Is *Science*

Science Process Skill 4: Reading

Purpose: To have youngsters recognize how reading is an integral part of science and science is an integral part of reading. Reading and science are thus interrelated and should be taught as such.

Teaching Tips: Teach youngsters how science and reading are interrelated with the use of the activities on the following four pages. Make copies of the four pages for each youngster. Read and discuss the title of each card. Do card 1 with the youngsters. Emphasize importance of each individual in the class. Have youngsters complete the *clue* and *start* activities on the remaining fifteen cards. Cut apart pages to make sixteen individual cards. If possible, laminate the cards for lasting durability. Have youngsters complete the matching stretch activities, one per card, found on the student activity page.

Special Tip: Integrate science and reading whenever possible by correlating card activities with skills found in basic reader or use as a review of such skills. Cards may be enlarged to allow additional space for answers.

Card Answers: (1) youth, pupil, group, us, bunch, produce, adult, clue, success; (2) fir, fur, elm, maple, oak, tiger, deer, horse; (3) A2 (buck), B1 (mole), C4 (palm), D3 (seal) (4) weather map, balloon, weigh, fuel, cough, muscle; (5) answers will vary; (6) auto, gas, sub, cuke, lab, phone; (7) National Aeronautics and Space Administration, Light Amplification by Stimulated Emission of Radiation, Sound Navigation Ranging, Radio Detecting and Ranging, Television, Unidentified Flying Object, Long Playing phonograph record, Medical Doctor, Fahrenheit, Video Terminal; (8) girl-boy, on-off, day-night, young-old; (9) speak, hand, hive, stop, foot, dog, sun; (10) grass, feather, rock, night, rose, bear, turtle, fox, mouse, bee, snow; (11) "I'm going to blow my top." "Break the ice." "Eat your heart out." "You get my goat." "Hit the hay." "Let off steam." "We don't see eye to eye on this." "Turn over a new leaf." "Put your foot down." (12) aerodynamics—air, anthropology—man, astronomy—star, barometer—weight, biologist—life, cardiologist—heart, geology—earth, hydroelectric—water, optometrist—eye, tripod—three, pediatrician—child, telescope—far; (13) degree, ohm, sun, earth, new moon or rain, snow, female, no smoking, hail, fog, male, greater than; (14) 1. he, 2. log, 3. gill, 4. goggles, 5. shell, 6. bee, 7. bill, 8. she; (15) pop, level, radar, toot, pup, eye, peep, noon; (16) birth, male, prescription, female, first aid, poison, no smoking, death, caduceus [emblem of the medical profession]

Student Activity Page Answers: (1) just between you and me; (2) white oak leaves are rounded, red oak leaves are pointed; (3) variable; (4) completed project; (5) variable; (6) simple microscope has one lens, compound has two lenses; (7) completed activity; (8) completed activity; (9) lunar eclipse: moon, earth, sun; solar eclipse: earth, moon, sun; (10 completed activity; (11) completed project; (12) completed activity; (13) E = volts, I = current in amps, R = resistance in ohms; (14) average lifespan of male = 68 years, average lifespan of female = 76 years; (15) pupil size gets smaller in lighted areas; (16) completed activity

Wild Card Answers: (A) nervous, (B) skeletal, (C) muscular (D) endocrine, (E) digestive, (F) lymphatic, (G) respiratory, (H) circulatory

Extending Source: Edward B. Fry, et al. *The New Reading Teacher's Book of Lists* (Englewood Cliffs, N.J.: Prentice-Hall, Inc., 1985).

PSST: The Word Is *Science* Cards

1

You Are Indispensable

U cannot spell YO _____ TH without U.

U cannot spell P _____ PIL without U.

U cannot spell GRO _____ P without U.

U cannot spell _____ S without U.

U cannot spell B _____ NCH without U.

U cannot spell PROD _____ CE without U.

U cannot spell AD _____ LT without U.

U cannot spell CL _____ E without U.

U cannot spell S _____ CCESS without U.

2

Homonyms

Homonyms are words that sound the same but are spelled differently.

Clue: F _ _ a kind of tree

F _ _ an animal covering

Start: Circle the names of three trees and three animals in the puzzle below.

E	A	R	T	U	X	D	Z
N	L	H	O	R	S	E	O
O	M	M	A	P	L	E	P
T	E	B	K	C	K	R	T
D	P	O	E	T	L	E	A
T	I	G	E	R	G	R	M

3

Homographs

Homographs are words that look and sound alike but have different meanings.

Clue:

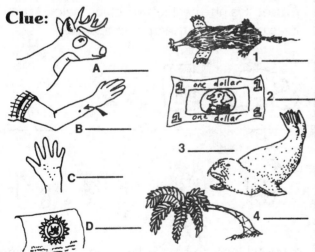

A _____

B _____

C _____

D _____

1 _____

2 _____

3 _____

4 _____

Start: Draw lines that connect pictures of words that look and sound alike but have different meanings. Print each word under its picture.

4

Frequently Misspelled Science Words

Clue: Below are pictures of science objects whose names are often misspelled. Name each object.

Start: On the blank below each picture, write the correct spelling of the name of the science object.

_____ _____ _____

_____ _____ _____

GA1150

PSST: The Word Is *Science* Cards

5
Compound Words

Compound words are joined together to make a new word.

Clue: black, bull, cut, copper, dragon, eye, ball, frost, gold, moon, red, down, pipe, wind, splash, fly, bite, fish, ship, wood, star, snow, bird, out, dog, cup, tall, head, fall

Start: On a separate page, write all the compound words that you can make by using the words above.

6
Shortened Science Words

Little words can be made from big words.

Clue: These long words can be made into shorter words: automobile, gasoline, submarine, cucumber, laboratory and telephone.

Start: To discover the shorter words, write the numbered letters of the alphabet on the blanks to the right.

For example: A-1, B-2, etc.

```
1 21 20 15 = ____ ____ ____ ____
7 1 19 = ____ ____ ____
19 21 2 = ____ ____ ____
3 21 11 5 = ____ ____ ____ ____
12 1 2 = ____ ____ ____
16 8 15 14 5 = ____ ____ ____
```

7
Acronyms

Acronyms are new words made from initials.

Clue: Use the clue words to identify the terms below.

Clue Word	Acronym
Space	NASA
Fast Light	LASER
Sound Subs	SONAR
Airplanes	RADAR
Antenna	TV
Unknown	UFO
Recess	LP
"What's Up Doc?"	MD
Hot and Cold	F
Look, Then See	VT

Start: On a separate piece of paper, write the full name for what the acronym means.

8
Antonyms

Antonyms are words that mean the opposite or nearly the opposite.

Clue: Using the picture clues below, draw lines connecting the opposite words.

Start: Unscramble the letters of the following words. Then write each word on the blank under the correct picture. RILG, OYB, NO, FOF, YAD, GHINT, GOUNY, DLO.

GA1150

PSST: The Word Is *Science* Cards

9

Analogies

Analogies show relationships between words.

Clue: hand, dog, speak, sun, hive, stop, foot

Start: Using the clue words, write the correct word in the blank that shows the correct relationship.

ear: hear—mouth: _____

finger: _____—toe: foot

bear: den—bee: _____

engine: go—brake: _____

wrist: hand—ankle: _____

paw: _____—fin: fish

moon: earth—earth: _____

10

Similes

Similes are words that explain something by making a comparison.

Clue: theafre, oser, asgrs, kocr, ignht, ebe, arbe, ofx, uttelr, oumse, onsw

Start: Unscramble each clue word above to make a word that best completes each simile.

As green as __ __ __ __ __

As light as a __ __ __ __ __ __

As hard as a __ __ __ __

As dark as __ __ __ __ __

As lovely as a __ __ __ __

As hungry as a __ __ __ __

As slow as a __ __ __ __ __

As sly as a __ __ __

As quiet as a __ __ __ __ __

As busy as a __ __ __

As white as __ __ __ __

11

Idioms

Idioms are expressions that have different meanings from the literal.

Clue: blow, put, turn, see, eat, break, hit, get, let

Start: Write the saying below the picture. The first one is done for you.

I'm going to blow my top! _____

_____

_____

_____

_____

_____

12

Word Combinations

New words are often formed by combining separate words, each with its own meaning.

Clue: heart, man, child, earth, weight, air, star, eye, far, water, three, life

Start: The words below consist of two different parts, each with a distinct meaning. Underline the first part of the word once and the second part twice. Then, selecting from the clues above, choose the correct meaning for the first part of each word and place to the right of the word. The first one is done for you.

Word	Meaning of First Part
aerodynamics	air
anthropology	_____
astronomy	_____
barometer	_____
biologist	_____
cardiologist	_____
geology	_____
hydroelectric	_____
optometrist	_____
tripod	_____
pediatrician	_____
telescope	_____

GA1150

PSST: The Word Is *Science* Cards

13

Science Symbols

Science symbols are pictures that stand for something.

Clue: degree, ohm, new moon or rain, sun, fog, no smoking, greater than, male, female, snow, earth, hail

Start: Write the clue word in the blank under each symbol.

_____ _____ _____ _____

_____ _____ _____ _____

_____ _____ _____ _____

14

Calculator Words

Read science words using a calculator.

Clue: (1) male _____ (2) tree _____ (3) part of a fish _____ (4) chemist _____ (5) sea _____ (6) busy _____ (7) part of a bird _____ (8) female _____

Start: Enter the numerals below into display on your calculator. Turn calculator upside down. Read word. Write word after clue word above. Make other science words.

(1) 34, (2) 907, (3) 7719, (4) 5379909, (5) 77345, (6) 338, (7) 7718, (8) 345

15

Palindromes

Palindromes are words that read the same backward and forward.

Clue:

Pop _____ _____

_____ _____ _____

Start: Write the name of each palindrome on the line below each object above. The first one is done for you.

16

The Signs of Science

Signs give messages.

Clue: female, male, poison, first aid, no smoking, prescription, birth, death, caduceus (bonus)

Start: Write the clue word in the blank under each sign of science.

_____ _____ _____

_____ _____ _____

_____ _____ _____

GA1150

Student Activity Page
PSST: The Word Is *Science*

Card Number	Activity
1	You $\frac{J}{S}$ me. Where are you? Where is just? How about me?
2	Stretch: Find out the difference between the shapes of white and red oak leaves.
3	Stretch: Draw a picture of the palm of your hand. Study different kinds of creases and fingerprints.
4	Stretch: Clip out the weather map from your newspaper today. Make a note of the high and low temperatures.
5	Stretch: Observe the moon tonight. Draw a picture of the moon.
6	Stretch: In a science laboratory, find out the difference between a simple and compound microscope.
7	Stretch: Write a letter to NASA, Educational Publications Services, LFC-9, Washington, D.C. 20546, and request information on future space trips.
8	Stretch: Using two bar magnets, put the opposite ends (N + S) together. What happens? How are magnets like people?
9	Stretch: Make a drawing that shows the relationship between the moon, earth and sun during solar and lunar eclipses.
10	Stretch: Find and study the features of a rock that match your personality.
11	Stretch: Find out how to do a leaf print. Then do a leaf print of your favorite leaf. (If there are no leaves in your area at this time, do this activity in the spring.)
12	Stretch: Draw a picture of a tree. Trace the path of water from roots to stems to leaves.
13	Stretch: Find out information on Ohm's Law. Write the letters that stand for volts, amps and ohms in Ohm's Law.
14	Stretch: Using a calculator, add the numbers below to find the average life spans of a male and female. ♂ 10 + 25 + 15 + 8 + 7 + 3 = □ yrs. _____ ♀ 14 + 11 + 20 + 16 + 10 + 5 = □ yrs. _____
15	Stretch: Look at the size of the pupils in your eyes. Spend several minutes in a dark room. Come out of the dark room. Look at the size of your pupils. Compare. What does light do to the size of the pupils in your eyes?
16	Stretch: Write a story about what you would do if an accident occurred in your science classroom.

GA1150

Wild Cards: Systems on the Go

Read the clue and name the system.

A Clue

S
E
N
S
E

O
R
G
A
N
S

_____

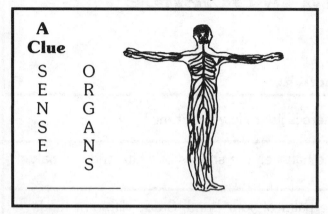

B Clue

2
0
6

B
O
N
E
S

_____

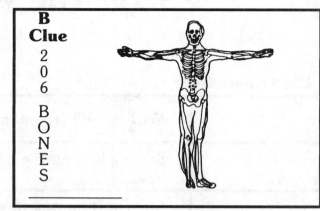

C Clue

F
I
B
E
R
S

_____

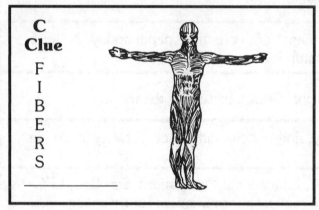

D Clue

H
O
R
M
O
N
E
S

_____

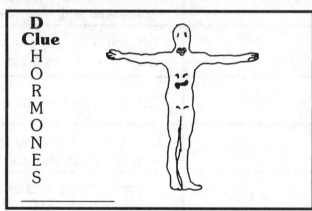

E Clue

S
A
L
I
V
A

_____

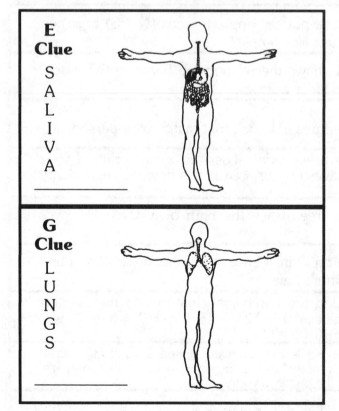

F Clue

L
Y
M
P
H

_____

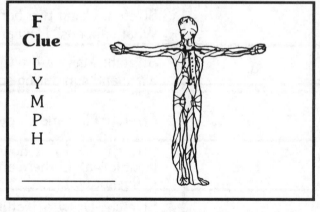

G Clue

L
U
N
G
S

_____

H Clue

C
A
R
D
I
A
C

_____

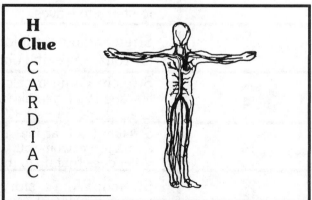

GA1150

Science Process Skill 5:
Observing

GA1150

Teacher/Parent Page

Learning Activity Packet 8: Overhead Science Recipes

Science Process Skill 5: Observing

Purpose: Observing is the process by which youngsters use their senses to identify objects and their properties by taking note of any changes in the object system. Using their senses, youngsters should be able to describe an object and any changes in the object or its properties. Observation is basic to all experiences in science and youngsters are encouraged to develop this process to the fullest extent possible.

Teaching Tips: The overhead projector is an excellent medium to use to enhance the observational skills of youngsters. The following pages include fourteen conveniently labeled science recipe cards which can be used on the overhead projector with ease. The cards feature cutouts, punch outs, transparencies or experiments. Cut out each card. Laminate each card. Follow the directions on each card. Use a single-edge razor blade or X-acto knife for cutouts. Move overhead projector closer to or farther away from screen to decrease or increase the size of objects. Use projector "out of focus" technique for "fade outs" and other interesting side effects. Store science recipe cards in a handy 3″ x 5″ file card box. Keep near your desk. Add additional cards to the file as more activities are discovered. Excellent for use as time fillers during periods of inactivity or for motivation and stimulation of scientific inquiry.

Special Tips: Read and discuss Recipe for Life I. Make transparency for overhead. Do same for Recipe for Life II. Place in science notebook.

Card Answers: (1) bear; (2) variety of creatures available; (3) variable; (4) pigeon; (5) variable; (6) magenta; (7) purple; (8) A = attract, B = repel; (9) surface tension; (10) Roy G. Biv = red, orange, yellow, green, blue, indigo, violet are colors of the visible spectrum; (11) a. test tube, b. beaker, c. Erlenmeyer flask, d. funnel, e. boiling flask, f. graduated cylinder; (12) answers are as shown; (13) approximately 360 stars; (14) completed project

Extending Source: For ideas, read the book *501 Ways to Use the Overhead Projector* by Lee Green and Don Dengerink (Littleton, CO: Libraries Unlimited, 1982).

GA1150

Overhead Science Recipe Cards

1

Biology: Animals

Cutout: Cut out shaped area. Place on overhead projector. Have youngsters identify animal.

3

Biology: Leaves

Transparency: Make transparency of this grid card. Place over small leaf on overhead. With an erasable pen, draw around leaf onto transparency. Count number of square inches of square area in leaf. One square equals .25 inches.

Recipe for Life I

I

AMONLYONE

BUTSTILLIAMONE

ICANNOTDOEVERYTHING

BUTICANSTILLDOSOMETHING

ANDBECAUSEICANNOTDOEVERYTHING

IWILLNOTREFUSETODOTHESOMETHING

THATICANDO

2

Biology: Animals

Experiment: Place clear plastic or glass container of warm water on overhead. Add one capsule of sea creature* to container. Have youngsters observe and act out the actions of the organism as it appears on the screen.

Identify creature.

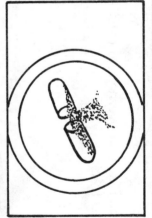

Capsule

*Instant Products, Inc., P.O. Box 33068, Louisville, KY 40232

GA1150

Overhead Science Recipe Cards

5

Physical Science: Heat and Temperature

Transparency: Make "target" transparency from this card. Place clear shallow dish of warm water over target on overhead. Drop one drop of food coloring onto bull's-eye. Time how long it takes for color to reach outer ring. Repeat using alcohol and then mineral oil. Then try with cold water. Compare results.

7

Physical Science: Light and Color

Experiment: Place clear plastic or glass container of regular tap water on overhead. Drop several drops of blue food coloring into water. Add several drops of red food coloring. Mix. Have youngsters identify new color. Then use drops of mineral oil and food coloring to observe new colors.

4

Biology: Animal Tracks

Cutout: Cut out shaded area. Place on overhead projector. Have youngsters identify animal track.

6

Physical Science: Light and Color

Cutout: Cut out two of these cards with square hole in center. Tape red cellophane over hole on card A and blue cellophane over hole on card B. Place card B on overhead and cover with card A. Have youngsters identify new color.

Tip: 2" x 2" slide frame holders can also be used effectively for this activity.

64

GA1150

Overhead Science Recipe Cards

Physical Science: Properties of Liquids — 9

Experiment: Place clear plastic or glass container of regular tap water on overhead. Drop one drop of DUCO or airplane cement into water. Have youngsters observe and then act out the movements of the living creature. Add one drop of liquid soap to container. Ask youngsters why all movements end when the soap is added to water.

General: Science Equipment — 11

Cutout: Cut out dark shaded areas. Place on overhead projector. Have youngsters identify each piece of science equipment.

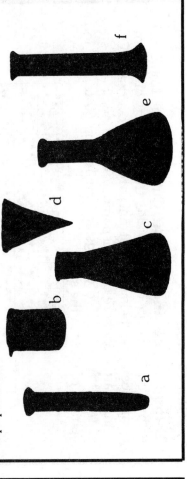

a
b
c
d
e
f

Physical Science: Magnetism — 8

Experiment: Place two bar magnets on overhead as shown below (opposite poles). Place sheet of glass or transparency film over magnets. Sprinkle iron filings onto glass. Have youngsters observe and then draw lines of force. Reverse poles (like poles). Note and draw lines of force. Compare.

Unlike poles (attract)

Like poles (repel)

(A) N S

(B) N N

Physical Science: Visible Spectrum — 10

Transparency: Make transparency out of this card. With markers, color in as marked. Place on overhead. Have youngsters identify colors of spectrum. Reinforce concept with name Roy G. Biv, the colors of the visible spectrum.

Red
Orange
Yellow
Green
Blue
Indigo
Violet

GA1150

Overhead Science Recipe Cards

13 — Space Science: Star Sampling

Transparency and Cutout: Cut out 2 cm² frame card with 1 cm² hole in center. Make transparency of 10 cm x 6 cm gridstar sky below. Place transparency on overhead. Drop frame card anywhere on transparency. Count number of stars in 1 cm² frame. Have youngsters multiply by 60 to find total number of stars in the sky.

1 cm
1 cm
2 cm
2 cm

Framing Card
Grid

Recipe for Life II

Eat less, _____ breathe more;
Talk less, _____ think more;
Ride less, _____ walk more;
Waste less, _____ give more;
Talk less, _____ practice more;
Frown less, _____ laugh more;
Boast less, _____ build more;
Condemn less, _____ cheer more;
Hate less, _____ love more;

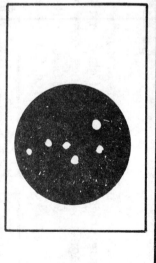

12 — Space Science: Moon Phases

Cutout: Cut out white areas of circles. Place on overhead. Have youngsters identify moon phases: waxing crescent, first quarter, waxing gibbous and full moon. Rotate card 180 degrees. Have youngsters identify remaining moon phases: waning gibbous, last quarter and waning crescent. Point out that the new moon is not visible.

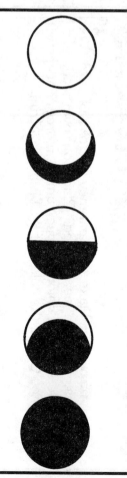

14 — Space Science: Constellations

Punch Out: Make a mini planetarium from dark, plastic panty hose container. With a heated nail or ice pick, punch holes into dome-shaped container to represent star constellations. Place on overhead. Have youngsters identify constellation(s).

Tip: Black plastic 35 mm film cans may also be used for this activity.

GA1150

Teacher/Parent Page

Learning Activity Packet 9: Comet Halley

Science Process Skill 5: Observing

Purpose: To observe the path of Comet Halley, a famous comet. To identify the parts of a comet: nucleus, coma and tail

Teaching Tips: This exercise features twelve activity cards that when cut apart and stapled together will make a useful flip book that shows the path of Comet Halley. Before movies were made, people made it look like pictures were moving. They did this by taking many slightly different pictures and stapling them together. When one flipped the pictures quickly, the objects in the pictures appeared to move. This activity uses this method. Make copies of the pages for each youngster or make one classroom set. Have youngsters cut apart cards. Glue to cardboard. Place number one on top. Staple cards together in upper left corner. Hold deck in left hand. With right thumb on top of the deck, have youngsters flip through the deck. Youngsters should observe Comet Halley as it orbits around the sun and then travels back into outer space. Discuss how this cycle occurs every seventy-six years. Identify the three parts of the comet: nucleus, coma and tail. Extend activity further with a discussion of various myths about the effects of comets on life.

Special Tip: Cut out Comet picture on page 71. Place small piece of magnetic tape on the reverse side of cutout comet. Place thin strip of magnetic tape on the path of Comet Halley on page 71. Have youngsters move magnetic comet along magnetic path accordingly.

Card Answers: completed project

Student Activity Page Answers: November 15, Pleiades; December 1, Pisces; January 1, Crosses equator for first time; March 1, Capricornus; April 1, Sagittarius; April 5, Scorpius; April 25, Hydra; May 1, Crosses equator for second time

Extending Source: R.D. Chapman, and R. Lynn Bondurant, Jr., *Comet Halley Returns* (National Aeronautics and Space Administration, Educational Programs, Office of Public Affairs, Goddard Space Flight Center, Greenbelt, MD 20777).

GA1150

Comet Halley Cards

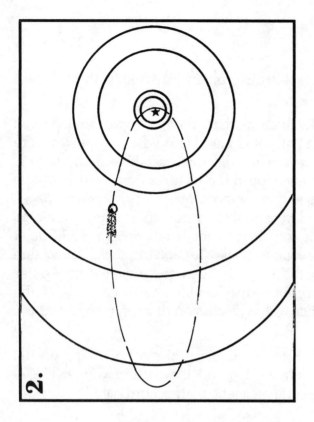

2.

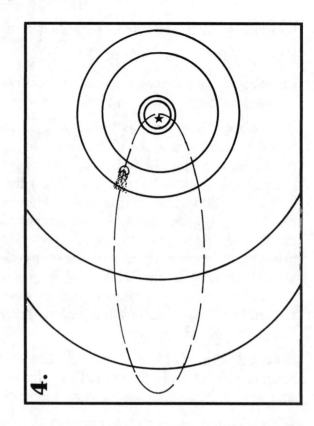

4.

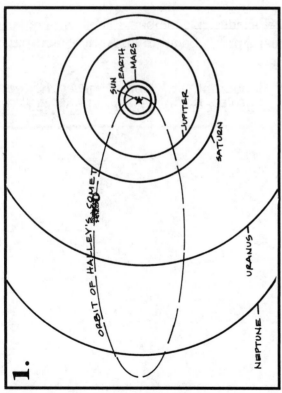

1.

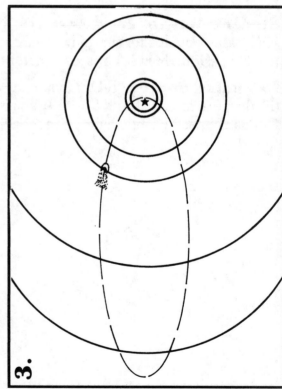

3.

68

GA1150

Comet Halley Cards

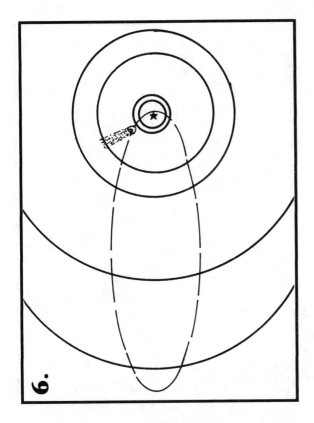

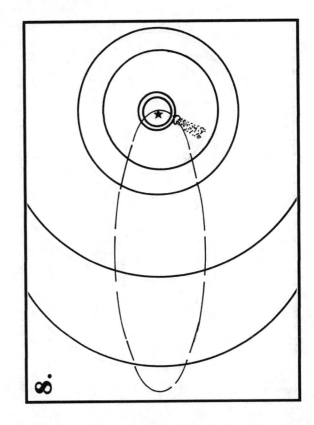

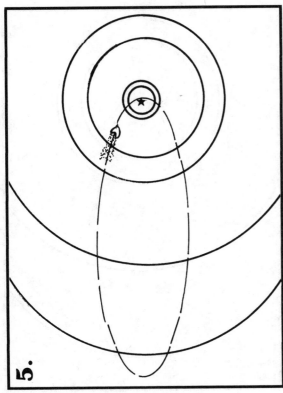

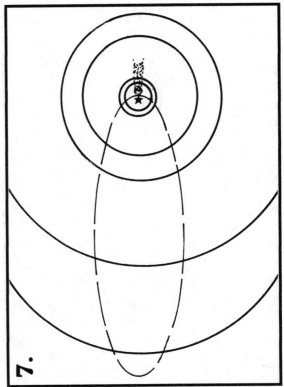

GA1150

Comet Halley Cards

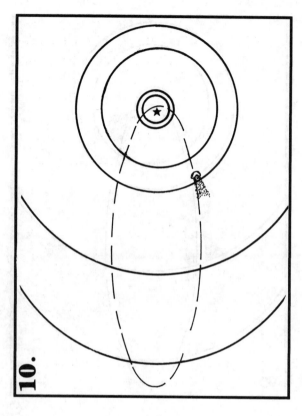

10.

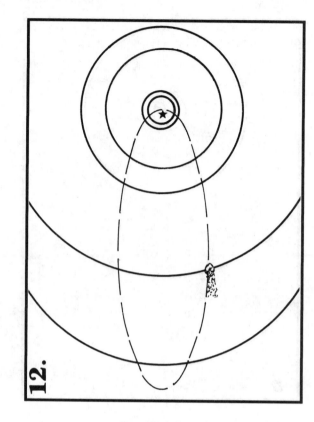

12.

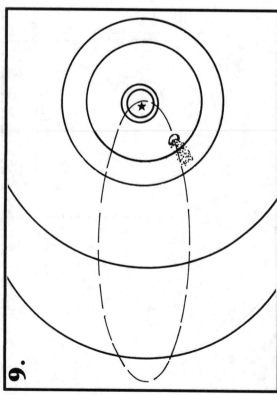

9.

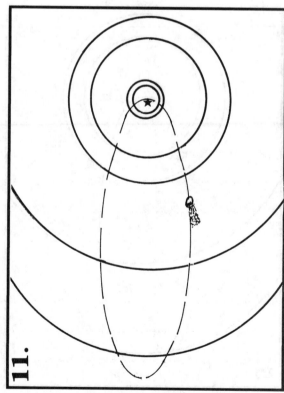

11.

GA1150

Student Activity Page: Comet Halley

A comet is like a dusty snowball that races around the sun. Halley's Comet is the most famous of all comets. The Chinese observed Halley's Comet in 240 B.C. Since then, Comet Halley has repeated its cycle about every seventy-six years, the last time being in 1986. Re-create this historical event. Below is a picture of the path Comet Halley took in 1986. Cut out the comet. Place on start, November 1. Move comet along path. End at May 1. Fill in the chart below. Pretend that you are Comet Halley. Make a tape recording of what you might see on your voyage around the sun. Be sure to include information on when you will return.

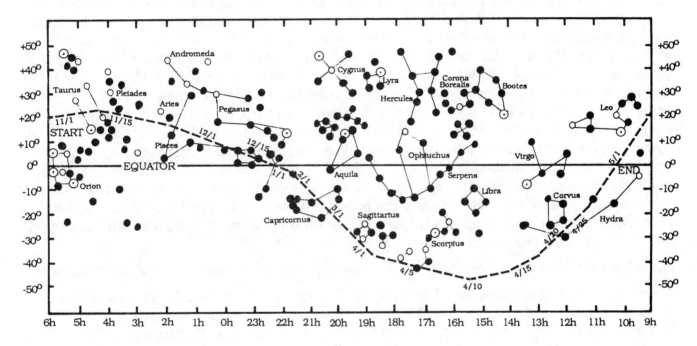

Date	Nearest Constellation
Nov. 15	
Dec. 1	
	Crosses equator for first time
March 1	
April 1	
April 5	
April 25	
	Crosses equator for second time

Halley's Comet

GA1150

Teacher/Parent Page

Learning Activity Packet 10: Constellations

Science Process Skill 5: Observing

Purpose: To identify twelve major constellations and infer the mythological character of each

Teaching Tips: These pages feature drawings of twelve major constellations and twelve matching mythological characters. Make copies of the pages for each youngster. Have youngsters cut out each card and match the constellation card to the mythological character card. Mount cards on small pieces of cardboard. Laminate. Play concentration and matching games. In school have youngsters carefully observe the position of each star in each constellation; then go outside at night in an attempt to locate each constellation. After observing the stars, have youngsters study the mythological character and legend related to each constellation. Here is one such legend, "The Legend of Cassiopeia." Cassiopeia is known as "The Woman in the Chair." She and Cepheus were queen and king of ancient Ethiopia. According to legend, Cassiopeia, while combing her hair on the seashore, said she was fairer than the Ethiopian sea nymphs. The nymphs asked a sea monster to ravage the seacoast. To prevent this from happening, the queen and king were told that they had to expose their daughter Andromeda to the ravages of the monster. Perseus, who was returning from his victory over Gorgon, saw Andromeda chained to the coast. To save her, Perseus used the head of Medusa and turned the monster to stone. He then carried off Andromeda as his wife. At death they both were placed with Cassiopeia and Cepheus in the sky.

Special Tip: *Neighbors in Space* by W. B. White is an excellent reference book for the activity.

Card Answers: 1. Cassiopeia—The Queen of Ethiopia, 2. Andromeda—Princess of Ethiopia, 3. Lyra—The Harp, 4. Draco—The Dragon, 5. Pegasus—The Horse, 6. Cygnus—The Swan, 7. Ursa Major—The Big Bear, 8. Sagittarius—The Archer, 9. Scorpius—Scorpion, 10. Capricorn—The Sea Goat, 11. Ursa Minor—The Little Bear, 12. Cepheus—King of Ethiopia

Student Activity Page Answers: Across—1. ram, 2. crow, 3. giraffe, 4. virgin, 5. crab, 6. fishes, 7. dolphin, 8. king, 9. queen, 10. hare, 11. sea goat, 12. archer, 13. big bear, 14. scales, 15. lion, 16. eagle, 17. water bearer, 18. princess, 19. northern crown, 20. great hunter; Down—1. river, 2. charioteer, 3. dragon, 4 herdsman, 5. winged horse, 6. herd, 7. big dog, 8. scorpion, 9. swan, 10. twins, 11. little bear, 12. bull, 13. arrow

Extending Source: Jerry DeBruin and Don Murad, *Look to the Sky* (Carthage, IL: Good Apple, Inc., 1988).

GA1150

Constellation Cards

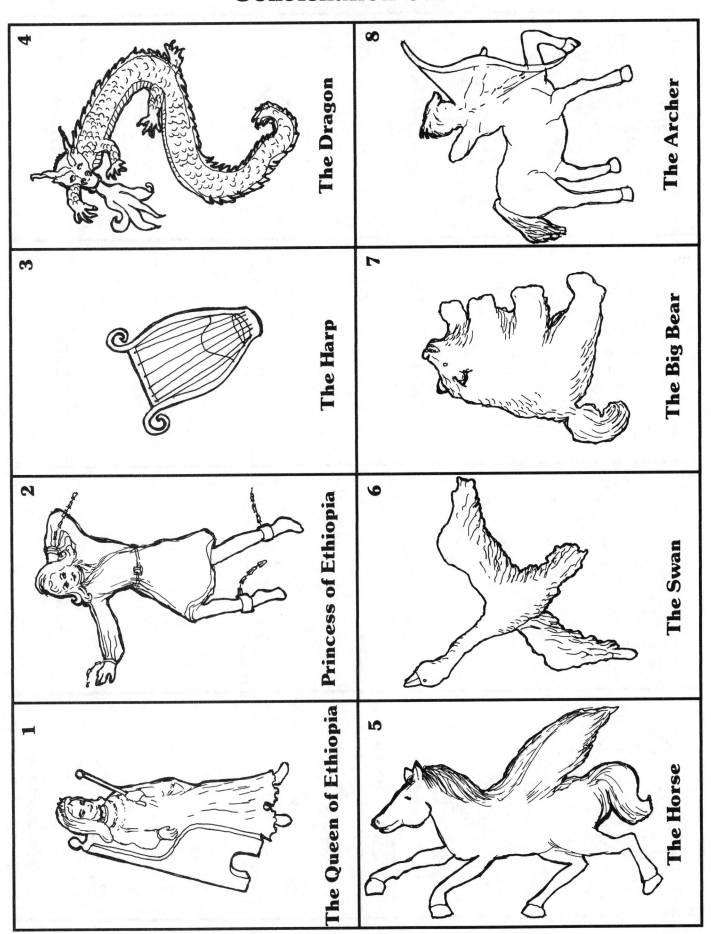

4 The Dragon

3 The Harp

2 Princess of Ethiopia

1 The Queen of Ethiopia

8 The Archer

7 The Big Bear

6 The Swan

5 The Horse

73

Constellation Cards

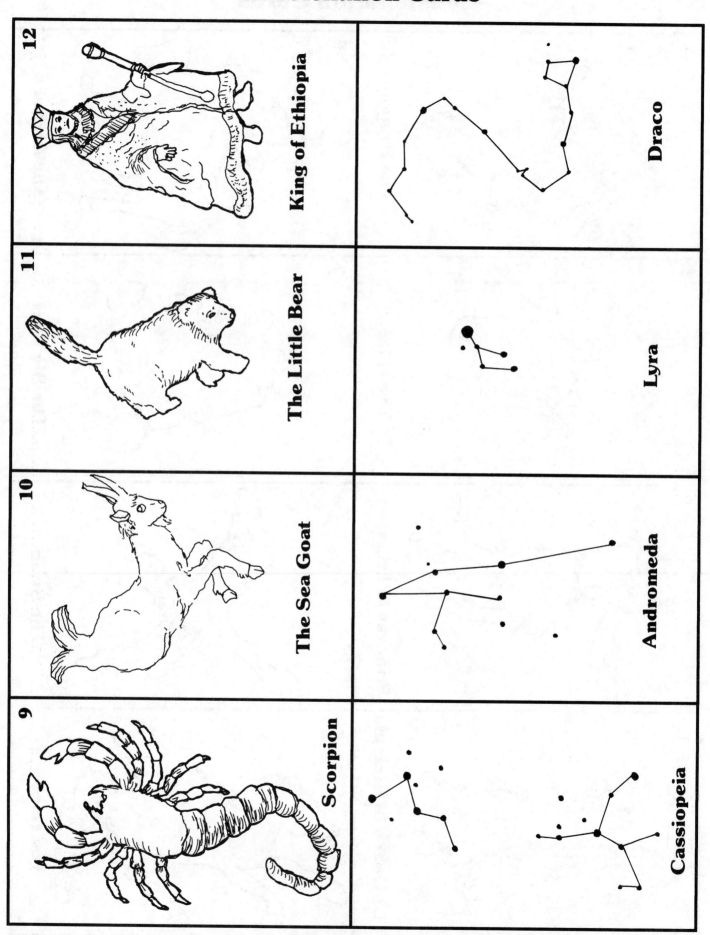

12 King of Ethiopia

Draco

11 The Little Bear

Lyra

10 The Sea Goat

Andromeda

9 Scorpion

Cassiopeia

74

GA1150

Constellation Cards

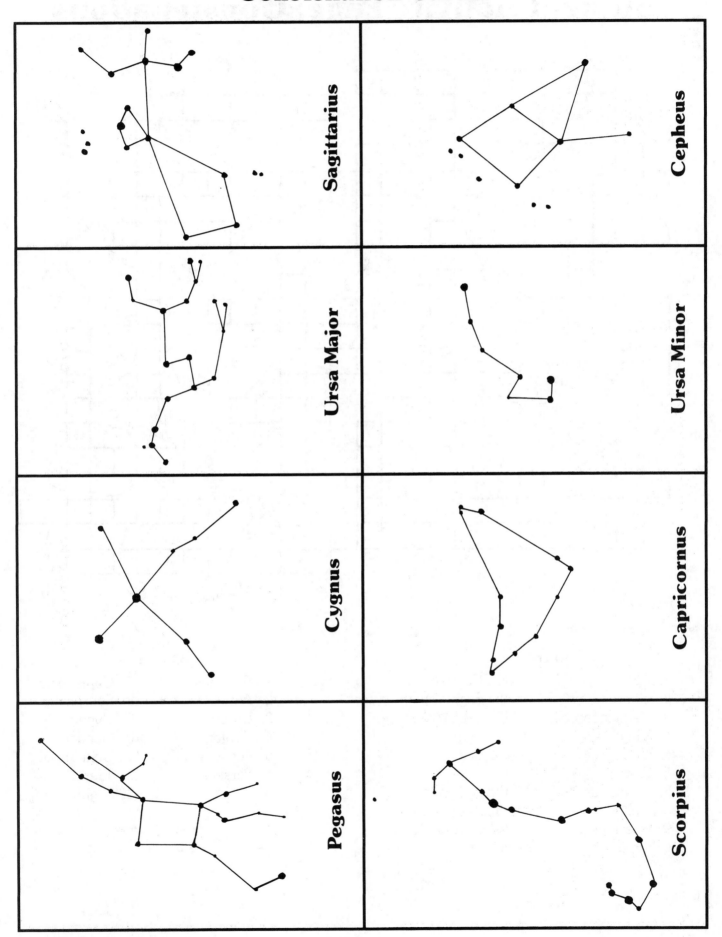

Sagittarius

Cepheus

Ursa Major

Ursa Minor

Cygnus

Capricornus

Pegasus

Scorpius

GA1150

Student Activity Page: Constellations

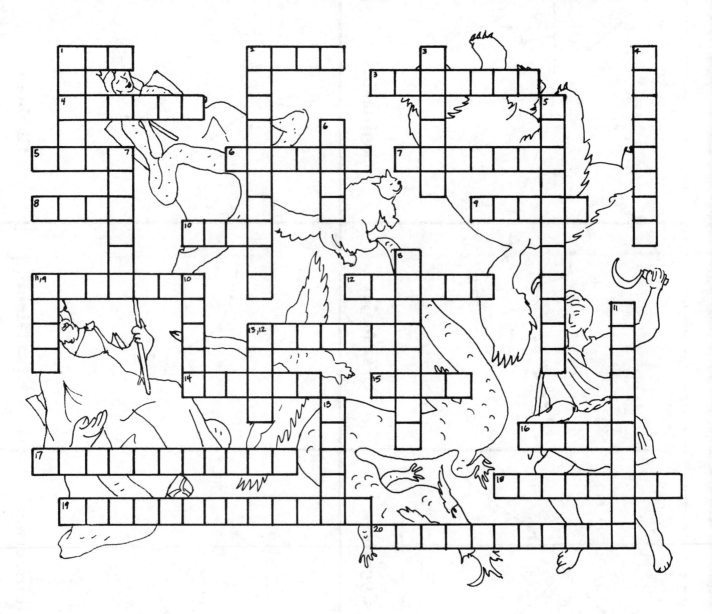

Across

1. Aries
2. Corvus
3. Camelopardalis
4. Virgo
5. Cancer
6. Pisces
7. Delphinus
8. Cepheus
9. Cassiopeia
10. Lepus
11. Capricornus
12. Sagittarius
13. Ursa Major
14. Libra
15. Leo
16. Aquila
17. Aquarius
18. Andromeda
19. Corona Borealis
20. Orion

Down

1. Eridanus
2. Auriga
3. Draco
4. Bootes
5. Pegasus
6. Perseus
7. Canis Major
8. Scorpius
9. Cygnus
10. Gemini
11. Ursa Minor
12. Taurus
13. Sagitta

GA1150

Teacher/Parent Page

Learning Activity Packet 11: Fall Frolics

Science Process Skill 5: Observing

Purpose: Using their senses, youngsters will be able to describe a scientific phenomenon as part of a scientific system and how systems change with the passage of time.

Teaching Tips: Observing is a science process skill that is basic to all science process skills. Youngsters need to develop the scientific process skill of observing early in the school year in the fall. Make copies of the following four pages for each youngster. Have youngsters observe closely the fall-related object/event on each card. Using the clues, help them identify the object/event and write the names in the appropriate blanks. After youngsters have completed all exercises, have them cut apart the four pages and place individual cards into a booklet of cards. Youngsters can add additional pages to these booklets as they discover more of nature's wonders. Conclude the study by having youngsters do the extending activities on the Student Activity Page.

Special Tip: Color leaves different colors and ask the youngsters to name the matching season.

Card Answers: Student Activity Page answers, when applicable, are found in parentheses.

Card 1—white oak leaves
Card 2—film, George Eastman
Card 3—sun, earth, equinox (September 22nd)
Card 4—nutrition label on cereal box, cereal (Answers will vary depending on cereal eaten.)
Card 5—baseball, baseball
Card 6—dog, dog (Answers will vary.)
Card 7—*Sputnik, Sputnik*
Card 8—Smokey the Bear
Card 9—$E = MC^2$, Albert Einstein, relativity (E = Energy, M = Mass, C = Velocity of light)
Card 10—tree, tree (Answers will vary.)
Card 11—incandescent light bulb, Thomas Edison (parts of light bulb are filament, support wires, lead-in wires, exhaust tube, solder, base)
Card 12—microscope, Anton Van Leeuwenhoek (Letters are larger.)
Card 13—no smoking sign, pollution
Card 14—(1) Cassiopeia, (2) Pegasus, (3) Little Dipper, (4) Constellation
Card 15—pumpkin, pumpkin, Halloween
Card 16—(Answers will vary—daylight saving time, standard time, standard time, daylight saving time)

Extending Source: June Zinkgraf and Toni Bauman, *Fall Fantasies* (Carthage, IL: Good Apple, Inc., 1980).

GA1150

Fall Frolics Cards

1 Happy Fall

Name of Object: _____

Clue: Rounded tips

My name is __ __ __ __ __ __

__ __ __ __ __ __ __ __ __ __ __

2 Smile

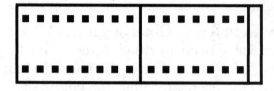

Name of Object: _____

Clue: I patented the first roll camera in the fall, 1888. I use a lot of the object above. I am a man from the East. My

name is __ __ __ __ __ __ __

__ __ __ __ __ __ __ __ __

3 Stay Close

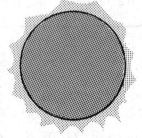 

Name of Object: Name of Object:

_____   _____

Clue: When I rise on September 22nd, I signal the first day of fall. I tilt the Northern Hemisphere away from the sun in fall and winter. The first day of fall is called the fall

__ __ __ __ __ __ __ __

4 Stay Healthy

PERCENTAGE OF U.S. RECOMMENDED
DAILY ALLOWANCES (U.S. RDA)

	1 oz.	With ½ cup Skim Milk**
Protein	4	15
Vitamin A	*	4
Vitamin C	*	*
Thiamine	4	8
Riboflavin	*	10
Niacin	8	8
Calcium	*	15
Iron	8	8
Vitamin D	*	15
Phosphorus	10	25
Magnesium	10	15
Zinc	8	10
Copper	6	8

*Contains less than 2% of the U.S. RDA of these nutrients.
**Vitamins A & D fortified.
INGREDIENTS: 100% natural whole wheat and wheat bran.

Name of Object: _____

Clue: September is Better Breakfast Month. You look at me each morning. I give you information on vitamins and minerals. I can be found on a breakfast __ __ __ __ __ __ __ box.

78

Fall Frolics Cards

5 Fly High

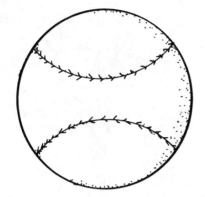

Name of Object: _____

Clue: Babe Ruth hit me for his 60th home run on September 30, 1927. Roger Maris hit me for his record-breaking 61st home run on October 1, 1961.

I am a __ __ __ __ __ __ __ __ .

6 Be a Friend

Name of Object: _____

Clue: I am often called a person's best friend. In September, a week's celebration is held in my honor.

I am a __ __ __ .

7 Spaced Out

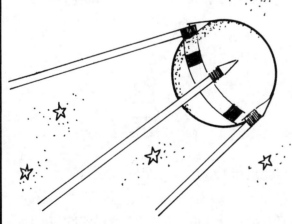

Name of Object: _____

Clue: On October 4, 1957, I was the first artificial satellite to orbit the earth. My name is

__ __ __ __ __ __ __ __ . I come from the country USSR (Russia).

8 Gentle Advice

Name of Object: _____

Clue: I am from the Bruin family, which means "bear." I signal the start of Fire Prevention Week. Find out the week in October when Fire Prevention Week occurs.

GA1150

Fall Frolics Cards

9 Faster Than Light

$$\begin{array}{ccc} e & e & q \\ u & a & l \\ s & m & c^2 \end{array}$$

Name of Object: _____

Clue: This scientific theory was discovered on October 17, 1933, by a refugee from Germany who *came* to the U.S. His name is

___ ___ ___ ___ ___

___ ___ ___ ___ ___ ___ ___ ___

The name of his theory is the theory of

___ ___ ___ ___ ___ ___ ___ ___ ___

10 Ageless Wonder

Name of Object: _____

Clue: My home is in the forest. People will honor me during National Forest Product Week in October. I am a ___ ___ ___ ___ and provide many useful products for people to use.

11 See the Light

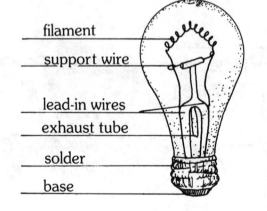

filament

support wire

lead-in wires

exhaust tube

solder

base

Name of Object: _____

Clue: On October 21, 1879, this object was first discovered by

T ___ ___ ___ ___ E ___ ___ ___ ___ ___

so we could see in the dark.

12 Expand Your Horizons

Name of Object: _____

Clue: I was born in the fall on October 24, 1632. I made this object which helps us to see small things that we've never seen before with the human eye. My name is

A ___ ___ ___ ___ ___ V ___ ___

L ___ ___ ___ ___ ___ ___ ___ ___ ___ ___

GA1150

Fall Frolics Cards

13 Breathe Deeply

Name of Object: _____

Clue: In the fall in October, we celebrate National Clean Air Month, a time to draw attention to efforts to keep our air clean. Smoke is a form of

__ __ __ __ __ __ __ __ __ .

14 Look to the Sky

Name of Object:

(1) C __ __ __ __ __ __

(2) P __ __ __ __ __ __

(3) L __ __ __ __ __ __

    D __ __ __ __ __ __

Clue: My name is the name given to a group of stars found in the fall sky. I am called a

(4) C __ __ __ __ __ __ __ __ __ __ __ .

15 Treat; Don't Trick

Name of Object: _____

Clue: In October, you will use me to celebrate a special day with treats. I am a __ __ __ __ __ __ __ __ .

My special day is called

__ __ __ __ __ __ __ __ __ __

16 Use Time Wisely

Name of Event: _____

Clue: In the fall, we sleep one hour more than we usually do. ST replaces DST.

ST is _____ _____ .

DST is _____ _____ _____ .

GA1150

Student Activity Page: Fall Frolics

Card Number	Extending Activity
1	Make a list of as many words that you can think of that have the word *fall* in them.
2	The camera is similar to the human eye. Find out how the cones in your eyes help you see beautiful fall colors.
3	Place an *x* on an analemma on a globe that shows the location of the sun on the first day of fall.
4	Make a list of vitamins and minerals eaten in one serving of breakfast cereal. Include the percentage of U.S. recommended daily allowances for each.
5	Hold flat piece of paper in front of mouth. Blow over top side of paper. Paper should lift upward or fly. The principle that causes an object to fly is Bernoulli's principle.
6	Write the name of your favorite type of dog on a picture of a doghouse. Then write a story about a time when you were "in the doghouse."
7	Research the topic "Space Travel: Artificial Satellites" in an encyclopedia. Name several satellites and the accomplishments of each.
8	Make a class poster that shows ways in which you can prevent fires. Show your poster to a fire fighter and then to members of your class.
9	Find out what each letter means in Einstein's $E = MC^2$ theory.
10	Count the number of annual rings in a log from a tree. Stick a pin in the yearly ring that represents your present age. Then find out how old the tree was when it was cut down.
11	Place a burned-out incandescent light bulb in a paper sack. Rap over table to break the bulb. Carefully remove parts. Trace the path of electricity through the light bulb. Find out what the little pieces of solder are for on every bulb.
12	A drop of water can act as a lens in a microscope. Lay a sheet of clear plastic or waxed paper over words in a newspaper. Place several drops of water on the plastic directly over letters on newspaper. Make a "before and after" drawing of what you see.
13	Pretend you are a molecule of air. Take a trip through your body. Be sure to identify the major organs in your body that you visit while on your trip. Describe what happens at each stop.
14	With a pencil, connect the stars in the "w" constellation. Name the constellation. Tell something about what the constellation represents.
15	Take a pumpkin seed apart. Find the seed coat, tiny plant and plant food. Tape a sample of each of these to a piece of cardboard and display in your room.
16	Count the number of hours you sleep in one week. Write a story about why our bodies need sleep. Find out what the letters *DST* and *ST* mean.

GA1150

Science Process Skill 6:
Hypothesizing and Predicting
Learning Activity Packet 12:
Sink or Float (p. 84)
Learning Activity Packet 13:
Batteries and Bulbs (p. 90)

H_o

Teacher/Parent Page

Learning Activity Packet 12: Sink or Float

Science Process Skill 6: Hypothesizing and Predicting

Purpose: To make predictions (guesses) based on data collected and then test the predictions made by using manipulative materials

Teaching Tips: As scientists, it is important for youngsters to make guesses or predictions about an intended outcome without fear of failure. Encourage youngsters to make guesses or predictions and thus learn from their trials and *original* mistakes. Stress how a vast amount of knowledge is gained as a result of making predictions and how many famous scientists use information gained from *wrong* predictions to make major discoveries. Sink or Float allows youngsters to gain such experiences. Make copies of the sixteen cards on the four pages for use in an activity center in your classroom. Laminate the cards. Teach youngsters how to use the cards. For nonreaders, have youngsters study the pictures carefully. With a nonpermanent marker, have youngsters circle an *S*, *F* or *SF* in the My Guess row on whether they feel the object will sink, float or both sink and float. Note: The words *top* and *bottom* or *up* and *down* can also be used. In a container filled with regular tap water, have youngsters place the object in the water and then circle the *S*, *SF* in the Try Out row. Have youngsters record whether their predictions were correct or incorrect by circling the C's or I's in the appropriate row. It is important to have youngsters first guess, try out and record their results much like a real scientist does. Emphasize that youngsters should do one card at a time and use the results from the first card to make a more accurate prediction for the second card. Emphasize that both correct and incorrect answers give scientists more information on which to base the next, more valid prediction. Use the student activity page on page 89 as an optional activity for youngsters who can read.

Special Tips: Encourage youngsters to make a system of two or more objects and predict whether the total system will sink or float.

Card Answers: (1) SF-debate, (2) S, (3) F, (4) SF-debate, (5) SF-debate, (6) S, (7) S, (8) F, (9) SF-debate, (10) F, (11) S, (12) F, (13) SF-debate, (14) SF-debate, (15) SF-debate, (16) your choice

Extending Source: Jerry DeBruin, *Young Scientists Explore the World of Water* (Carthage, IL: Good Apple, Inc., 1985).

GA1150

Sink or Float Cards

1. Apple	Sink (S)	Float (F)	Both Sink and Float (SF)
My Guess (prediction)	S	F	SF
Try Out (trial)	S	F	SF
Correct (record)	C	C	C
Incorrect (record)	I	I	I

2. Marble	Sink (S)	Float (F)	Both Sink and Float (SF)
My Guess (prediction)	S	F	SF
Try Out (trial)	S	F	SF
Correct (record)	C	C	C
Incorrect (record)	I	I	I

3. Styrofoam	Sink (S)	Float (F)	Both Sink and Float (SF)
My Guess (prediction)	S	F	SF
Try Out (trial)	S	F	SF
Correct (record)	C	C	C
Incorrect (record)	I	I	I

4. Wood	Sink (S)	Float (F)	Both Sink and Float (SF)
My Guess (prediction)	S	F	SF
Try Out (trial)	S	F	SF
Correct (record)	C	C	C
Incorrect (record)	I	I	I

GA1150

Sink or Float Cards

5. Soap	Sink (S)	Float (F)	Both Sink and Float (SF)
My Guess (prediction)	S	F	SF
Try Out (trial)	S	F	SF
Correct (record)	C	C	C
Incorrect (record)	I	I	I

6. Scissors	Sink (S)	Float (F)	Both Sink and Float (SF)
My Guess (prediction)	S	F	SF
Try Out (trial)	S	F	SF
Correct (record)	C	C	C
Incorrect (record)	I	I	I

7. Pins	Sink (S)	Float (F)	Both Sink and Float (SF)
My Guess (prediction)	S	F	SF
Try Out (trial)	S	F	SF
Correct (record)	C	C	C
Incorrect (record)	I	I	I

8. Pencil	Sink (S)	Float (F)	Both Sink and Float (SF)
My Guess (prediction)	S	F	SF
Try Out (trial)	S	F	SF
Correct (record)	C	C	C
Incorrect (record)	I	I	I

GA1150

Sink or Float Cards

9. Pen

	Sink (S)	Float (F)	Both Sink and Float (SF)
My Guess (prediction)	S	F	SF
Try Out (trial)	S	F	SF
Correct (record)	C	C	C
Incorrect (record)	I	I	I

10. Paper Cup

	Sink (S)	Float (F)	Both Sink and Float (SF)
My Guess (prediction)	S	F	SF
Try Out (trial)	S	F	SF
Correct (record)	C	C	C
Incorrect (record)	I	I	I

11. Eraser

	Sink (S)	Float (F)	Both Sink and Float (SF)
My Guess (prediction)	S	F	SF
Try Out (trial)	S	F	SF
Correct (record)	C	C	C
Incorrect (record)	I	I	I

12. Aluminum Foil

	Sink (S)	Float (F)	Both Sink and Float (SF)
My Guess (prediction)	S	F	SF
Try Out (trial)	S	F	SF
Correct (record)	C	C	C
Incorrect (record)	I	I	I

GA1150

Sink or Float Cards

13. Plastic Jar	Sink (S)	Float (F)	Both Sink and Float (SF)
My Guess (prediction)	S	F	SF
Try Out (trial)	S	F	SF
Correct (record)	C	C	C
Incorrect (record)	I	I	I

14. Ruler	Sink (S)	Float (F)	Both Sink and Float (SF)
My Guess (prediction)	S	F	SF
Try Out (trial)	S	F	SF
Correct (record)	C	C	C
Incorrect (record)	I	I	I

15. Paper Clip	Sink (S)	Float (F)	Both Sink and Float (SF)
My Guess (prediction)	S	F	SF
Try Out (trial)	S	F	SF
Correct (record)	C	C	C
Incorrect (record)	I	I	I

16. Your Choice	Sink (S)	Float (F)	Both Sink and Float (SF)
My Guess (prediction)	S	F	SF
Try Out (trial)	S	F	SF
Correct (record)	C	C	C
Incorrect (record)	I	I	I

GA1150

Name _____

Date _____

Student Activity Page: Sink or Float

Directions: Which of the objects will sink and which of the objects will float? Predict (guess), try out and then record your results. S = sink, F = float

Name of Object	Predict (guess) (S or F)	Try Out (trial) (S or F)	Correct or Incorrect (C or I)
1. Apple	_____	_____	_____
2. Marble	_____	_____	_____
3. Styrofoam	_____	_____	_____
4. Wood	_____	_____	_____
5. Soap	_____	_____	_____
6. Scissors	_____	_____	_____
7. Pins	_____	_____	_____
8. Pencil	_____	_____	_____
9. Pen	_____	_____	_____
10. Paper Cup	_____	_____	_____
11. Eraser	_____	_____	_____
12. Aluminum Foil	_____	_____	_____
13. Plastic Jar	_____	_____	_____
14. Ruler	_____	_____	_____
15. Paper Clip	_____	_____	_____
16. Your Choice:	_____	_____	_____

Number Correct _____

Number Incorrect _____

Percent Correct _____

Stumpers

1. Design an experiment in which you make a piece of Styrofoam sink.

2. Develop an experiment in which you can make a marble float.

3. Try placing objects in *salt* water. Do the objects float easier in salt water or regular tap water? Then try soapy water. Keep a record of your results in your science notebook.

4. Design an experiment that would show your friends that you can swim easier in salt water than in regular water.

89

GA1150

Teacher/Parent Page

Learning Activity Packet 13: Batteries and Bulbs

Science Process Skills: Hypothesizing and Predicting

Purpose: To make predictions based on data collected and then test the predictions that they have made

Teaching Tips: Hypotheses and predictions are inferences that have been improved upon by observation and testing. Youngsters need to learn that the more observations and tests that they do, the more valid their inferences will be. Make copies of the three pages of prediction cards. Laminate if possible. With erasable pens, have the youngsters try out their predictions. Youngsters circle whether it lit or didn't light and circle whether the results of their predictions were correct or incorrect. Tell youngsters they should use the data gathered from an initial trial to make a more valid prediction for the second trial. Stress also that a closed circuit is needed to make the bulb light and that metal must touch the bulb in two places, side and bottom, for this to occur.

Special Tip: Electric utilities will sometimes donate unused electrical wire, bulbs and dry cells for this activity.

Card Answers: (A) won't light, (B) will light, (C) will light, (D) won't light (debate), (E) will light, (F) won't light, (G) won't light (debate), (H) won't light, (I) won't light, (J) will light, (K) won't light, (L) will light, (M) won't light, (N) will light, (O) won't light (debate), (P) won't light

Student Activity Page Answers: Found in column 4 on page 94.

Extending Source: Jerry DeBruin, *Young Scientists Explore Electricity & Magnetism* (Carthage, IL: Good Apple, Inc., 1985).

GA1150

Batteries and Bulbs Cards

Scientists predict or guess when or how something might happen. You can do the same. Use dry cells, flashlight bulb and piece of wire to find out if the bulb will or won't light in each drawing below. Guess first by circling *will light* or *won't light*. Then try to light the bulb. Circle whether *it lit* or *didn't light*. Record your total score in the blanks on page 93.

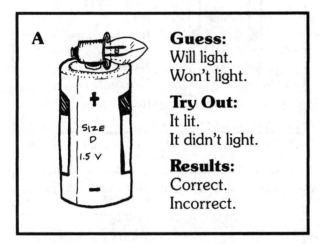

A

Guess:
Will light.
Won't light.

Try Out:
It lit.
It didn't light.

Results:
Correct.
Incorrect.

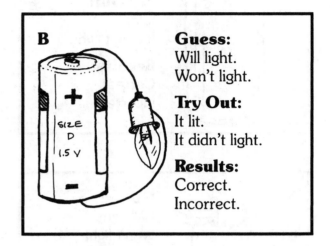

B

Guess:
Will light.
Won't light.

Try Out:
It lit.
It didn't light.

Results:
Correct.
Incorrect.

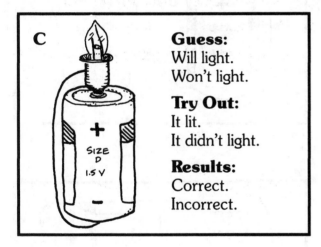

C

Guess:
Will light.
Won't light.

Try Out:
It lit.
It didn't light.

Results:
Correct.
Incorrect.

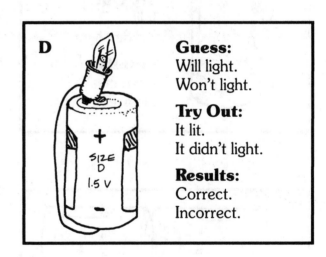

D

Guess:
Will light.
Won't light.

Try Out:
It lit.
It didn't light.

Results:
Correct.
Incorrect.

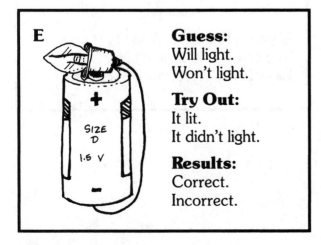

E

Guess:
Will light.
Won't light.

Try Out:
It lit.
It didn't light.

Results:
Correct.
Incorrect.

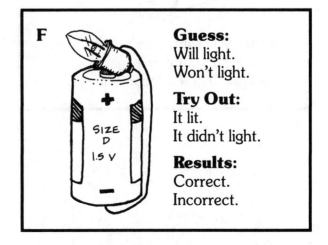

F

Guess:
Will light.
Won't light.

Try Out:
It lit.
It didn't light.

Results:
Correct.
Incorrect.

GA1150

Batteries and Bulbs Cards

G

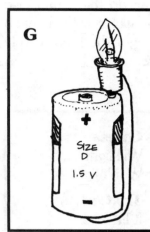

Guess:
Will light.
Won't light.

Try Out:
It lit.
It didn't light.

Results:
Correct.
Incorrect.

H

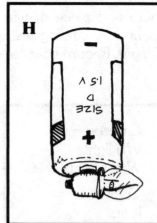

Guess:
Will light.
Won't light.

Try Out:
It lit.
It didn't light.

Results:
Correct.
Incorrect.

I

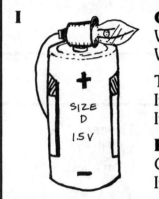

Guess:
Will light.
Won't light.

Try Out:
It lit.
It didn't light.

Results:
Correct.
Incorrect.

J

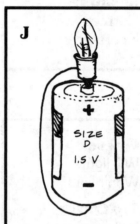

Guess:
Will light.
Won't light.

Try Out:
It lit.
It didn't light.

Results:
Correct.
Incorrect.

K

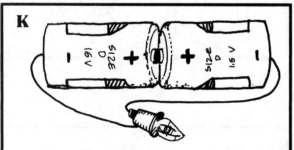

Guess: Will light. Won't light.
Try Out: It lit. It didn't light.
Results: Correct. Incorrect.

L

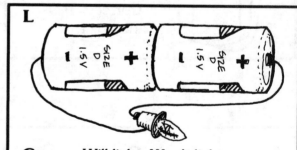

Guess: Will light. Won't light.
Try Out: It lit. It didn't light.
Results: Correct. Incorrect.

GA1150

Batteries and Bulbs Cards

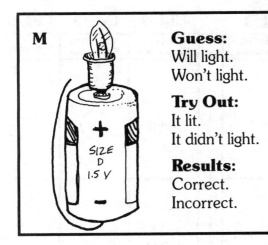

M

Guess:
Will light.
Won't light.

Try Out:
It lit.
It didn't light.

Results:
Correct.
Incorrect.

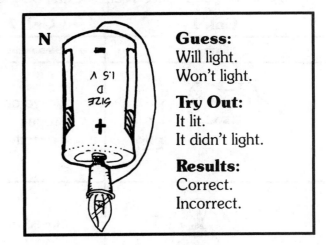

N

Guess:
Will light.
Won't light.

Try Out:
It lit.
It didn't light.

Results:
Correct.
Incorrect.

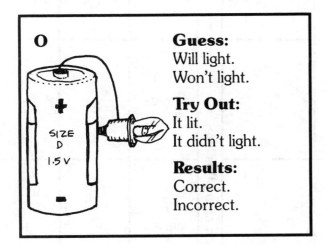

O

Guess:
Will light.
Won't light.

Try Out:
It lit.
It didn't light.

Results:
Correct.
Incorrect.

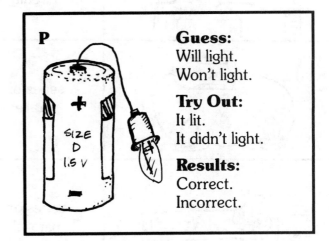

P

Guess:
Will light.
Won't light.

Try Out:
It lit.
It didn't light.

Results:
Correct.
Incorrect.

Number Correct: _____

Number Incorrect: _____

Percent Correct: _____

GA1150

Student Activity Page: Batteries and Bulbs

Fold page on dotted line. Observe the picture in column 1 at the left. Read the statement in column 2. Write your prediction in column 3. Unfold the page to see if your prediction was correct. Circle *C* if correct, *I* if incorrect. The first one is done for you.

Col. 1 Picture	Col. 2 Statement	Col. 3 Prediction (my guess)	Col. 4 Correct Response	Col. 5 Correct Response	Col. 6 Incorrect
	closed or open circuit	open	open	Ⓒ	I
	closed or open circuit		closed	C	I
	series or parallel		series	C	I
	series or parallel		series	C	I
	incandescent or fluorescent		fluor-escent	C	I
	dry cell or wet cell		wet cell	C	I
	magnetic or nonmagnetic		magnetic	C	I

Fold back along this line.

Science Process Skill 7: Experimenting

Learning Activity Packet 14: Pocket Card Science (p. 96)

Learning Activity Packet 15: Film Can Science (p. 103)

95

GA1150

Teacher/Parent Page

Learning Activity Packet 14: Pocket Card Science

Science Process Skill 7: Experimenting

Purpose: To describe how free and inexpensive materials can be used to involve youngsters in "hands-on" science activities and enhance the learning of major science concepts

Teaching Tips: Educators know that people learn most effectively by *doing* science, that is by manipulating and experimenting with materials. Pocket Card Science features sheets of pocket cards that, when duplicated and cut apart, make a convenient Pocketbook of Science that slips into a youngster's pocket. Make copies of the pages. Have youngsters cut out the sixteen pocket cards. The front (Pocket 1) and back (Pocket 16) covers of the Pocketbook can be mounted on cardboard, laminated and fastened together at the top with paper fasteners so pages can be flipped or new pages added at any time. The free and inexpensive materials needed to do the activities on the cards can be easily collected by you and your youngsters. Store all materials in a small sneaker box or hamburger container. Have youngsters complete Pocket Cards 1 and 16. Introduce Card 2. Inform youngsters that Pocket Card 2 features key words that will be encountered in the activities. Pocket Card 3 is a recording card for sketches and ideas. Card 4 provides space for the youngsters' very best ideas and experiments. Do card five together as a class. Youngsters should see happy face move inside the circle. Introduce word *parallax*. With both eyes open, have youngsters line up their index finger with a vertical line on the chalkboard. Have them close one eye, open both eyes, then close the other eye. The apparent shifting of the finger against the background is called parallax. Have youngsters do Cards 6-15 individually noting the results of their experiments on extra log pages.

Special Tip: A pocket-shaped carrying case for the pocket cards can be made from discarded items of clothing.

Card Answers: (1) completed card; (2) completed activity; (3) completed page; (4) completed page; (5) face moves in circle; (6) completed list, old woman, young woman; (7) completed experiment; (8) completed project; (9) Roy G. Biv represents colors of the visible spectrum; (10) completed page; (11) less cargo when soap added; (12) completed project; (13) completed project; (14) completed project; (15) completed project; (16) completed activity

Student Activity Page 2 Answers: Rocks: Igneous—Granite (F), Basalt (I), Obsidian (R), Diorite (E), Secret Word: FIRE. Sedimentary—Conglomerate (W), Sandstone (O,) Limestone (R), Shale (N), Secret Word: WORN. Metamorphic—Slate (H), Schist (E), Marble (A), Quartzite (T), Secret Word: HEAT

Extending Source: Jerry DeBruin, *Young Scientists Explore Rocks & Minerals* (Carthage, IL: Good Apple, Inc., 1986).

GA1150

Pocket Card Science Cards

(front cover)

My Pocketbook of Science

Name: _____

_____

School: _____

Address: _____

Phone: _____

Top Secret Science Dreams and Experiences

1

My Pocket Dictionary of Science Terms and Formulas

adhesion
buoyancy
center of gravity
cohesion
cones
constellation
lift

optical illusion
parallax
persistence of vision
rods
spectra
surface tension

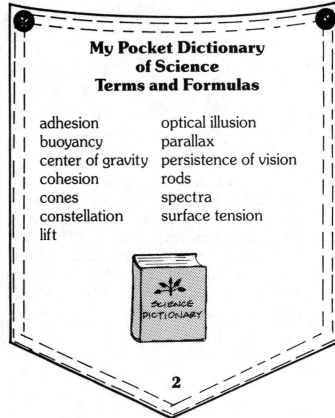

2

My Little Log of Science Sketches and Ideas

3

My Very Best Science Ideas and Experiments

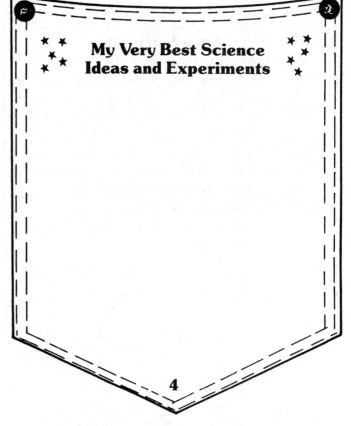

4

GA1150

Pocket Card Science Cards

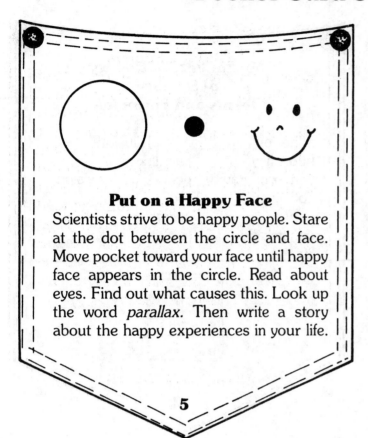

Put on a Happy Face

Scientists strive to be happy people. Stare at the dot between the circle and face. Move pocket toward your face until happy face appears in the circle. Read about eyes. Find out what causes this. Look up the word *parallax*. Then write a story about the happy experiences in your life.

5

The eyes sometimes trick you into seeing something that is really hidden or not like it really is. In your little log, make a list of all the things that you can see in the picture to the right. Then read about and make your own optical illusions.

A Picture Is Worth a Thousand Meanings

6

I Am a Scientist

With colored pens or crayons, color the designated area that shows the amount of liquid in the flask below. Stare at this liquid for forty-five seconds. Shift eyes to a white piece of paper or wall. What color liquid do you see? Can you change the color of the liquid back to its original color? Write a story about what you think causes the liquid to change colors. Be sure to look up information on rods and cones in your eyes.

7

Centering Gives Balance

Cut out three of these from single-layered cardboard. Glue together. Amaze your friends at how you can balance this and a belt on the tip of your finger. Write a story about how the center of gravity is important in athletics and in the design of automobiles.

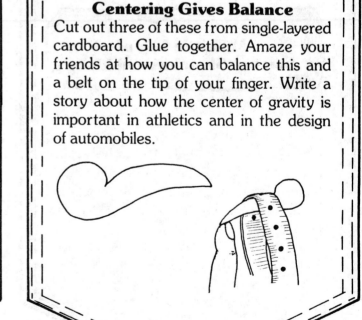

8

Pocket Card Science Cards

Bubble Blower

Save a pop top from a soda container and use as a bubble blower. Place several drops of dish soap in water in a small container. Dip pop top into solution. Blow bubbles. Carefully observe the size and color of each bubble. Name the colors in each bubble. Can you see Roy G. Biv in your bubbles?

9

A Sinking Feeling

Remove the center part of a plastic food coloring container by using a hammer and nail. Fill leftover container with mineral oil. Add one drop of food coloring. Put cap on. Observe the drop of food coloring. Time how long it takes the drop to go to the bottom. Turn upside down. What happens? Pretend that the drop of food coloring is actually a bathysphere and that you are its pilot. Describe your descent and ascent to the surface of the water in an ocean. Are you under pressure? Tell about your feelings in your log.

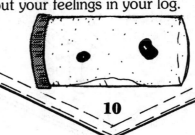

10

Buoyant Boat

Study how a boat floats and sinks with the use of a small sauce container from a fast food place. Put it in regular tap water. Add pennies for cargo. Count number of pennies before boat sinks. Sketch what the water looks like around edges of boat before boat sinks. Repeat. Add one drop of soap to water. Does the boat hold more cargo in regular water or soapy water? Make a sketch in your log book of each boat, its cargo and the areas surrounding each boat.

11

Motor Car Magic

Punch holes in ends of plastic film can acquired from a film processing center. Tie nut on rubber band and stretch through can. Tie knots on each end of rubber band or insert small nails or toothpicks. Roll motor car forward and backward. Write a story about your experiences.

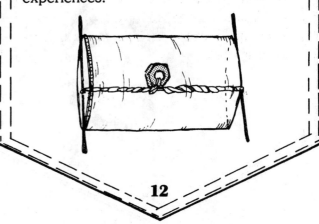

12

GA1150

Pocket Card Science Cards

Helicopter Hype

Cut out helicopter pattern and fold into helicopter. Drop helicopter from different heights. Time. Observe the direction of spin. Can you make the helicopter spin in the opposite direction? Tell someone about how you accomplished this task.

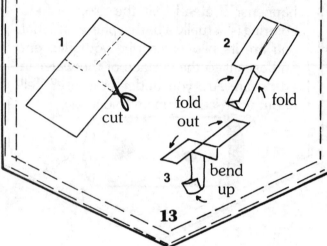

1 cut

2 fold fold

fold out

3 bend up

13

Constellation Viewer

Obtain black film containers from photo processing place. With a nail, punch holes in the bottom of the film can to represent your favorite constellation pattern. Look through the other end of film can toward light to view constellation. Write a story in your little log about the history of your constellation.

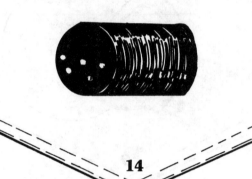

14

Science Puzzle

Cut out pieces on pocket below. Rearrange pieces to make completed picture. Mount on cardboard. Look up information on the next space shuttle flight and what it hopes to accomplish.

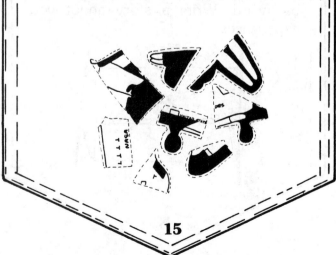

15

(back cover)

© By:

Name: _____

Address: _____

Copyright Registry Number: _____

All rights reserved. Author will share the contents of this publication with others if they take time to listen.

16

GA1150

Student Activity Page 1: Pocket Card Science

Here are drawings of three pockets that you can make to store the pictures of rocks on the next page. The pockets are named after the three main classes of rocks: igneous, sedimentary and metamorphic. Cut out each pocket. Fold on dark, solid lines. Glue to cardboard to make pocket card holder. Place matching pictures of rocks on the next page in correct pockets. Then go outside and pick your own pocketful of rocks to study.

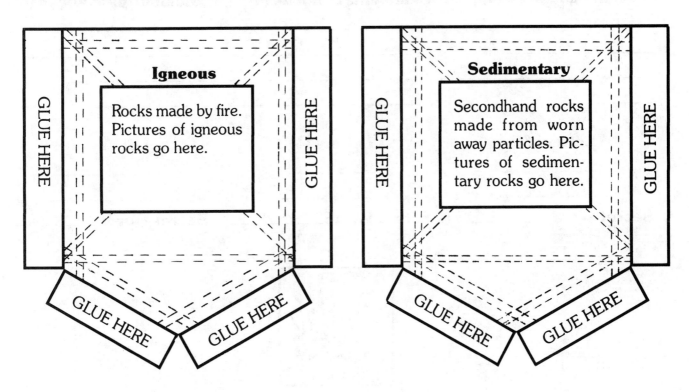

Igneous

Rocks made by fire. Pictures of igneous rocks go here.

GLUE HERE · GLUE HERE · GLUE HERE · GLUE HERE

Sedimentary

Secondhand rocks made from worn away particles. Pictures of sedimentary rocks go here.

GLUE HERE · GLUE HERE · GLUE HERE · GLUE HERE

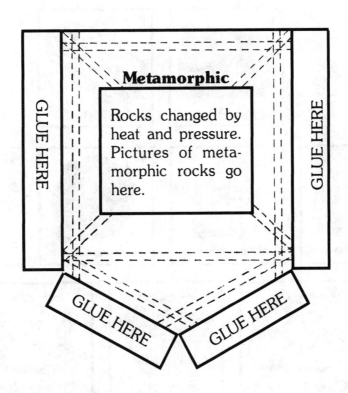

Metamorphic

Rocks changed by heat and pressure. Pictures of metamorphic rocks go here.

GLUE HERE · GLUE HERE · GLUE HERE · GLUE HERE

GA1150

Student Activity Page 2: Pocket Card Science

Collect and study the twelve rocks below. Then cut out each picture on this page. Place the picture in the correct pocket made from page 101. Rearrange the cards in each pocket so that the letters on each card, when placed in the correct order, will make a secret word that tells something about each class of rocks: igneous, sedimentary and metamorphic. Record these secret words in the blanks below.

Igneous Rocks (4)	**Sedimentary Rocks (4)**	**Metamorphic Rocks (4)**
_____	_____	_____
_____	_____	_____
_____	_____	_____
_____	_____	_____

Letters (4)	**Letters (4)**	**Letters (4)**
____ ____	____ ____	____ ____
____ ____	____ ____	____ ____

Secret Word:_____ **Secret Word:**_____ **Secret Word:**_____

A Marble

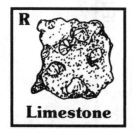
R Obsidian

N Shale

R Limestone

O Sandstone

I Basalt

H Slate

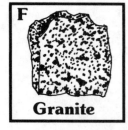
F Granite

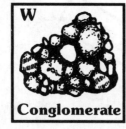
W Conglomerate

E Schist

T Quartzite

E Diorite

102

GA1150

Teacher/Parent Page

Learning Activity Packet 15: Film Can Science

Science Process 7: Experimenting

Purpose: To demonstrate how youngsters can make inexpensive science equipment and then actively participate in scientific investigations using such equipment

Teaching Tips: The development of skills in construction and experimentation is basic to the role that scientists play in society. This activity features the construction of simple science equipment and the use of such equipment in scientific experimentation featuring "hands-on" activities. You and your youngsters can make science equipment using 35 mm cans which can be acquired free from photo processing centers. Take a grocery bag or small box to such center and ask the manager to save the cans and any discarded 35 mm film for you. The cans often come in three types: black plastic cans with snap-on grey covers (U.S.), clear plastic cans with snap-on covers (usually foreign film available in U.S.) and silver-colored metal cans with screw-on lids. Make copies of the four pages of cards of film can science experiments for each youngster. Have youngsters cut out individual cards. If possible, laminate the cards. Give youngsters one film can. Do Card 1 on Student Activity Page together as a class noting different types of film cans. Have youngsters become actively involved in the remaining fifteen cards and record their responses on the Student Activity Page. Have the class make a book or deck of film can science experiments and add more cards as new experiments are discovered. Use as an individual, small group or large group activity.

Student Activity Page Answers: (1) three; (2) length of film is 66 mm, width of actual film is 35 mm, number of holes per side on actual 35 mm film is 8, weight (mass) of actual film can is 8 grams, height of actual film can is 50 mm, circumference of actual film can is 100 mm; (3) will vary; (4) length of stream is 45 mm; (5) will vary; (6) thicker rubber band will make can move faster and farther; (7) Cassiopeia; (8) foil moves together (Van de Graaff) (9) will vary; (10) The dam is thicker and stronger at the bottom because pressure is greatest where water is the deepest; (11) will vary; (12) will vary; (13) heavier; (14) pressure; (15) 3 volts; (16) arrow points in opposite direction—B

Extending Source: Send for a copy of "Photo Reports Make It Happen," Eastman Kodak Company, 343 State Street, Rochester, NY 14650.

Film Can Science Cards

Film Can Science   1

How many cans?

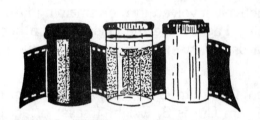

Metric Measurements   2

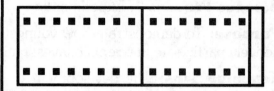

Directions: Fill in the blanks below.

The length of the film above is _____ mm.
The width of actual film is _____ mm.
Each complete negative of actual film has _____ holes on a side.
A film can weighs _____ grams.
The height of a film can is about _____ mm.
The circumference of a film can is about _____ mm.

½ actual size

Metric Film Can Weights 3

Weigh film can with cover on balance. Add sand to film can until can, cover and sand weigh 30 grams. Glue cover onto can. Have friend(s) guess the weight (mass) of film can in grams. Record results of your friends' guesses. Make other weights by adding different amounts of sand to film cans.

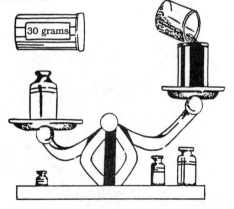

30 grams

Trundle Wheel   4

Scientists use a trundle wheel to measure the length of things like a stream. Measure distance around the film can. With a permanent marker, draw a line through the center of base of can. Place end of line on *start*. Roll can to *finish*. Find the length of the stream below by using your film can trundle wheel.

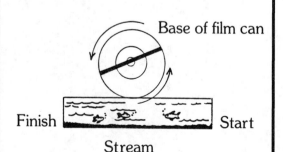

Base of film can

Finish   Start

Stream

GA1150

Film Can Science Cards

Can of Mysteries   5

Place penny, paper clip, washer or other similar objects in black film can. Secure cover. Ask your friends to guess what is inside the film can. After objects are identified, tell them a detective story which includes clues used to identify objects in the can.

Motor Car   6

Punch two holes in two lids and bottom of film can. Position lids on ends of can. Cut one end of a long rubber band and pass it through the four holes in a figure eight. Tie the cut ends of rubber band together. Tie nut or bolt to center of rubber band inside can. Glue lids in place to ends of film can. Roll can away from you and it will return faithfully to you. Try thicker rubber band.

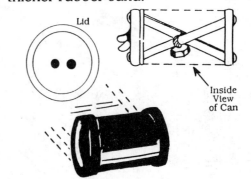

Lid

Inside View of Can

Constellation Viewer   7

With a nail or ice pick, punch holes in bottom of black film can that represents stars in your favorite constellation. Remove cover. Look through film can toward light to view constellation. Identify the constellation below. Write a story about the history of your constellation.

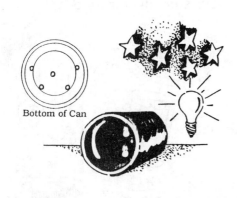

Bottom of Can

Electroscope   8

Straighten paper clip and bend one end into *L* shape. Place narrow folded piece of aluminum foil over *L*. Punch straight end of paper clip through cover of transparent film can. Snap on cover with paper clip to film can. Rub comb through hair and touch end of paper clip. What happens to foil? Find out about static electricity— both positive and negative charges.

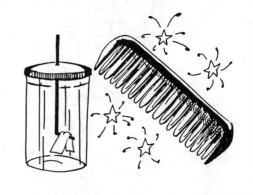

GA1150

Film Can Science Cards

Bathysphere 9

Fill transparent film can with mineral oil. Add one drop of food coloring. Place cap on tightly. Observe drop of food coloring. Time how long it takes the drop to go to the bottom. Turn upside down. What happens? Pretend the drop of food coloring is a bathysphere and you are its pilot. Describe your descent and ascent to surface of ocean. Find out about pressure and "the bends."

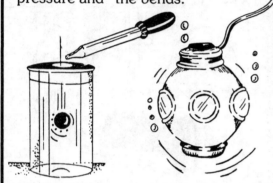

Water Pressure Dam 10

With paper punch, punch three holes at various levels in plastic film can as shown. Hold the can just far enough under a steady stream of water to keep it full. Measure or draw how far the water shoots out of each hole. Through which hole does water shoot the farthest? Why? Answer this question in your science log. Why is a dam which holds back river water thicker and stronger at the bottom?

Air Takes Up Space 11

Remove film can cover. Fill can half full with crumpled paper. Turn can upside down and firmly press film can into glass of water. Find out why the crumpled paper does not get wet. Make a list of other places where air takes up space.

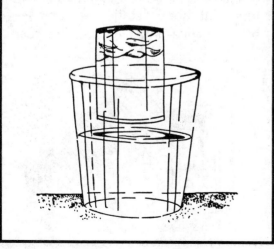

Growing Seeds 12

Remove cover from clear film can. Punch holes in bottom of film can. Glue cover to bottom of can. Pour enough water into film can to fill reservoir in film can cover. Add soil. Plant several marigold, grass or radish seeds in soil. Water lightly. Observe growth of roots, stems and leaves. Keep a record of your findings on your student activity page.

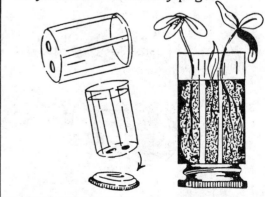

GA1150

Film Can Science Cards

Momentum Movers 13

Glue a film can cover to the bottom of each of two film cans. Fill one can with plaster of Paris. Leave the other can empty. Snap on covers. Roll cans down a ramp. Find out which one, the heavier or lighter, wins by traveling a greater distance. Make a record of your findings on your student activity page.

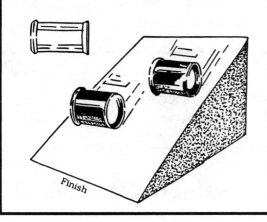

Under Pressure 14

Fill film can with water. Over a sink, place index card over top of film can. Turn film can upside down. What happens? Write a story that tells why the water stays in the can.

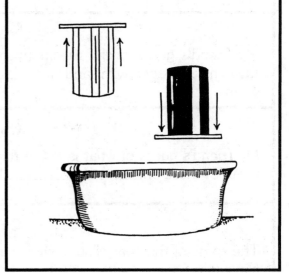

Film Can Flashlight 15

Take two film cans and place one on top of the other. The bottom can should not have a lid. With help from your teacher or parents, cut out bottom of top film can container as shown. With a pencil, punch hole in lid. Screw in light bulb. Punch two holes as shown for switch. Insert a paper fastener through each hole from the inside out. Attach one wire from top paper fastener to side of bulb, and tape another wire from bottom of C-size dry cell to the bottom paper fastener. Slip C-size dry cells into film cans. Touch paper fasteners together to make the bulb light. Make a drawing of what your flashlight looks like.

Which Way Now? 16

Draw an arrow on an index card as shown. Note direction in which arrow points. Fill clear film can with water. Stand card with arrow behind can. Look through can at arrow. In which direction does the arrow now point? Study how this experiment is like a camera, your eye or a mirror.

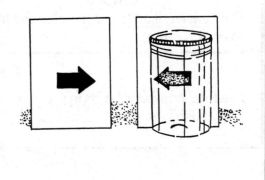

GA1150

Student Activity Page: Film Can Science

Record your answers in the boxes below after you have constructed your equipment and done your experiment.

Card 1

The number of film cans shown on Card 1 is _____.

Card 2

Length of film shown on Card 2 is _____ mm.
Width of actual film is _____ mm.
Number of holes per frame on one side is _____
Weight (mass) of film can is _____ grams.
Height of actual film can is _____ mm.
Circumference of actual film can is _____ mm.

Card 3

My friend's guess of the weight (mass) of the film can loaded with sand is _____ grams.

Card 4

The length of the stream is _____ mm.

Card 5

My friend's guess of what is inside the can includes these objects _____.

Card 6

The farthest distance that my wound-up film can car travels is _____ cm.

Card 7

The name of the constellation shown in the film can is _____.

Card 8

Name the generator that allows one's hair to stand up. _____

Card 9

The length of time that it takes the drop of food coloring to go from top to bottom is _____ seconds.

Card 10

Through which hole will water shoot out the farthest? _____

Card 11

List three places or things smaller than a film can where air takes up space. _____
_____

Card 12

The height of my tallest growing plant in the film can container is _____ cm.

Card 13

Circle one.
The <u>heavier</u>, <u>lighter</u> car traveled the farthest down the ramp.

Card 14

Air p __ __ __ __ __ __ __ on the card causes water to stay in the film can.

Card 15

The total number of volts in my two batteries in my flashlight is _____ volts.

Card 16

Circle the arrow below that shows which way the arrow points after you have done the experiment.   A ➡→   B ←◄

GA1150

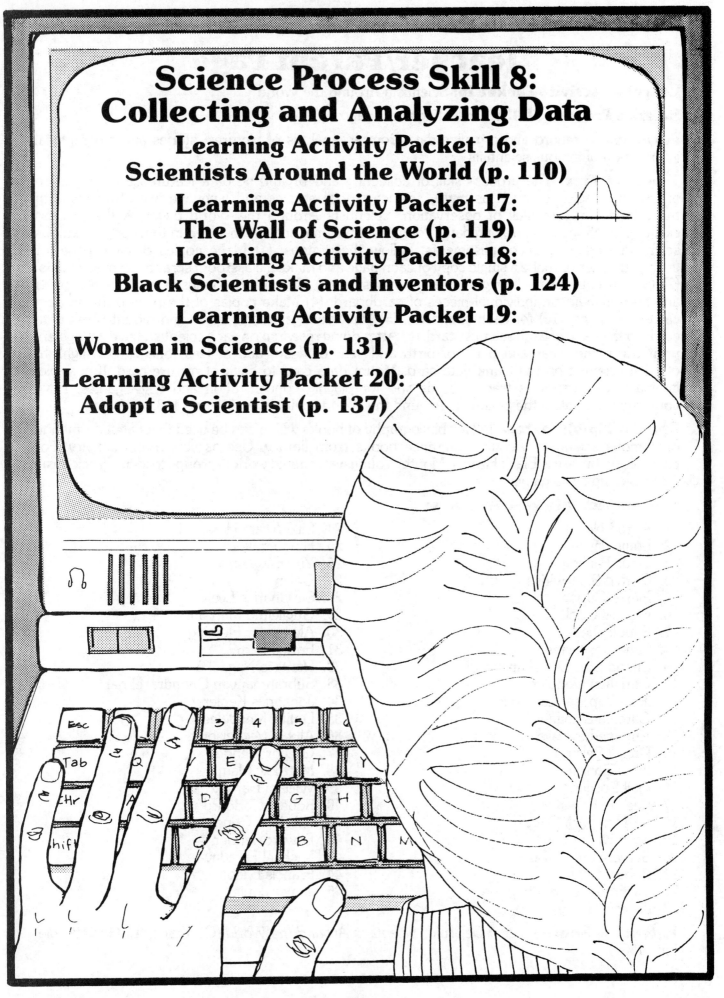

Science Process Skill 8: Collecting and Analyzing Data

GA1150

Teacher/Parent Page

Learning Activity Packet 16: Scientists Around the World

Science Process Skill 8: Collecting and Analyzing Data

Purpose: To record and organize data from an analysis of pictures, stories and biographical information of famous scientists

Teaching Tips: The process skill of collecting and organizing data features the integration of various disciplines such as math, science, social studies and language arts. Starting with the science process skill of observation, Scientists Around the World develops the process skill of collecting and analyzing data. Youngsters become actively involved in the study of famous scientists and their accomplishments. Follow these steps: (1) Make copies of each page for each youngster or make a single copy of each page and make a classroom scrapbook of scientists. (2) Give a copy of each page to each youngster. (3) Have each youngster cut out the cards and mount them on individual pieces of cardboard. (4) Make copies of the page of blank data cards (see page 116) for each youngster. (5) Have youngsters cut apart and mount blank data cards to the back of each scientist card. (6) After doing research on each scientist, have youngsters print the name, year and place of birth and year of death and at least one career highlight of each scientist on the blank data card. Mount data card to back of picture card. If possible, laminate. Use cards as trading cards and for playing concentration and trivia games. Have youngsters complete the Scientists Around the World trivia pages 117 and 118.

Special Tip(s): See page 142 for bibliography of books which can be used to locate information on famous scientists. Acquire reference books from library. Use as year-round activity. For example, February is Black History Month. Youngsters should work in groups to identify scientists and make up trivia games.

Student Activity Page Answers:

1. Alfred Nobel
2. Louis Pasteur
3. Linus Pauling
4. Gerald S. Hawkins
5. Pierre Curie
6. Francis Crick
7. Rudolf Diesel
8. René Descartes
9. Theodosius Dobzhansky
10. Christian Doppler
11. Jean Baptiste Lamarck
12. Carolus Linnaeus
13. Antoine Lavoisier
14. Daniel Bernoulli
15. Niels Bohr
16. Gail Borden
17. Lee De Forest
18. Sir Humphry Davy
19. John Dalton
20. Satyendranath Bose
21. Robert Boyle
22. Sir Frederick Banting
23. Joseph Henry
24. Sir William Herschel
25. Hippocrates
26. Yuri Gagarin
27. Galen
28. Sir Charles Lyell
29. Guglielmo Marconi
30. Alexander Fleming
31. Enrico Fermi
32. Hantaro Nagaoka
33. Subrahmanyan Chandrasekhar
34. Johannes Kepler
35. Dmitri Mendeleev
36. Albert Michelson
37. Gregor Mendel
38. Matthew Maury
39. William Harvey
40. Robert Goddard
41. Nicolaus Copernicus
42. Edward Jenner
43. Michael Faraday
44. Francis Bacon
45. James Joule

Extending Source: Jerry DeBruin, *Scientists Around the World* (Carthage, IL: Good Apple, Inc., 1987).

GA1150

Scientists Around the World Cards

Francis Bacon
1561-1626

Sir Frederick Banting
1891-1941

Daniel Bernoulli
1700-1782

Niels Bohr
1885-1962

Gail Borden
1801-1874

Satyendranath Bose
1894-1974

Robert Boyle
1627-1691

Subrahmanyan Chandrasekhar
1910-

Nicolaus Copernicus
1473-1543

GA1150

Scientists Around the World Cards

Francis Crick
1916-

Pierre Curie
1859-1906

John Dalton
1766-1844

Sir Humphry Davy
1778-1829

Lee De Forest
1873-1961

René Descartes
1596-1650

Rudolf Diesel
1858-1913

Theodosius Dobzhansky
1900-1975

Christian Doppler
1803-1853

GA1150

Scientists Around the World Cards

Michael Faraday
1791-1867

Enrico Fermi
1901-1954

Alexander Fleming
1881-1955

Yuri Gagarin
1934-1968

Galen
130-200

Robert Goddard
1882-1945

William Harvey
1578-1657

Gerald Hawkins
1928-

Joseph Henry
1797-1878

Scientists Around the World Cards

Sir William Herschel
1738-1822

Hippocrates
460 B.C.-377 B.C.

Edward Jenner
1749-1823

James Joule
1818-1889

Johannes Kepler
1571-1630

Jean Saptete Lamarck
1744-1829

Antoine Lavoisier
1743-1794

Carolus Linnaeus
1707-1778

Sir Charles Lyell
1797-1875

GA1150

Scientists Around the World Cards

Guglielmo Marconi
1874-1937

Matthew Maury
1806-1876

Gregor Mendel
1822-1884

Dmitri Mendeleev
1834-1907

Albert Michelson
1852-1931

Hantaro Nagaoka
1865-1950

Alfred Nobel
1833-1896

Louis Pasteur
1822-1895

Linus Pauling
1901-

GA1150

Scientists Around the World Blank Data Cards

Name _____

_____

Year of birth _____

Year of death _____

Place of birth _____

_____

Career highlights _____

_____

_____

_____

Name _____

_____

Year of birth _____

Year of death _____

Place of birth _____

_____

Career highlights _____

_____

_____

_____

Name _____

_____

Year of birth _____

Year of death _____

Place of birth _____

_____

Career highlights _____

_____

_____

_____

Name _____

_____

Year of birth _____

Year of death _____

Place of birth _____

_____

Career highlights _____

_____

_____

_____

Name _____

_____

Year of birth _____

Year of death _____

Place of birth _____

_____

Career highlights _____

_____

_____

_____

Name _____

_____

Year of birth _____

Year of death _____

Place of birth _____

_____

Career highlights _____

_____

_____

_____

Name _____

_____

Year of birth _____

Year of death _____

Place of birth _____

_____

Career highlights _____

_____

_____

_____

Name _____

_____

Year of birth _____

Year of death _____

Place of birth _____

_____

Career highlights _____

_____

_____

_____

Name _____

_____

Year of birth _____

Year of death _____

Place of birth _____

_____

Career highlights _____

_____

_____

_____

GA1150

Student Activity Pages: Scientists Around the World

Below are some statements about scientists. Read each carefully. Write the correct name of the scientist in the blank after each statement. Check your answers with the answer key. Then make up your own trivia questions.

1. I invented dynamite. I am _____

2. I prevented rabies in Joseph Meister, a boy bitten by a rabid dog. I am _____

3. I believe that vitamin C prevents and speeds up a person's recovery from a common cold. I am
_____

4. I am famous for my research studies on an ancient monument called Stonehenge in England. I am _____

5. I did a dangerous experiment when I put radium on my arm and got burned. The experiment did show, however, the tremendous energy in the atom. I am _____

6. I discovered the DNA molecule was a double helix. Thus, I named my house the Golden Helix. I am _____

7. I invented an automobile engine that does not have spark plugs. A fuel used in cars and trucks is named after me. I am _____

8. Because of ill health, I was often allowed to stay home from school and do my work in bed. I taught a Swedish ruler. This eventually led to my death. I am _____

9. I came to the United States from the Soviet Union. I like to study genes and how humans came into being. I am _____

10. I discovered a law that says the pitch of a sound gets higher as the source of the sound moves closer and lower as the source of the sound moves away. I am _____

11. I am a French naturalist who classified eight-legged spiders and six-legged insects. I used the terms *vertebrate* and *invertebrate* in my work. I am _____

12. I am known as the Little Botanist. I discovered a system for classifying living things. I am _____

13. I am known as the Father of Chemistry. I wrote the first chemical equation. I also showed that there are three states of matter: solid, liquid and gas. I am _____

14. I discovered how gases are made up of tiny particles. My principle is used to explain how airplanes fly and baseballs curve. I am _____

15. I worked with the hydrogen atom and learned that it gave off radiation. I won the first Atoms for Peace Award because I believed that nuclear energy should be used for peaceful purposes. I am
_____

16. I am famous for developing many instant foods that we have today including condensed milk, fruit juices and various beverages. I made evaporated milk, which was used by soldiers in the Civil War. I am _____

17. I am an American scientist interested in radio broadcasting. I made the first musical broadcast in history in 1910. I am _____

18. I studied gases and liked to breathe them into my lungs. I discovered a gas called laughing gas and had laughing gas parties for my friends. I am _____

19. I became a teacher at age 12. I was color-blind. I studied the weights of atoms and kept weather records for over fifty-seven years. I am _____

20. I am from India and like to work with numbers. I worked with Albert Einstein and studied tiny atomic particles. I am _____

21. I am often called the Father of Chemistry as I was the first chemist to collect a gas. I built my own air pump, vacuum pump and studied pressure with a J tube. I am _____

22. I am a Canadian physician who discovered insulin which is taken daily by millions of people who suffer from diabetes. I am _____

23. I got interested in science as a youngster by reading a science book. Later I built and measured the strength of an electromagnet. Eventually I became the first secretary of the Smithsonian Institution in Washington, D.C. I am _____

GA1150

24. My parents smuggled me from Germany to England. I became an astronomer and discovered the planet Uranus. I always thought that there were people on the moon and planets. I am _____.

25. I am often called the Father of Medicine because I began the first school of medicine. My name is used as an oath that medical doctors take even to this day. I am _____.

26. I am a Russian cosmonaut who became the first human to fly in space. I died in an airplane crash and the ashes from my body were placed in the Kremlin Wall in Moscow, Soviet Union. I am _____.

27. My nickname is Claudius. I like to work with the human body. I learned that muscles work in pairs. I was the first person to feel a pulse made by the beating heart and could tell if something was wrong with the person by feeling the pulse. I am _____.

28. I am called the Founder of Modern Geology. I love to study rocks, especially very old fossils. I believe changes on Earth occur very slowly. I am _____.

29. I invented the wireless telegraph. I sent the first telegraph message across the English Channel, then across the Atlantic Ocean from England to Newfoundland. I am _____.

30. I was born on a farm in Scotland. By doing an experiment on moldy bread, I discovered penicillin. I received the Nobel prize for medicine with two others in 1945. I am _____.

31. I am called the Father of the Atomic Pile. I produced the world's first nuclear chain reaction under the stands in a football stadium in 1942. I am _____.

32. I am from Japan and like to work with atoms. I compared the model of the atom with its electron shells to the planet Saturn and its rings. I am _____.

33. I am from India and like astronomy especially white dwarf stars. I found out that if a star gets bigger than the sun, it may blow up into a supernova. I am _____.

34. I was three years old when I got smallpox which crippled my hands and damaged my eyesight. I became an astronomer and liked to study how the planets moved. I wrote a science fiction story in the 1600's about a person who travels to the moon. My story came true over 300 years later when Neil Armstrong stepped on the surface of the moon. I am _____.

35. I am a Russian chemist. I designed the Periodic Table of Elements. Even though I did not know how to fly a balloon, I went up in one to take a picture of a solar eclipse. Luckily, I landed the balloon safely. I am _____.

36. I came to the United States from Germany at age 4. I went to the U.S. Naval Academy and was *good* at science but only *fair* at being a sailor. I studied and discovered how fast light travels. I am _____.

37. I became a priest at age 25. I am called the Father of Genetics because I worked with peas to study what characteristics are passed down to the next generation of peas. I am _____.

38. I am known as the Father of Oceanography. I study ocean winds and currents. I became lame in a stagecoach accident but overcame this handicap to become a fine scientist. I am _____.

39. I found out that the heart is a muscle that pushes blood throughout the body in a closed loop or curve. I also like to study how a chick grows inside an egg. I am _____.

40. I am known as the Father of the Space Age and the Father of Rocketry because of my work with rockets. In 1919, I wrote a story which told about sending a rocket to the moon. I earned over 200 patents for my works. I am _____.

41. I am from Poland and love astronomy. After many years, I discovered that the sun, not the earth, is the center of the universe. I am _____.

42. I discovered a vaccination against smallpox by putting smallpox vaccine into an 8-year-old boy, James Phipps. The boy did *not* get smallpox. My vaccine saved thousands of lives from the dreaded smallpox disease. I am _____.

43. As a youngster, I liked to read books which got me interested in electricity. Later I often did science lectures and experiments with youngsters at Christmas. I built the first electric generator and discovered lines of force in a magnet. I am _____.

44. I believe that the mind can discover truth and gain power over nature. I am _____.

45. I have a unit of work or energy named after me. I founded a law that says that energy used up in one form reappears in another form and is never lost. I am _____.

Teacher/Parent Page

Learning Activity Packet 17: The Wall of Science

Science Process Skill 8: Collecting and Analyzing Data

Purpose: To collect, record and analyze data by studying pictures of famous scientists and analyzing their accomplishments

Teaching Tips: This activity features portraits of twenty-seven famous scientists with matching name/contribution tags designated as bricks for the wall. In addition to using the cards as trading cards and for playing concentration and trivia exercises, these pages can be used by following these steps: (1) Make copies of each of the four pages for each youngster or one set of the four pages for a classroom wall of scientists. (2) Have youngsters glue or tape Tab B on page 121 to Tab A on page 120 and Tab D on page 122 to Tab C on page 121. By doing this, the wall of twenty-seven scientists will be made. (3) After doing research on each scientist, have youngsters cut out the matching brick for each scientist and tape or glue the correct brick under the picture of the matching scientist. If possible, laminate the wall for lasting durability. The wall can also be mounted on single-layered cardboard before lamination. In lieu of gluing or taping the brick to the wall, a small piece of magnetic tape can be placed on the reverse side of the brick and under the picture of the scientist. Youngsters can then select a magnetic brick and place it under the matching scientist. (The magnetic tape will hold the brick to the portrait.) Thus, the wall can be used over and over again. In addition, as youngsters use reference materials, have them design an experiment or make a drawing or cartoon which is related to the scientist's contribution. Visit The Wall of Science often.

Special Tip(s): Give youngsters clues as to the names and accomplishments of each scientist, for example, Edison (light bulb). When done correctly, the names on the wall are in alphabetical order ranging from Archimedes to Watson.

Card Answers: Page 120, Row 1: Archimedes, Isaac Asimov, Christiaan Barnard; Row 2: Luther Burbank, Thomas Edison, Henry Ford; Row 3: Benjamin Franklin, Galileo Galilei, John Glenn. Page 121, Row 1: Charles Goodyear, Samuel Morse, Sir Isaac Newton; Row 2: Joseph Priestley, Walter Reed, Wilhelm Konrad Roentgen; Row 3: Ernest Rutherford, Carl Sagan, Jonas Salk. Page 122, Row 1: Alan Shepard, Igor Sikorsky, Edward Teller; Row 2: Nikola Tesla, Benjamin Thompson, Anton van Leeuwenhoek; Row 3: Andres Vesalius, Alessandro Volta, James Watson

Extending Source: Jerry DeBruin, *Scientists Around the World* (Carthage, IL: Good Apple, Inc., 1987).

GA1150

The Wall of Science

GA1150

Tab A

The Wall of Science

GA1150

The Wall of Science

GA1150

The Wall of Science

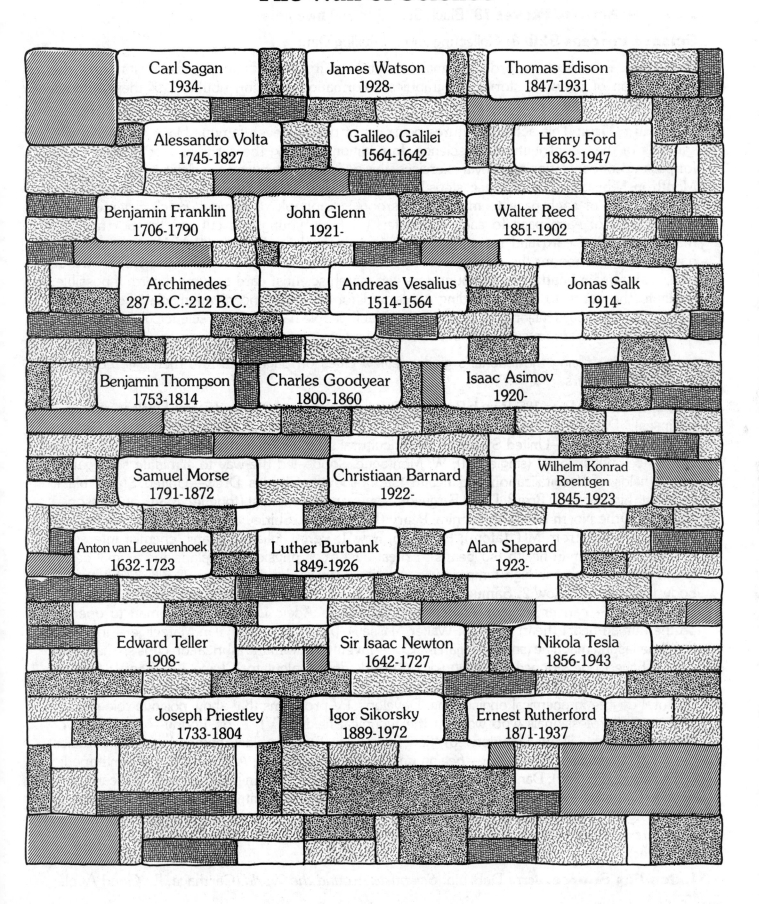

Carl Sagan
1934-

James Watson
1928-

Thomas Edison
1847-1931

Alessandro Volta
1745-1827

Galileo Galilei
1564-1642

Henry Ford
1863-1947

Benjamin Franklin
1706-1790

John Glenn
1921-

Walter Reed
1851-1902

Archimedes
287 B.C.-212 B.C.

Andreas Vesalius
1514-1564

Jonas Salk
1914-

Benjamin Thompson
1753-1814

Charles Goodyear
1800-1860

Isaac Asimov
1920-

Samuel Morse
1791-1872

Christiaan Barnard
1922-

Wilhelm Konrad
Roentgen
1845-1923

Anton van Leeuwenhoek
1632-1723

Luther Burbank
1849-1926

Alan Shepard
1923-

Edward Teller
1908-

Sir Isaac Newton
1642-1727

Nikola Tesla
1856-1943

Joseph Priestley
1733-1804

Igor Sikorsky
1889-1972

Ernest Rutherford
1871-1937

GA1150

Teacher/Parent Page

Learning Activity Packet 18: Black Scientists and Inventors

Science Process Skill 8: Collecting and Analyzing Data

Purpose: To collect, record and analyze data about famous minority scientists from the investigation of pictures, stories, biographical information and contributions of these famous scientists to science

Teaching Tips: This activity features portraits of twenty-seven famous black scientists with symbols of their contributions to science. In addition to using the cards as trading cards and for playing concentration and trivia exercises, this activity can be used to celebrate Black History Month in February. Follow these steps: (1) Make copies of each page for each youngster or make a copy of each page to make a classroom scrapbook of Famous Black Scientists. (2) Give a copy of each page to each youngster. (3) Have youngsters cut out the portrait and matching symbol card and mount each on single-layered cardboard. (4) Using tape or glue, have youngsters mount the symbol card to the reverse side of the matching scientist card or cards can remain unattached so youngsters can match scientist card to symbol card. If possible, laminate the cards to use as trading cards and for playing concentration, classification and trivia games. Discuss major contributions that black people have made to science. Add additional scientists to a classroom collection of minority scientists.

Special Tip: Using the teacher's guide, review clues on pages 128-130; then give copies of cards to youngsters.

Card Answers: Page 125, Row 1: Benjamin Banneker, important United States black astronomer (eclipses); David Blackwell—pioneer in the field of statistics (bell-shaped curve); George Washington Carver—United States black agricultural scientist (peanuts); Row 2: Jewel Plummer Cobb—cell physiologist (single cell); W. Montague Cobb—led the way to eliminate segregation in the fields of hospitalization and health (stethoscope); Charles Drew—United States black biologist (blood bank); Row 3: Lloyd Ferguson—outstanding chemist (tongue); Matthew Henson—discovered the North Pole with Admiral Peary (North Pole); Shirley Jackson—first black woman to receive Ph.D. from MIT (atom); Page 126, Row 1: Percy Julian—organic chemist interested in the field of human health (soybeans); Ernest Just—cell physiologist (plant and animal cells); Reatha King—expert in high temperature chemistry (three degrees above 98.6°F, 37°C) human body temperature; Row 2: Samuel Kountz—performed over 500 kidney transplants (kidneys); Lasalle Leffall—cancer surgeon (cancer symbol); Myra Adele Logan—first woman to operate on the human heart (heart); Row 3: Walter Massey—physicist (atom); Jan Matzeliger—invented the shoe-lasting machine (shoes); Elijah McCoy—invented automatic lubrication cups so machines do not have to be stopped for oiling (*oil* on upside-down calculator); Page 127, Row 1: Garrett Morgan—invented stoplight (stop sign); Jennie Patrick—first black woman in U.S. to earn a doctoral degree in chemical engineering. Develops TV programs that show positive role models of minority professionals who work in the technical fields (TV); Leon Roddy—identified over 600 spiders in his lifetime (spiderweb); Row 2: Charles Turner—black entomologist who studies bees, ants and wasps (calculator—*bee* on upside-down calculator); Augustus White—orthopedic spinal surgeon (spine); Daniel Williams—first successful pericardium heart surgery (pericardium); Row 3: Granville Woods—railroad signals. Wizard in railway communications (railway switch); Jane Wright—chemotherapist interested in a cure for cancer (cancer symbols); Louis Wright—first person to experiment with Aureomycin, an antibiotic for humans (more than 100 types of cancer)

Extending Source: Jerry DeBruin, *Scientists Around the World* (Carthage, IL: Good Apple, Inc., 1987).

GA1150

Black Scientists and Inventors Cards

Benjamin Banneker
1731-1806

David Blackwell
1919-

George Washington Carver
1864-1943

Jewel Plummer Cobb
1924-

W. Montague Cobb
1904-

Charles Drew
1904-1950

Lloyd Ferguson
1918-

Matthew Henson
1866-1955

Shirley Jackson
1946-

Black Scientists and Inventors Cards

Percy Julian 1899-1975	**Ernest Just** 1883-1941	**Reatha King** 1938-
Samuel Kountz 1930-1981	**Lasalle Leffall** 1930-	**Myra Adele Logan** 1908-1977
Walter Massey 1938-	**Jan Matzeliger** 1852-1889	**Elijah McCoy** 1844-1929

Black Scientists and Inventors Cards

Garrett Morgan
1877-1963

Jennie Patrick
1949-

Leon Roddy
1921-

Charles Turner
1861-1946

Augustus White
1936-

Daniel Williams
1856-1931

Granville Woods
1856-1910

Jane Wright
1919-

Louis Wright
1891-1952

GA1150

Black Scientists and Inventors Cards

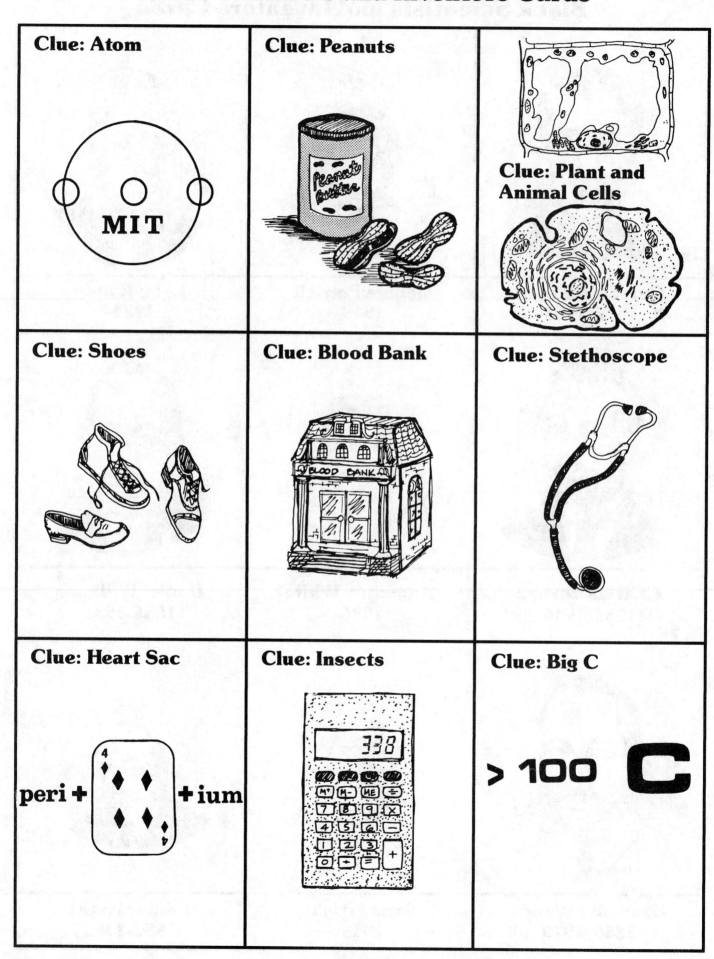

Clue: Atom

MIT

Clue: Peanuts

Peanut Butter

Clue: Plant and Animal Cells

Clue: Shoes

Clue: Blood Bank

BLOOD BANK

Clue: Stethoscope

Clue: Heart Sac

peri + 4 + ium

Clue: Insects

338

Clue: Big C

> 100 C

GA1150

Black Scientists and Inventors Cards

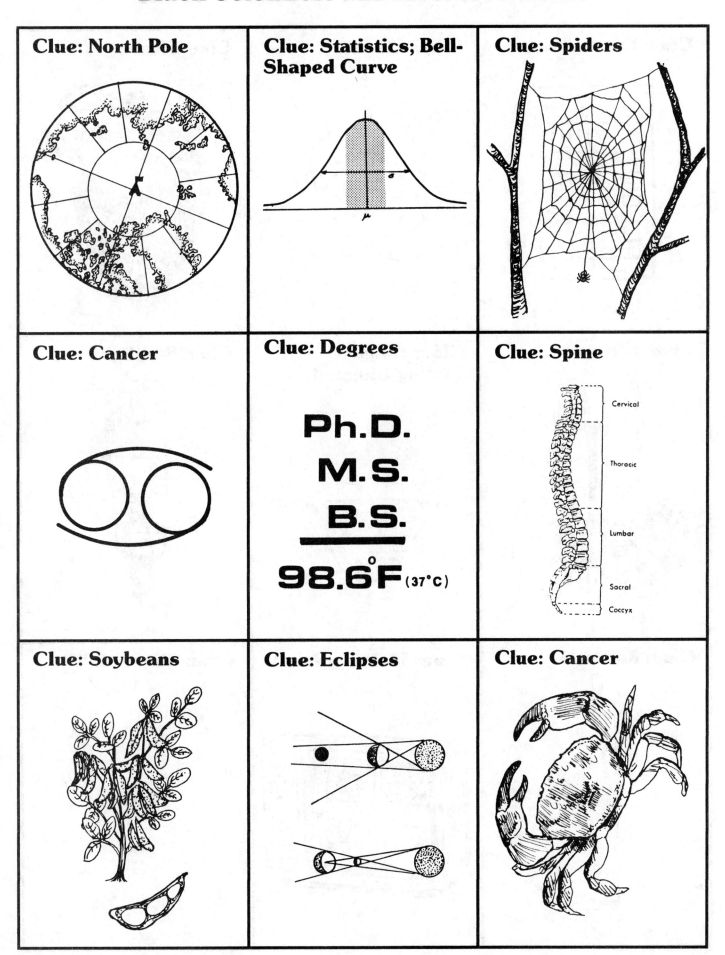

Clue: North Pole

Clue: Statistics; Bell-Shaped Curve

Clue: Spiders

Clue: Cancer

Clue: Degrees

Ph.D.
M.S.
B.S.
——————
98.6°F (37°C)

Clue: Spine

Cervical

Thoracic

Lumbar

Sacral

Coccyx

Clue: Soybeans

Clue: Eclipses

Clue: Cancer

GA1150

Black Scientists and Inventors Cards

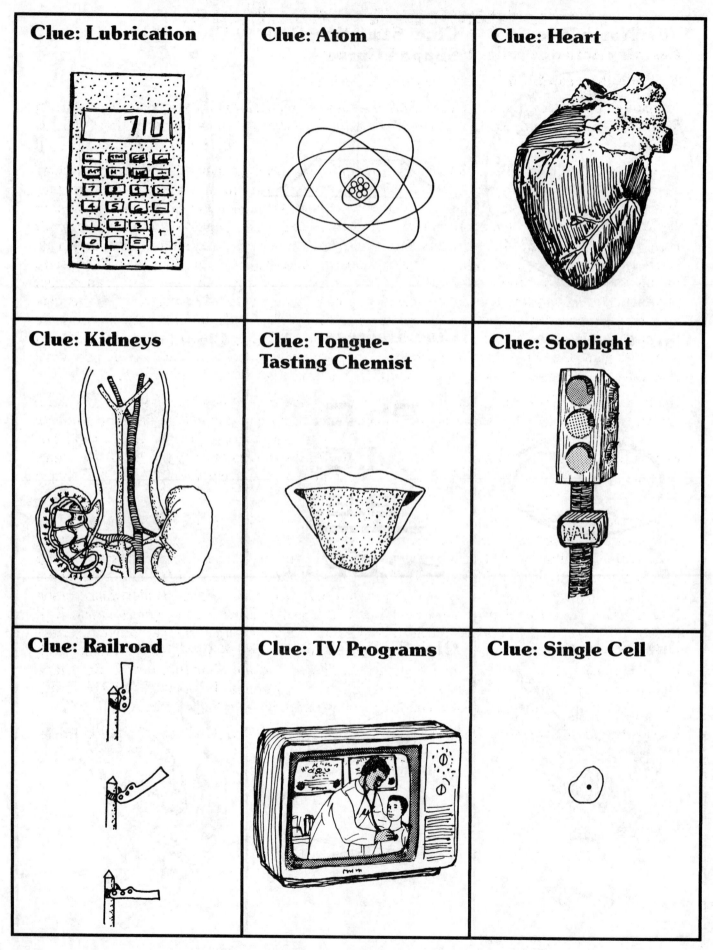

Clue: Lubrication

Clue: Atom

Clue: Heart

Clue: Kidneys

Clue: Tongue-Tasting Chemist

Clue: Stoplight

Clue: Railroad

Clue: TV Programs

Clue: Single Cell

GA1150

Teacher/Parent Page

Learning Activity Packet 19: Women in Science

Science Process Skill 8: Collecting and Analyzing Data

Purpose: To collect, record and analyze data about famous women scientists by analyzing pictures, stories, biographical information and contributions to science made by these famous women

Teaching Tips: This activity features portraits of twenty-seven women scientists with matching symbols or messages of their contributions to science. Follow these steps: (1) Make copies of each page for each youngster or make a single copy of each page to be used as a classroom scrapbook of Famous Women Scientists. (2) Give copies of the pages to the youngsters. (3) Have youngsters cut out the portraits and matching symbol cards, and mount these on single-layered cardboard such as oaktag or poster board. (4) Using tape or glue, have youngsters mount the matching symbol card to the reverse side of the scientist card, or cards can remain unattached so youngsters can match scientist card to symbol card. (The portraits of scientists and their symbols can be mounted on pizza wheels for a class collection.) If possible, laminate the cards which can then be used as trading cards or for playing concentration, classification and trivia games. Discuss major contributions that women have made to science. Add additional scientists to a classroom collection of women scientists as study is extended further.

Special Tip(s): (1) Review clues on page 135 before introducing activity cards to youngsters. Assign two youngsters to work as a team to investigate a single scientist, then have the students report on their findings to the class. Optional: Use activity as a total class activity. (2) For information on how to promote the concept of sex equity in education, write to the Women's Educational Equity Act (WEEA) Publishing Center, Education Development Center, 55 Chapel St., Suite 200, Newton, MA 02160.

Card Answers: Page 132, Row 1: Jacqueline Auriol (I'd Rather Be Flying; It's Safer), Clara Barton (Red Cross symbol), Mary Ann Bickerdyke (herbal tea); Row 2: Elizabeth Blackwell (Ms. Women of the Year), Rachel Fuller Brown (mushroom), Rachel Carson (postage stamp of the environment); Row 3: Edith Cavell (YORC postage stamp), Marie Curie (radium), Genevieve De Galard (beaver); Page 133, Row 1: Amelia Earhart (airplane), Gladys Anderson Emerson (nutritionist), Alice Hamilton (Safety First); Row 2: Dorothy Crawford Hodgkin (vitamin B_{12}), Elizabeth Kenny (muscles), Maria Mayer (energy); Row 3: Barbara McClintock (jumping genes), Margaret Mead (banner of man), Sylvia Earle Mead (diver); Page 134: Lise Meitner (radioactive), Maria Mitchell (telescope), Florence Nightingale (Blessed Are the Merciful); Row 2: Sally Ride (space shuttle), Princess Tsahai H. Selassie (Ethiopia), Valentina Tereshkova (USAF-USSR); Row 3: Lillian Wald (nurse), Chien-Shiung Wu (cobalt-beta), Rosalyn Yalow (message)

Extending Source: Jerry DeBruin, *Scientists Around the World* (Carthage, IL: Good Apple, Inc., 1987).

GA1150

Women in Science Cards

Jacqueline Auriol
1917-

Clara Barton
1821-1912

Mary Ann Bickerdyke
1817-1901

Elizabeth Blackwell
1821-1910

Rachel Fuller Brown
1898-1980

Rachel Carson
1907-1964

Edith Cavell
1865-1915

Marie Curie
1867-1934

Genevieve De Galard
1925-

GA1150

Women in Science Cards

Amelia Earhart
1898-1937(?)

Gladys Anderson Emerson
1903-1986

Alice Hamilton
1869-1970

Dorothy Crawford Hodgkin
1910-

Elizabeth Kenny
1886-1952

Maria Mayer
1906-1972

Barbara McClintock
1902-

Margaret Mead
1901-1978

Sylvia Earle Mead
1935-

Women in Science Cards

Lise Meitner
1878-1968

Maria Mitchell
1818-1889

Florence Nightingale
1820-1910

Sally Ride
1951-

Princess Tsahai H. Selassie
1919-1942

Valentina Tereshkova
1937-

Lillian Wald
1867-1940

Chien-Shiung Wu
1912-

Rosalyn Yalow
1921-

GA1150

Women in Science Cards

CAUTION:
Wear goggles!

YORC

Volunteer
lend a hand

USA 20c

Personal Message from Rosalyn Yalow

"I'm a scientist because even at this stage I love investigation. Even after the Nobel prize, the biggest thrill is to go to my laboratory and hope that day I will know something nobody ever knew before. There are very few days when it happens, but the dream is still there. That's what it means to be an investigator."

Sincerely,

Rosalyn S. Yalow

Ms.
WOMEN
OF
THE
YEAR

HERBAL TEA

COBALT
NUCLEI

BETA
PARTICLE

I'D RATHER
BE FLYING;
IT'S SAFER

Radium

1 2 3 (Y) 4 5 6 7 8 (X) 9 10

GA1150

Student Activity Page:
Women in Science

In the box at the bottom of the page, design a bumper sticker that would show how women have made efforts to obtain equal rights. Here are two such bumper stickers to get you started on your task.

  The Best Man for the Job Is a Woman

  A Woman's Place Is in the House . . . and the Senate

136

GA1150

Teacher/Parent Page

Learning Activity Packet 20: Adopt a Scientist

Science Process Skill 8: Collecting and Analyzing Data

Purpose: To collect, record and analyze data in booklet form about famous scientists by analyzing pictures and symbols of contributions made by these famous scientists to science

Teaching Tips: This activity features twelve mini booklets of famous scientists. The booklets include portraits of the scientists and a matching picture of each scientist's contribution to science. Follow these steps: (1) Make copies of each booklet for each youngster. Consider making one complete set for the class as a class scrapbook of scientists. (2) Have youngsters cut out each booklet on the solid, black lines. (3) Have youngsters fold each booklet on the dotted lines with the name and portrait of each scientist on the *front* cover of the booklets. (4) Make copies of the matching symbol card for what that scientist is famous. (5) Have youngsters mount the symbol card to the *back* cover of the matching booklet. (6) Open the booklets and have youngsters print pertinent information about the scientists inside the booklets as pages are needed. Extend activity by having youngsters do science fair projects based on the works of their famous scientists.

Special Tip(s): Before beginning this activity, alert the school librarian that youngsters will be searching for information on famous scientists, some of which are *not* found in encyclopedias. *National Geographic* can be used for such scientists as Eugenie Clark. Correlate this activity with Learning Activity Packet 42, Library Science Cards, found on pages 304-309.

Booklet Answers: Page 138: Neil Armstrong (man on moon), John J. Audubon (bird), Alexander Graham Bell (telephone), Eugenie Clark (shark); Page 139: Charles Darwin (monkeys), Albert Einstein ($E = MC^2$), Susan Picotte (feather in headband), Florence Sabin (I thank you for not smoking); Page 140: Orville Wright (airplane), Wilbur Wright (bicycle), Chen Ning Yang (mirror message), Hideki Yukawa (K capture)

Extending Source: Jerry DeBruin, *Scientists Around the World* (Carthage, IL: Good Apple, Inc., 1987).

 GA1150

Adopt a Scientist Booklets

Neil Armstrong
1930-

John J. Audubon
1785-1851

Alexander Graham Bell
1847-1922

Eugenie Clark
1922-

138

Adopt a Scientist Booklets

Charles Darwin
1809-1882

Albert Einstein
1879-1955

Susan Picotte
1865-1915

Florence Sabin
1871-1953

Adopt a Scientist Booklets

Orville Wright
1871-1948

Wilbur Wright
1867-1912

Chen Ning Yang
1922-

Hideki Yukawa
1907-1981

140

Adopt a Scientist Booklets

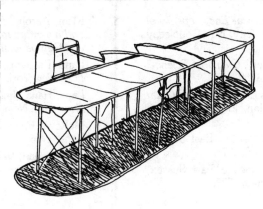

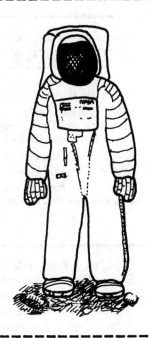

Dear Yang,
We love you
and are proud
of you. Hope
you have a
good day at
school.
Love,
Mom & Dad

Dear Yang,
We love you
and are proud
of you. Hope
you have a
good day at
school.
Love,
Mom & Dad

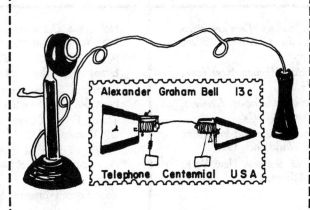

Alexander Graham Bell   13c

Telephone Centennial USA

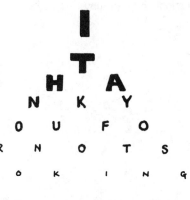

I
T
H   A
N   K   Y
O   U   F   O
R   N   O   T   S
M   O   K   I   N   G

$E = MC^2$

GA1150

Wild Card Scientists Bibliography

Asimov, Isaac. *Asimov's Biographical Encyclopedia of Science and Technology.* Garden City, NY: Doubleday and Company, Inc., 1982.

Cane, Philip and Samuel Nisenson. *Giants of Science.* New York: Grossett and Dunlap, 1959.

Clark, Donald. *The How It Works Encyclopedia of Great Inventors and Discoveries.* London, England: Marshall Cavendish Books Limited, 1978.

Clark, Paul. *Famous Names in Medicine.* East Sussex, England: Wayland Publishers Limited, 1978.

_____ *Famous Names in Science.* East Sussex, England: Wayland Publishers Limited, 1979.

Clark, Paul. *Famous Names in Space Exploration.* East Sussex, England: Wayland Publishers Limited, 1978.

Crichlow, Ernest. *Exceptional Black Scientists.* Ardsley, NY: Ciba-Geigy Corp., Ardsley, NY 10502.

DeBruin, Jerry. *Scientists Around the World.* Carthage, IL: Good Apple, Inc., 1987.

Feldman, Anthony and Peter Ford. *Scientists and Inventors.* London, England: Alous Books Limited, New York: Facts on File, 1979.

Giscard de'Estaing, Valerie-Anne. *The World Almanac Book of Inventions.* New York: Ballantine Books, a Division of Random House, 1985.

Graves, Curtis M. and Jane A. Hodges. *Famous Black Americans: Folder Games for the Classroom.* Silver Spring, MD: Bartleby Press, 1986.

Gridley, Marion E. *American Indian Women.* New York, NY: Hawthorn Books, Inc., 1974.

_____ *Contemporary American Indian Leaders.* New York: Dodd, Mead and Company, 1972.

Haber, Louis. *Black Pioneers of Science and Invention.* New York: Harcourt, Brace and World, Inc., 1970.

_____ *Women Pioneers of Science.* New York: Harcourt Brace Jovanovich Publishers, 1979.

Hayden, Robert C. *Eight Black American Inventors.* Reading, Mass: Addison-Wesley Publishing Co., 1972.

_____ *Seven Black American Scientists.* Reading, Mass: Addison-Wesley Publishing Co., 1970.

Hume, Ruth. *Great Women of Medicine.* New York: Random House, 1964.

Jenkins, Edward S. et al. *American Black Scientists and Inventors.* Washington: National Science Teachers Association, 1975.

Johnston, Johanna. *They Led the Way.* New York: Scholastic, Inc., 1973.

Klein, Aaron E. *Hidden Contributors: Black Scientists and Inventors in America.* Garden City, NY: Doubleday and Company, Inc., 1971.

Land, Barbara. *The New Explorers (Women in Antarctica).* New York: Dodd, Mead and Company, 1981.

Lane, Hana Umlauf. *The World Almanac Book of Who.* New York: Newspaper Enterprise Assocation, Inc., 1980.

McKown, Robin. *Heroic Nurses.* New York: G.P. Putnam's Sons, 1966.

McLenighan, Valjean. *Women and Science.* Milwaukee: Raintree Publishers, 1979.

Marzell, Ernst S. *Great Inventions.* Minneapolis: Lerner Publications Company, 1973.

Millard, Anne. *The Osborne Book of World History.* London, England: Osborne Publishing Ltd., 1985.

Newton, Clarke. *Famous Pioneers in Space.* New York: Dodd, Mead and Company, 1963.

Newton, David E. *Black Scientists.* Portland, Maine: J. Weston Walch Publishers, 1970.

Nisenson, Samuel and William A. Dewitt. *Illustrated Minute Biographies.* New York: Grossett and Dunlap, 1953.

Noble, Iris. *Contemporary Women Scientists of America.* New York: Messner Publishers, 1979.

Posin, Dan Q. *Dr. Posin's Giants: Men of Science.* Evanston, IL: Row, Peterson and Company, 1961.

Simmons, Sanford. *Great Men of Science.* New York: Hart Book Company, Inc., 1955.

Tharp, Edgar. *Giants of Invention.* New York: Grossett and Dunlap, 1971.

Toppin, Edgar. *A Biographical History of Blacks in America Since 1528.* New York: David McKay Company, 1971.

Yost, Edna. *Women of Modern Science.* New York: Dodd, 1959.

Your Choice: Additional Bibliography

GA1150

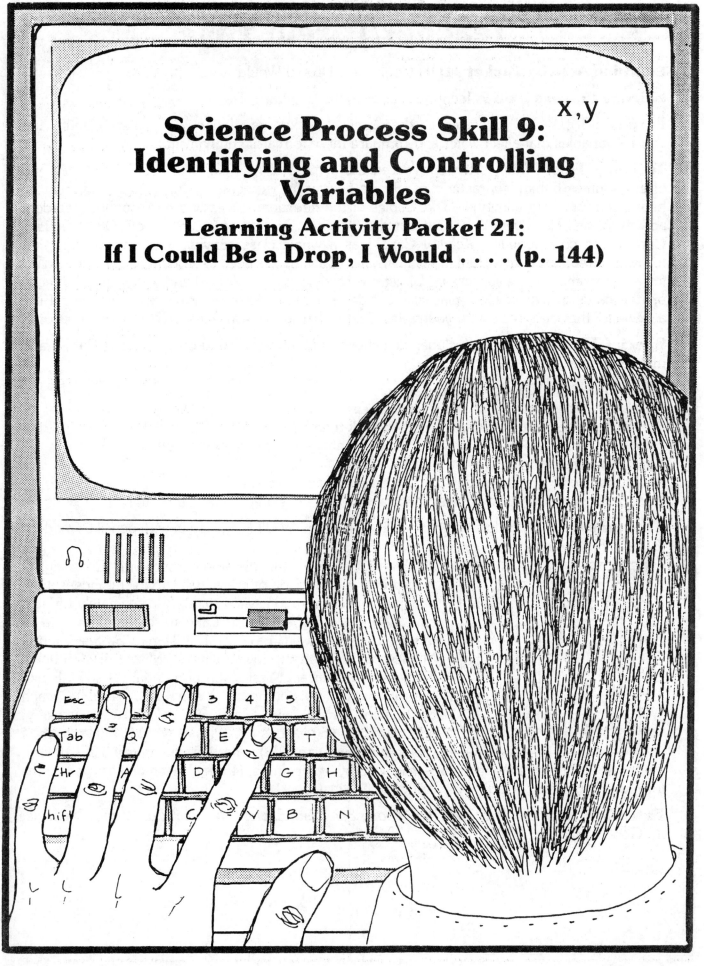

Science Process Skill 9:
Identifying and Controlling
Variables

Learning Activity Packet 21:
If I Could Be a Drop, I Would . . . . (p. 144)

x,y

Teacher/Parent Page

Learning Activity Packet 21: If I Could Be a Drop, I Would . . . .

Science Process Skill 9: Identifying and Controlling Variables

Purpose: To involve youngsters in the process of experimentation. Youngsters identify and control variables that affect water and compare these to real-life human situations.

Teaching Tips: Water, often considered the symbol of new life, is a necessity for life and often assumes human characteristics. Stress how water is necessary for growth and must be kept clean for life to continue. Make copies of the directions pages and corresponding student activity pages. Have youngsters cut out the 32 cards, 16 sets of 2 cards each. Do Directions Card 1 and corresponding Activity Card 1 as a whole class activity. Teach youngsters that following directions is important to scientists and that variables need to be identified and controlled for an experiment to be successful. Directions cards can be laminated and water placed directly on the cards in lieu of clear plastic. Consider making a book of water activities. Hopefully, a new life, that of a dedicated, young, budding scientist, will evolve as a result of your efforts.

Special Tip: The following includes definitions of key words found on Directions Card 4 and matching Activity Card 4.

Definitions for Words on Card 4:

Adhesion: Physical attraction of two substances
Bonds: A substance that causes objects to stick together
Cohesion: Mutual attraction by which the elements of a body are held together
Hard: Firm, resistant to pressure
Molecules: Configuration made up of atomic nuclei and electrons
Surface Tension: Cohesive force near surface of a liquid; skin-like effect on water

Card Answers: (1) Follow Directions; (2) The letters WATER shaded in with pencil or marker; (3) H_2O, H = hydrogen, O = oxygen, 23, 8, 15, 23;

4.

(5) B = SOAP, will vary; (6) A = barbed wire, B = twig, C = eyedropper, D = blade of grass, will vary; (7) condensation, precipitation, evaporation, will vary; (8) Approximately 1.5" (3.8 cm) 2348 mi. (3799 km) from Lake Itasca in Minnesota to mouth of Southwest Pass in Louisiana. States include Minnesota, Wisconsin, Iowa, Illinois, Missouri, Kentucky, Tennessee, Arkansas, Mississippi, Louisiana; (9) solid, liquid, gas, will vary; (10) southeast, 9 squares crossed to reach destination (H10), will vary; (11) Use water wisely. approximately 650 gallons (2470 l) per year; (54 gal. per mo.) (12) answers will vary; (13) water, approximately 2.0" (5.0 cm), 8 glasses; (14) Letters on penny are magnified by water drops; (15) hydrogen and oxygen atoms form water molecule colored blue, will vary; (16) water

Extending Source: Jerry DeBruin, *Young Scientists Explore the World of Water* (Carthage, IL: Good Apple, Inc., 1986).

Directions Cards: If I Could Be a Drop, I Would . . . .

1. Follow Directions:

Do activities and record results. Cut out each of the 16 directions and activity cards. Carefully read and follow the directions on the directions cards. Write your answers on the cards. Then cover each card with clear see-through plastic or slip each card into a small clear plastic bag. With an eyedropper and water, do the activities on the 16 cards found on the student activity pages. Mount activity cards to the back of the directions cards. Identify and control things that change water and you. Use often to discover the secrets that lie deep within water and yourself. Be sure to do Activity 1 found on the student activity page on page 146.

2. Identify Myself

Directions: With a pencil, shade in the letters and discover your name. Then cover this card with clear plastic. Do Activity 2 found on the student activity page on page 146.

3. Symbolize Myself

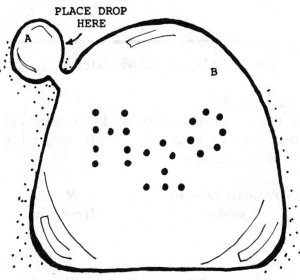

PLACE DROP HERE

Directions: With a pencil connect the dots and discover your symbol. Then cover this card with clear plastic or place card in small clear plastic bag. Do Activity 3 on the student activity page on page 146.

4. Identify Some of My Strengths

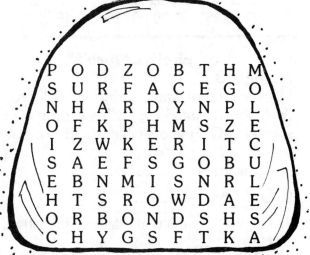

```
P O D Z O B T H M
S U R F A C E G O
N H A R D Y N P L
O F K P H M S Z E
I Z W K E R I T C
S A E F S G O B U
E B N M I S N R L
H T S R O W D A E
O R B O N D S H S
C H Y G S F T K A
```

Directions: Circle the words that describe my strengths: hard, molecules, bonds, adhesion, cohesion, surface tension. Cover this card with clear plastic or place card in small clear plastic bag. Do Activity 4 on the student activity page on page 146.

GA1150

Student Activity Page: If I Could Be a Drop, I Would . . . .
Activity Cards

Reminder: Now that you have read and followed the directions on each card, cover each card with clear plastic or slip the card inside a small, clear plastic bag. You are now ready to do the activities that are related to the directions cards. Write your answers on the cards below. Try to think of things that might affect your results. Then mount the activity card to the back of the appropriate directions card.

Do Activities and Record Responses

Activity 1
Use this code to decipher an important strategy that you can use to do your activities correctly.

A	B	C	D	E	F	G	H	I	J	K	L
1	2	3	4	5	6	7	8	9	10	11	12

M	N	O	P	Q	R	S	T	U	V
13	14	15	16	17	18	19	20	21	22

W	X	Y	Z
23	24	25	26

__ __ __ __ __ __
6 15 12 12 15 23

__ __ __ __ __ __ __ __ __ __
4 9 18 5 3 20 9 15 14 19

Identify Myself

Activity 2
Using an eyedropper or soda straw and a drop of water, trace your name by pulling the drop of water over each letter on the directions card. Try different types of water such as hot and cold water. Your name is

_____

Symbolize Myself
Activity 3
Place a drop of water in drop A. Pull drop A along path into drop B. Move drop over symbol H_2O. Find out what H and O mean.

1. H means <u>H</u> __ __ __ __ __ __

2. O means <u>O</u> __ __ __ __ __

3. Number of dots that make up the letters H_2O _____

4. Number of the letter H in the alphabet _____

5. Number of the letter O in the alphabet _____

6. Total _____

If you have controlled all your variables, your answers for questions 3 and 6 should match.

Identify Some of My Strengths

Activity 4
Write the *strength* words in alphabetical order and describe each. Then make a list of your strengths.

Strength Words of Water	My Strengths

GA1150

Directions Cards: If I Could Be a Drop, I Would . . . .

5. Identify a Secret Weakness

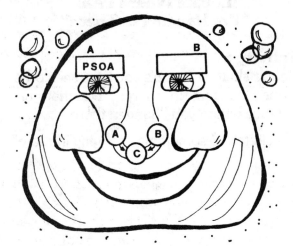

Directions: Rearrange the letters in box A to make a word that describes something weak. Write that word in box B. Cover this card with clear plastic or place card in a small clear plastic bag. Do Activity 5 on the student activity page on page 148.

6. Locate Where I Am
"I'm Hanging in There"

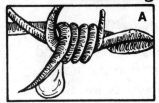 

 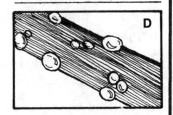

Directions: In the blank below each picture, print the name of the object from which each drop hangs. Then cover this card with clear plastic or place card in a small clear plastic bag. Do Activity 6 on the student activity page on page 148.

7. Recycle Myself

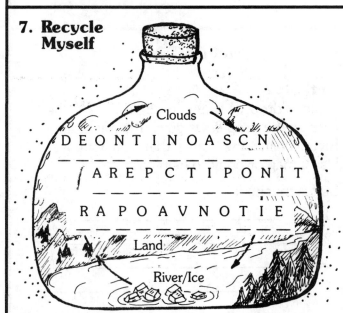

Directions: Unscramble the letters to identify the three stages in the water cycle. Then cover this card with clear plastic or place card in a small, clear plastic bag. Do Activity 7 on the student activity page on page 148.

8. Take a Trip

Directions: With a string, measure the length of the Mississippi River in inches (cm). Compare to miles (km). Then cover this card with clear plastic or place card in a small clear plastic bag. Do Activity 8 on the student activity page on page 148.

GA1150

Student Activity Page: If I Could Be a Drop, I Would . . . .
Activity Cards

Identify a Secret Weakness

Activity 5

Water drop A and soapy drop B meet and mix it up at drop C. Describe the action. Below, write the name of one of the things about yourself that you would like to change.

Drop A met drop B and this is what happened . . .

The one thing that I want to change about myself is _____.

To do this change, I'm going to control my
_____

Locate Where I Am
"I'm Hanging in There"

Activity 6

Make a sketch of where you have seen other drops "hanging in there." Describe one instance where you "hung in there."

My sketch of something "hanging in there"

I "hung in there" when I_____
_____
_____

Recycle Myself

Activity 7

Trace the path of a drop of water going through the water cycle in the bottle. Tell a friend about an uplifting experience.

A real uplifting experience for me was when I_____
_____
_____

Take a Trip

Activity 8

Place a drop of water in circle A. Tilt the card so the drop flows down the Mississippi River. Name the states that you touched. Use a map or book to help you.

States touched:

1. _____
2. _____
3. _____
4. _____
5. _____
6. _____
7. _____
8. _____
9. _____
10. _____

GA1150

Directions Cards: If I Could Be a Drop, I Would . . . .

9. Go Through Changes

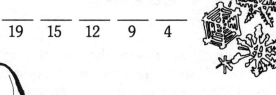

$$\overline{\quad}_{19} \; \overline{\quad}_{15} \; \overline{\quad}_{12} \; \overline{\quad}_{9} \; \overline{\quad}_{4}$$

$$\overline{\quad}_{12} \; \overline{\quad}_{9} \; \overline{\quad}_{17} \; \overline{\quad}_{21} \; \overline{\quad}_{9} \; \overline{\quad}_{4}$$

$$\overline{\quad}_{7} \; \overline{\quad}_{1} \; \overline{\quad}_{19}$$

Directions: Write the numbered letter of the alphabet in each blank to name three changes in water. Then cover this card with clear plastic or place card in a small, clear, plastic bag. Do Activity 9 on the student activity page on page 150.

10. Change My Course of Direction
Life Is a Maze

North

	A	B	C	D	E	F	G	H
1								
2								
3								
4								
5								
6								
7								
8								
9								
10								

West   East

South

Directions: You are in grid space A1. Draw a line through these squares to reach H10: B2, C2, D3, E4, E5, F6, G7, G8, H9, H10. In which direction did you travel? Then cover this card with clear plastic or place card in a small, clear plastic bag. Do Activity 10 on the student activity page on page 150.

11. Not Waste Myself

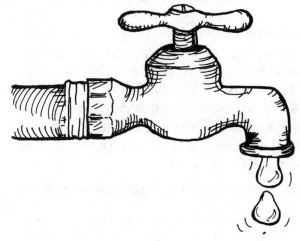

Directions: Print the symbol H_2O in the drops coming out of the faucet. Find out what *water conservation* means. Then cover this card with clear plastic or place card in a small, clear, plastic bag. Do Activity 11 on the student activity page on page 150.

12. Have Some Secrets

A
"A drop of water will evaporate by itself, but it will last forever if united in an ocean."

B
My Secret

Directions: In the blank water drop B above, write a message that would reveal a secret about yourself. Then cover this card with clear plastic or place card in a small, clear plastic bag. Do Activity 12 on the student activity page on page 150.

GA1150

Student Activity Page: If I Could Be a Drop, I Would . . . .
Activity Cards

Go Through Changes

Activity 9

Place a small piece of ice on the snowflakes. Time how long it takes to melt. Then name three changes that happened to you in your life.

Three changes in my life:

1. _____

2. _____

3. _____

Change My Course of Direction
Life Is a Maze

Activity 10

Pull a drop of water along the path through the maze. Count the number of squares crossed. Then describe one life experience in which you needed direction.

I needed a change in my life when I _____

_____

Not Waste Myself

Activity 11

Set a faucet so one drop leaks per second. With help from your parents, find out the number of gallons (liters) of water wasted per month at this rate.

1	Drop wasted per second
60	Drops wasted per minute
3600	Drops wasted per hour
86,400	Drops wasted per day
2,592,000	Drops wasted per month

Divide the number of drops wasted per month by 48,000 to get the number of gallons of water wasted per month.

Have Some Scerets

Activity 12

Pull a drop of water across the printed message in drop A. Add one drop for each letter (70 drops) in drop A. Pull water drops into B to make an ocean of unity and togetherness. Then make a list of factors that determine the size of the ocean of unity in drop B.

Things that determine the size of drop B.

1. _____

2. _____

GA1150

Directions Cards: If I Could Be a Drop, I Would . . . .

13. Be Humorous

Directions: The baby shouts the secret code H₂O. The baby really wants ___ ___ ___ ___ ___. Cover this card with a clear plastic bag. Do Activity 13 on the student activity page on page 152.

14. Expand My Horizons

Figure A

Figure B

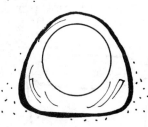

Figure C

Directions: Place a penny on Figure A. Observe print size in words, date and mint symbol. Then cover this card with a clear plastic bag. Do Activity 14 on the student activity page on page 152.

15. Learn About Togetherness The Water Molecule

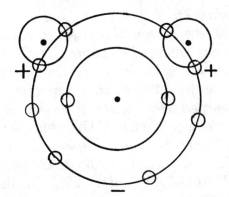

Directions: Color the hydrogen (+) atoms yellow and the oxygen atoms (–) green. Together they make the water molecule. Color entire molecule blue. Then cover this card with clear plastic or place card in a small, clear plastic bag. Do Activity 15 on the student activity page on page 152.

16. Read Books About Water

Water: A Field Trip Guide by Helen Ross Russell. Little, Brown and Co., 1973.

Water: Experiments to Understand It by Boris Armor. Lothrop, Lee & Shepard, 1980.

Clean Air and Sparkling Water: The Fight Against Pollution by Dorothy E. Shuttlesworth. Doubleday and Company, Inc., 1968.

Drip, Drop by Donald Carrick. Macmillan Publishing Company, Inc., 1973.

I Am a Raindrop by Joe Lewis Garcia. Sanchez Santillana Publishing Company, 1975.

Directions: Read the names of the books above. They all deal with the topic W ___ ___ ___ ___. Then do Activity 16 on the student activity page on page 152.

151

Student Activity Page: If I Could Be a Drop, I Would . . . .
Activity Cards

Be Humorous

Activity 13
Place several drops of water on the letters and number in H_2O. Gently tilt the card so the water runs into the baby's mouth. Measure the distance traveled by the water. Then with the help of your parents, write in the glass below the number of glasses of water a person should drink per day.

Expand My Horizons

Activity 14
Fill Figure B with drops of water. Remove card. Draw what your penny now looks like in Figure C. Water can expand horizons for both you and your penny. Then list below at least three things that you know get bigger and what causes them to get bigger.

Item	Cause
1. _____	1. _____
2. _____	2. _____
3. _____	3. _____

Learn About Togetherness

Activity 15
Bonds hold water molecules together. Form a bond of friendship with someone today. Write the name, address and telephone number of that person below. Then call or write a letter to that person.

Name _____

Street _____

City _____

State _____

Telephone _____

Read Books About Water

Activity 16
Go the the library and check out one of the books listed on Directions Card 16. Print the title of the book below. Then read the book carefully. Write a short report on what you learned about water. If you would like to do more experiments with water, see the book *Young Scientists Explore the World of Water* by Jerry DeBruin, available from Good Apple, Inc., Box 299, Carthage, IL 62321.

GA1150

Science Process Skill 10: Estimating
Learning Activity Packet 22: Joystick (p. 154)

153

GA1150

Teacher/Parent Page

Learning Activity Packet 22: Joystick

Science Process Skill 10: Estimating

Purpose: To involve youngsters in the process of estimation and describe how estimation is a useful practice in science; to introduce youngsters to the metric system of measurement

Teaching Tips: This activity involves youngsters in the estimation of linear measurements before doing actual measurements with various manipulatives. Make copies of the Student Activity Page: Joystick for each youngster. Have youngsters cut out the square decimeter and mount on Popsicle stick. Introduce SI metric system to youngsters by pointing out that a centimeter is about the width of their index finger. Tell youngsters that *centi* means 100 and *deci* means 10. Point out that there are 10 centimeters in a decimeter and 100 centimeters in a meter. Have youngsters measure five classroom objects that are longer and five that are shorter than a decimeter. Record the names of these objects on the back of the joystick. Make copies of the eight earthworm cards. Do Card 1 with the youngsters by having them first estimate the length of the earthworm; then using the joystick, accurately measure the earthworm in centimeters. Have youngsters record both estimates and actual measurements on the cards. Subtract to find the difference between an estimation and actual measurement. Stress how the ability to estimate gives one a rough figure of the actual measurement itself.

Card Answers: (1) 5.0 cm, (2) 2.6 cm, (3) 4.0 cm, (4) 5.4 cm, (5) 3.1 cm, (6) 3.6 cm, (7) 4.5 cm, (8) 2.0 cm

GA1150

Joystick Activity Cards

1

I estimate the earthworm to be _____ cm.

I measured the earthworm to be _____ cm.

Difference between estimate and actual measurement is _____ cm.

2

I estimate the earthworm to be _____ cm.

I measured the earthworm to be _____ cm.

Difference between estimate and actual measurement is _____ cm.

3

I estimate the earthworm to be _____ cm.

I measured the earthworm to be _____ cm.

Difference between estimate and actual measurement is _____ cm.

4

I estimate the earthworm to be _____ cm.

I measured the earthworm to be _____ cm.

Difference between estimate and actual measurement is _____ cm.

5

I estimate the earthworm to be _____ cm.

I measured the earthworm to be _____ cm.

Difference between estimate and actual measurement is _____ cm.

6

I estimate the earthworm to be _____ cm.

I measured the earthworm to be _____ cm.

Difference between estimate and actual measurement is _____ cm.

7

I estimate the earthworm to be _____ cm.

I measured the earthworm to be _____ cm.

Difference between estimate and actual measurement is _____ cm.

8

I estimate the earthworm to be _____ cm.

I measured the earthworm to be _____ cm.

Difference between estimate and actual measurement is _____ cm.

Student Activity Page: Joystick

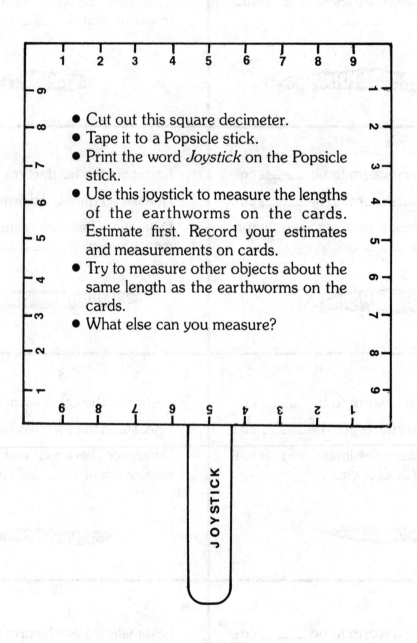

| 1 | 2 | 3 | 4 | 5 | 6 | 7 | 8 | 9 |

- Cut out this square decimeter.
- Tape it to a Popsicle stick.
- Print the word *Joystick* on the Popsicle stick.
- Use this joystick to measure the lengths of the earthworms on the cards. Estimate first. Record your estimates and measurements on cards.
- Try to measure other objects about the same length as the earthworms on the cards.
- What else can you measure?

JOYSTICK

156

Science Process Skill 11: Comparing

Learning Activity Packet 23:
Cycles: Beginning to Ending
to Beginning (p. 158)

Learning Activity Packet 24:
Spring's Seedlings (p. 167)

Teacher/Parent Page

Learning Activity Packet 23: Cycles: Beginning to Ending to Beginning

Science Process Skill 11: Comparing

Purpose: To help youngsters identify and compare natural cycles and to recognize the repetition of such cycles

Teaching Tips: In science, natural cycles can be seen everywhere by the keen observer. Youngsters need to be aware of these cycles and be able to compare the changes that have occurred over time. These pages feature a card deck of fifty-two playing cards that make up the following ten cycles: (1) mealworm, (2) butterfly, (3) frog, (4) grasshopper, (5) water cycle, (6) baby before birth, (7) moon, (8) food chain, (9) rock cycle, (10) seasons. Make a copy of each page for each youngster. Have youngsters cut out the fifty-two cards and mount on single-layered cardboard. Some teachers may want to mount the cards on the backs of blank plastic playing cards. If possible, laminate the cards. Have youngsters shuffle the deck. Lay cards faceup on the table. Youngsters place cards in order to represent the order in each of the ten cycles. Use cards in a learning center for work by individual, small group or large groups of youngsters or as a whole school project in the library. Emphasize the importance of cycles and how youngsters can predict when a cycle will repeat itself by observing and comparing the last card in the cycle followed by the first card in the cycle. The cycle goes on and on. Copy the following answers and mount on cardboard. Laminate and use as a self-checking answer key for youngsters to consult. Have youngsters store their card decks of cycles in small plastic containers similar to those in which baseball cards are stored.

Special Tip: When finished, have the youngsters color each cycle a different color. Cycles are then color-coded for easy reference and use.

Card and Student Activity Page Answers:

Cycle	Beginning to End of Cycle
Mealworm	D, C, B, A
Butterfly	H, G, F, E
Frog	L, K, J, I
Grasshopper	O, N, M
Water Cycle	R, Q, P
Baby Before Birth	X, W, V, U, T, S
Moon	Y, Z, FF, AA, DD, CC, BB, EE
Food Chain	PP, OO, NN, MM, LL, KK, JJ, II, HH, GG
Rock Cycle	VV, UU, TT, SS, RR, QQ
Seasons	ZZ, YY, XX, WW

Extending Source: Jerry DeBruin, *School Yard-Backyard Cycles of Science: A Guide to Science Concepts, Strategies and Hands-On Activities* (Carthage, IL: Good Apple, Inc., 1989).

GA1150

Cycles: Beginning to Ending to Beginning Cards

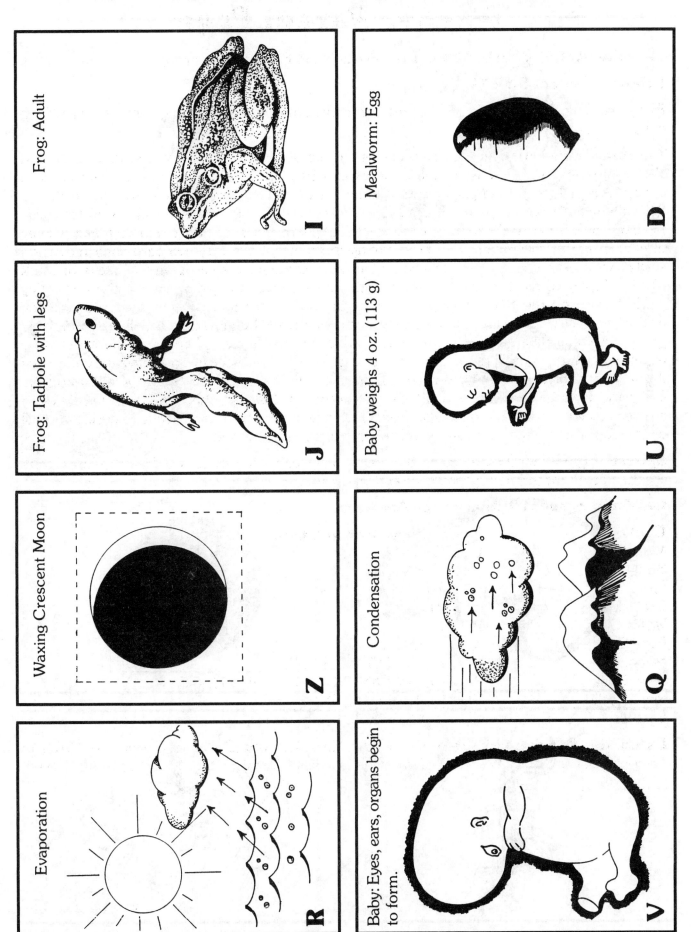

Frog: Adult **I**

Mealworm: Egg **D**

Frog: Tadpole with legs **J**

Baby weighs 4 oz. (113 g) **U**

Waxing Crescent Moon **Z**

Condensation **Q**

Evaporation **R**

Baby: Eyes, ears, organs begin to form. **V**

Cycles: Beginning to Ending to Beginning Cards

Hot sun, children swimming

YY

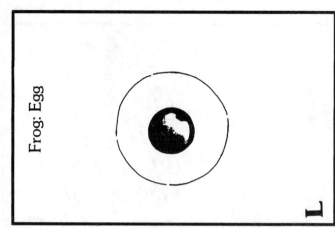

Frog: Egg

L

Igneous Rocks (crystals)

UU

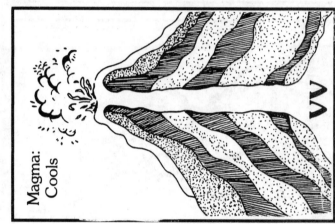

Magma: Cools

VV

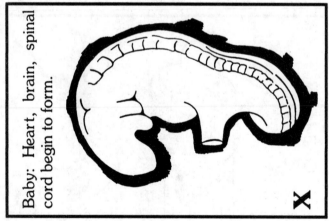

Baby: Heart, brain, spinal cord begin to form.

X

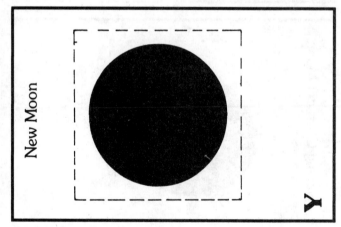

New Moon

Y

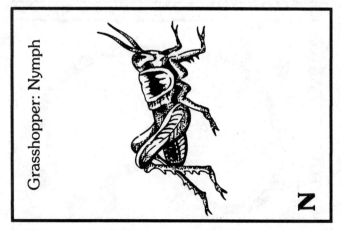

Grasshopper: Nymph

N

Farmer cultivates small corn plants.

OO

GA1150

Cycles: Beginning to Ending to Beginning Cards

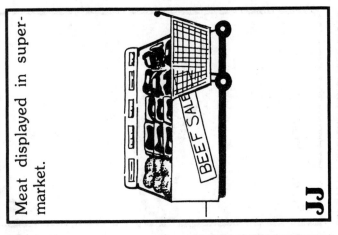

Baby weighs 21 oz. (970 g).

T

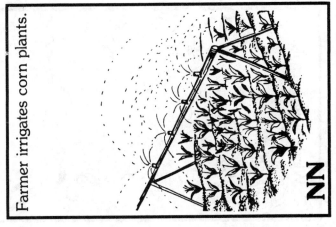

Farmer irrigates corn plants.

NN

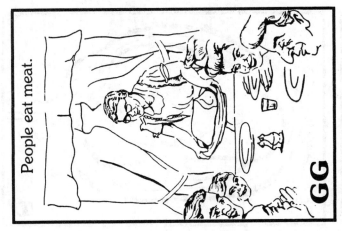

People eat meat.

GG

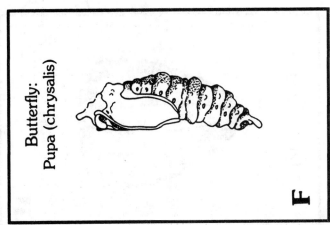

Meat displayed in super-market.

JJ

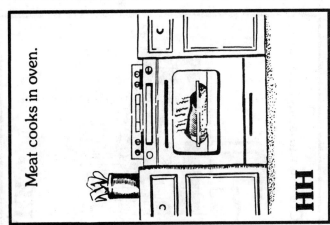

Butterfly: Pupa (chrysalis)

F

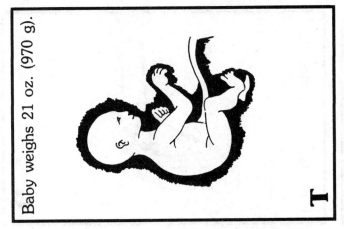

Meat cooks in oven.

HH

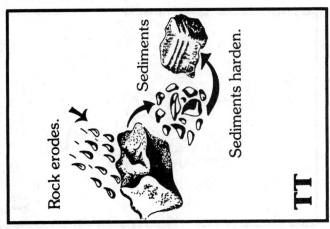

Rock erodes. Sediments Sediments harden.

TT

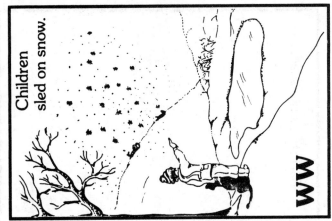

Children sled on snow.

WW

GA1150

Cycles: Beginning to Ending to Beginning Cards

Butterfly: Egg

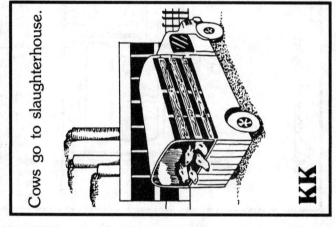

H

Frog: Tadpole without legs

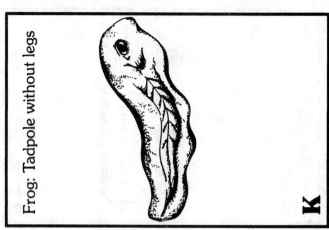

K

Cows go to slaughterhouse.

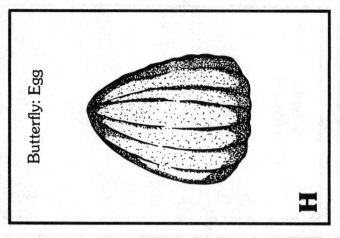

KK

Winds blow; kites fly.

ZZ

Mealworm: Pupa

B

Butterfly: Larva (caterpillar)

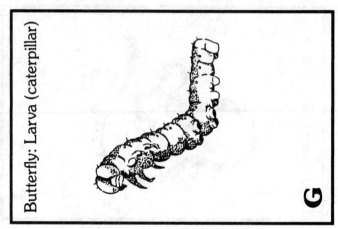

G

Farmer plants seeds.

PP

Baby is born.

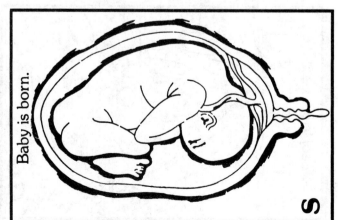

S

GA1150

Cycles: Beginning to Ending to Beginning Cards

Full Moon

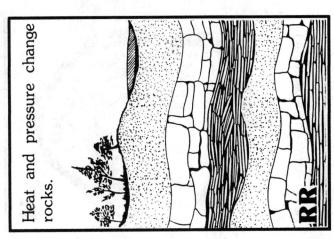

DD

Heat and pressure change rocks.

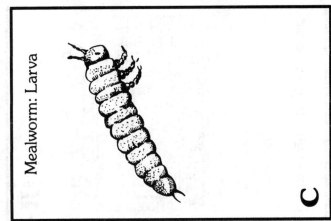

RR

Sedimentary Rocks (layers)

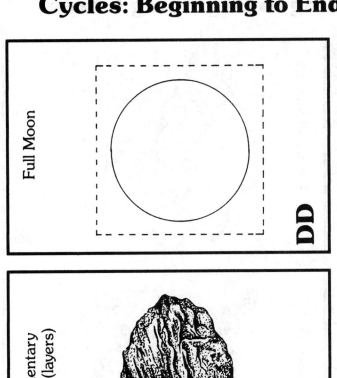

SS

Mealworm: Larva

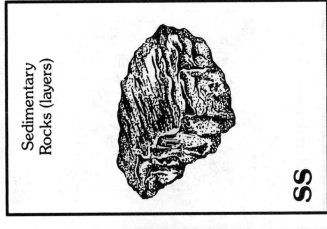

C

Cows eat corn.

LL

Last Quarter Moon

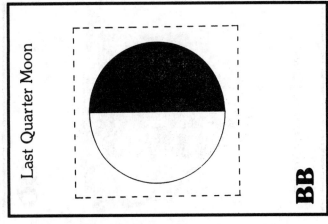

BB

Mealworm: Adult

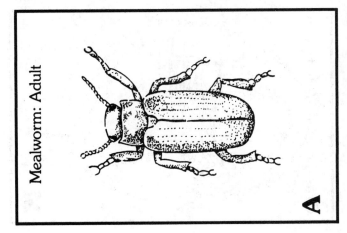

A

Butterfly: Adult

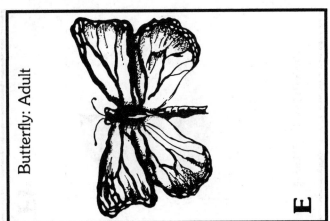

E

163

GA1150

Cycles: Beginning to Ending to Beginning Cards

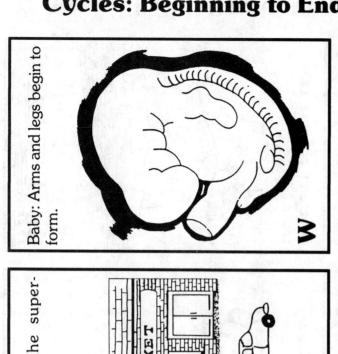

Baby: Arms and legs begin to form.

W

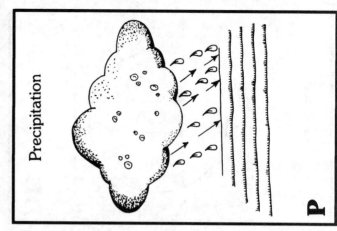

Precipitation

P

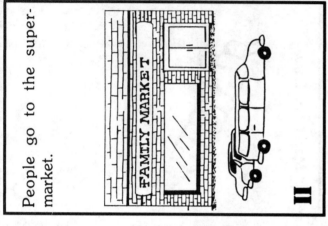

People go to the supermarket.

II

Grasshopper: Eggs

O

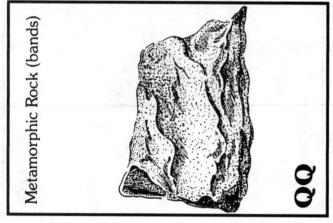

Metamorphic Rock (bands)

QQ

Leaves fall from trees.

XX

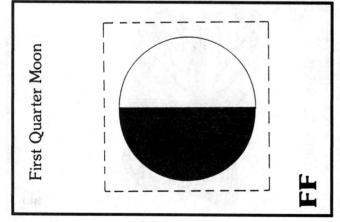

First Quarter Moon

FF

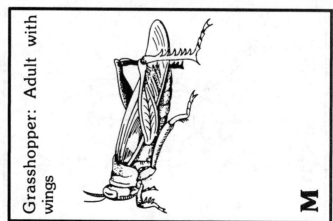

Grasshopper: Adult with wings

M

GA1150

Cycles: Beginning to Ending to Beginning Cards

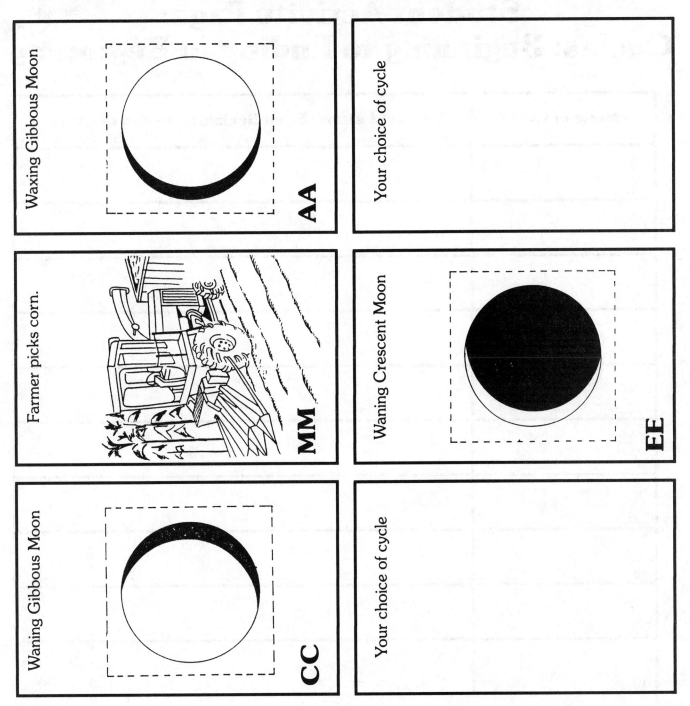

Waxing Gibbous Moon

AA

Your choice of cycle

Farmer picks corn.

MM

Waning Crescent Moon

EE

Waning Gibbous Moon

CC

Your choice of cycle

GA1150

Student Activity Page:
Cycles: Beginning to Ending to Beginning

Name of Cycle	Correct Letters: From Beginning to End of Cycle
1.	
2.	
3.	
4.	
5.	
6.	
7.	
8.	
9.	
10.	

GA1150

Teacher/Parent Page

Learning Activity Packet 24: Spring's Seedlings

Science Process Skill 11: Comparing

Purpose: To have youngsters identify and describe the stages in the life cycle of a plant from seed to fully matured plant, then to seed. In addition, youngsters will compare seedlings to mature plants and identify edible products that mature plants produce.

Teaching Tips: These pages feature thirty cards; fifteen have pictures of seedlings, fifteen pictures of edible products that mature plants produce. Make a copy of each page for each youngster or one set for classroom study preferably in the spring when spring planting occurs. Have youngsters cut out the thirty cards and mount on single-layered cardboard, oaktag or poster board. If possible, laminate the cards. Have youngsters lay cards faceup on their desks or on a table used in a learning center. Match the cards of seedlings with the respective cards of plant products. Have youngsters record the correct answers on the student activity page on page 172. Discuss the life cycle of a plant starting from seed to mature plant and the edible product it produces to seed again to begin a new cycle. Note how various plants both in and out of school go through this cycle. Obtain a watermelon to share with the class. Have youngsters save the seeds when eating the watermelon. After the seeds dry, plant a seed in a small container. Then give each youngster two seeds to take home to plant in small containers. Encourage youngsters to record information about their watermelon plants on the student activity page (page 172).

Special Tip(s): Plant seeds whose names are *unknown* to the youngsters. After seeds grow into plants, have youngsters identify each. Nonliving objects such as stones can also be planted to note the difference between living and nonliving things.

Card and Student Activity Page Answers:

Plant Product	Plant Product Card Number	Seedling Card Number
Asparagus	1	19
Bean	29	2
Celery	18	3
Tomato	4	17
Carrot	23	5
Corn	6	24
Peas	7	22
Cabbage	26	8
Onion	9	30
Lettuce	20	10
Cucumber	21	11
Broccoli	12	27
Radish	28	13
Watermelon	14	16
Beet	15	25

Extending Source: Jerry DeBruin, *Creative, Hands-On Science Experiences* (rev. ed., Carthage, IL: Good Apple, Inc., 1986).

GA1150

Spring Seedlings Cards

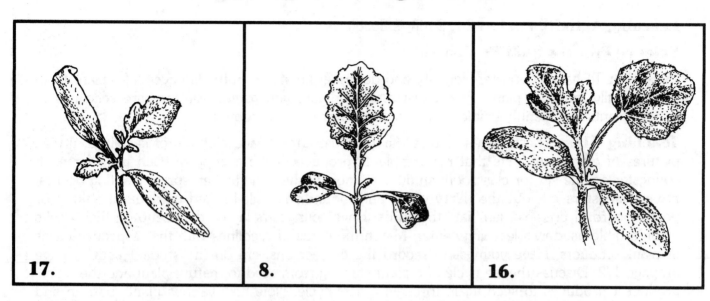

17.   8.   16.

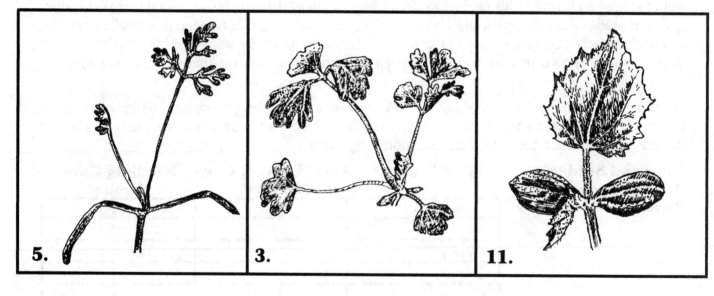

5.   3.   11.

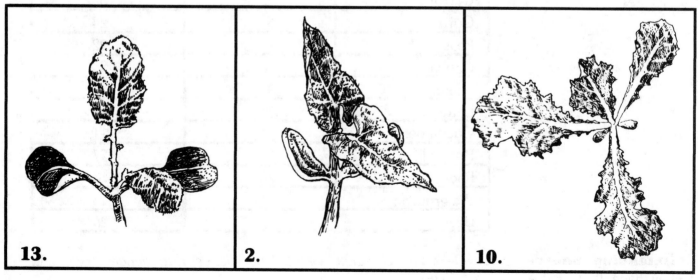

13.   2.   10.

Spring Seedlings Cards

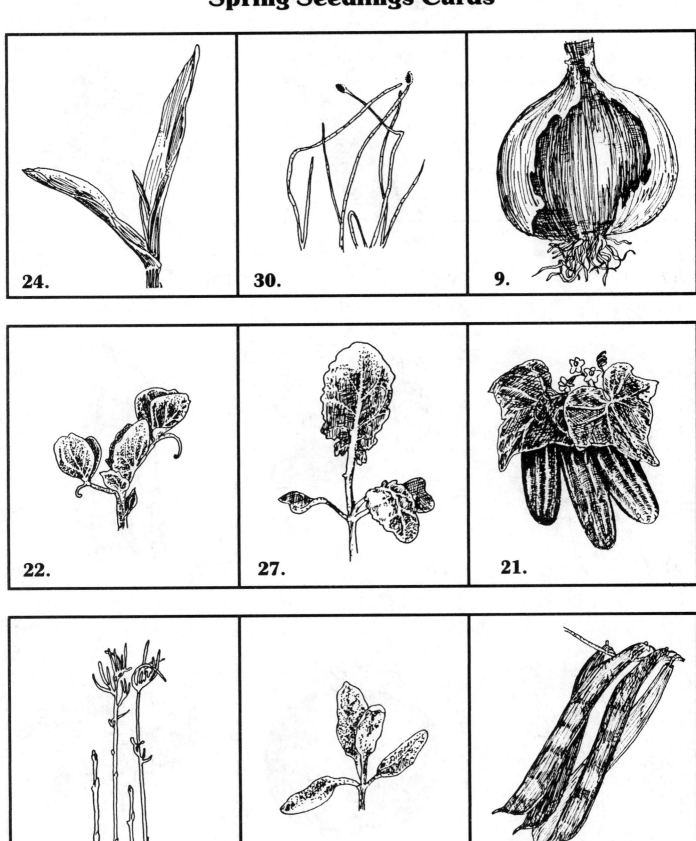

24.

30.

9.

22.

27.

21.

19.

25.

29.

Spring Seedlings Cards

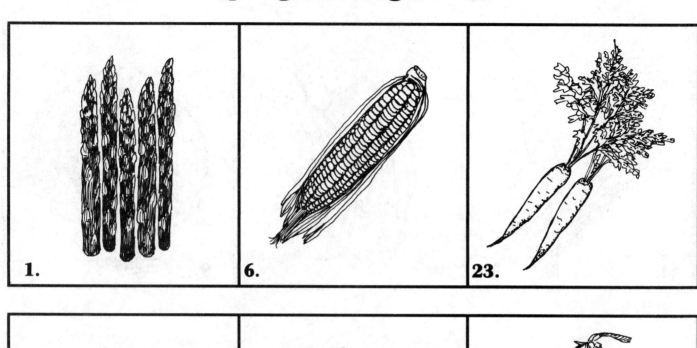

1.

6.

23.

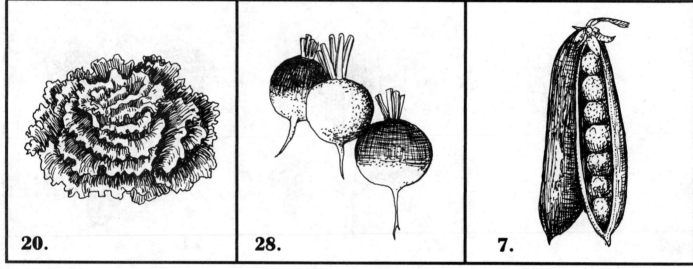

20.

28.

7.

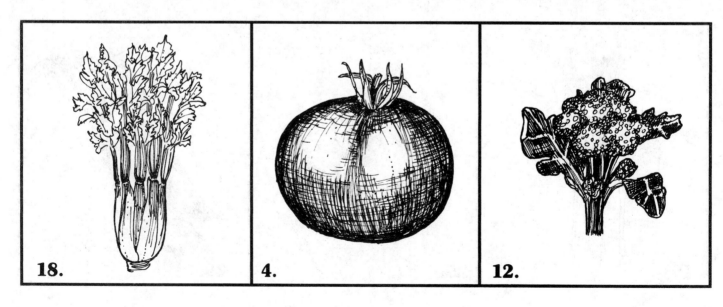

18.

4.

12.

GA1150

Spring Seedlings Cards

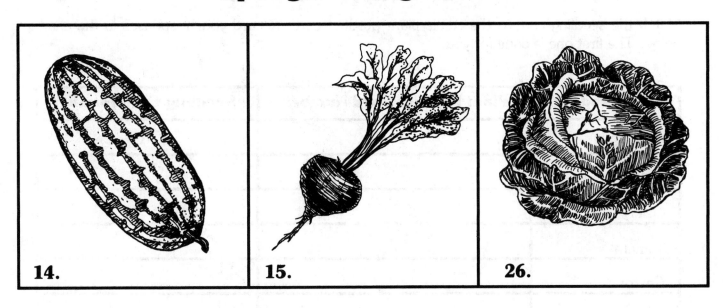

14.

15.

26.

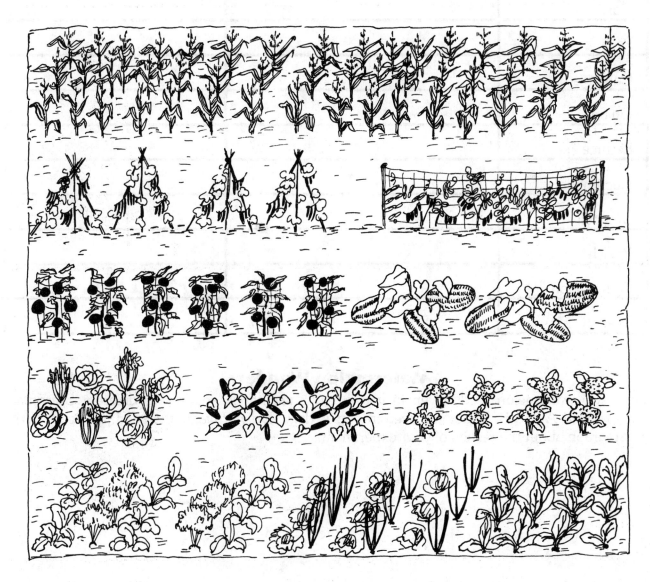

171

Student Activity Page: Spring's Seedlings

Match the seedling card to the edible plant product card. Record your responses in the chart below. The first one is done for you.

Plant Product	Plant Product Card Number	Seedling Card Number
Asparagus	1	19
Bean		
Celery		
Tomato		
Carrot		
Corn		
Peas		
Cabbage		
Onion		
Lettuce		
Cucumber		
Broccoli		
Radish		
Watermelon		
Beet		

Watermelon Wonders

Plant two watermelon seeds given to you by your teacher in soil in two different Styrofoam cups labeled A and B. Water the seed in cup A daily. Do *not* water the seed in cup B. Write a paragraph about the results of your experiment.

GA1150

Science Process Skill 12: Measuring

Learning Activity Packet 25:
Trip Cards of Science Activities (p.174)

Teacher/Parent Page

Learning Activity Packet 25: Trip Cards of Science Activities

Science Process Skill 12: Measuring

Purpose: To identify the location of major science points of interest and compute distances from a location to those sites

Teaching Tips: This activity features seventy-two activity cards divided into three sets of twenty-four cards per set: (1) national parks, geological wonders, and science centers and museums. Cards can be used throughout the year by individuals, small and large groups of youngsters and are particularly useful in late spring as youngsters plan their summer travels. Make copies of the card pages for classroom use. Have youngsters cut out cards and mount on single-layered cardboard. If possible, laminate the set of seventy-two cards. Youngsters use erasable pens or markers and write answers on the cards. Wipe off with damp cloth or towel when completed. Make copies of the three student activity pages on pages 184, 185 and 186. Have children use the map on each student activity page to identify each site and the state in which the site is found. Depending on age level, teach youngsters how to measure and calculate distances by using the distance scale on each student activity page. Follow these steps: (1) Have youngsters make an *X* on the maps to represent their hometown. (2) Write the name of the city and state on the chart. (3) Identify a site to which the youngsters would like to travel. (4) With a ruler, have youngsters measure the distance in inches (cm) on the map from their hometown to the site. (5) Using the scale, calculate the approximate distance in miles (km) from home to the site. Record on chart. Double the distance for round trip. (Alaska and Hawaii are not to scale.) (6) Have youngsters gather information about each site. Then have youngsters plan real trips to their favorite sites. Compute number of miles (km), costs for gas, food, lodging and incidental expenses.

Special Tip(s): (1) Alaska and Hawaii found on the maps on pages 184-186 are not drawn to scale. Use a scale map that includes these states or eliminate them from the activity. Emphasize group work while doing this activity. (2) Laminate pages 184-186. Using nonpermanent markers, have youngsters plot their trips; then erase for reuse of maps.

Card Answers: National Parks Map Numbers: 1, 6, 7, 9, 11, 12, 13, 14, 15, 16, 17, 18, 19, 20, 21, 22, 8, 5, 3, 4, 10, 2, 23, 24

Geological Wonders Map Numbers: 2, 1, 5, 3, 4, 7, 6, 8, 9, 10, 11, 12, 14, 15, 22, 16, 17, 18, 19, 20, 21, 13, 28, 23

Science Centers and Museums Map Numbers: 1, 2, 3, 4, 5, 6, 7, 8, 9, 10, 11, 12, 13, 14, 15, 16, 17, 18, 19, 20, 21, 22, 23, 24

Extending Source: See *Passport to Your National Parks 1986-1990*, Eastern National Park and Monument Association, Jamestown Visitor Center, Jamestown, VA 23081.

GA1150

Trip Cards: National Parks

Map Number _____

Name of Park: Denali National Park

State: _____

Distance from Home: _____ miles

_____ kms

Map Number _____

Name of Park: Hawaii Volcanoes National Park

State: _____

Distance from Home: _____ miles

_____ kms

Map Number _____

Name of Park: Mt. Rainier National Park

State: _____

Distance from Home: _____ miles

_____ kms

Map Number _____

Name of Park: Crater Lake National Park

State: _____

Distance from Home: _____ miles

_____ kms

Map Number _____

Name of Park: Yosemite National Park

State: _____

Distance from Home: _____ miles

_____ kms

Map Number _____

Name of Park: Glacier National Park

State: _____

Distance from Home: _____ miles

_____ kms

Map Number _____

Name of Park: Yellowstone National Park

State: _____

Distance from Home: _____ miles

_____ kms

Map Number _____

Name of Park: Grand Teton National Park

State: _____

Distance from Home: _____ miles

_____ kms

Trip Cards: National Parks

Map Number _____

Name of Park: Bryce Canyon National Park

State: _____

Distance from Home: _____ miles

_____ kms

Map Number _____

Name of Park: Zion National Park

State: _____

Distance from Home: _____ miles

_____ kms

Map Number _____

Name of Park: Grand Canyon National Park

State: _____

Distance from Home: _____ miles

_____ kms

Map Number _____

Name of Park: Rocky Mountain National Park

State: _____

Distance from Home: _____ miles

_____ kms

Map Number _____

Name of Park: Mesa Verde National Park

State: _____

Distance from Home: _____ miles

_____ kms

Map Number _____

Name of Park: Carlsbad Caverns National Park

State: _____

Distance from Home: _____ miles

_____ kms

Map Number _____

Name of Park: Big Bend National Park

State: _____

Distance from Home: _____ miles

_____ kms

Map Number _____

Name of Park: Wind Cave National Park

State: _____

Distance from Home: _____ miles

_____ kms

GA1150

Trip Cards: National Parks

Map Number _____

Name of Park: Hot Springs National
Park

State: _____

Distance from Home: _____ miles

_____ kms

Map Number _____

Name of Park: Everglades National Park

State: _____

Distance from Home: _____ miles

_____ kms

Map Number _____

Name of Park: Great Smoky Mountains National Park

State: _____

Distance from Home: _____ miles

_____ kms

Map Number _____

Name of Park: Mammoth Cave National
Park

State: _____

Distance from Home: _____ miles

_____ kms

Map Number _____

Name of Park: Acadia National Park

State: _____

Distance from Home: _____ miles

_____ kms

Map Number _____

Name of Park: Shenandoah National
Park

State: _____

Distance from Home: _____ miles

_____ kms

Map Number _____

Name of Park: Capitol Reef National
Park

State: _____

Distance from Home: _____ miles

_____ kms

Map Number _____

Name of Park: Kings Canyon National
Park

State: _____

Distance from Home: _____ miles

_____ kms

Trip Cards: Geological Wonders

Map Number _____

Name of Wonder: Mt. St. Helens

State: _____

Distance from Home: _____ miles

_____ kms

Map Number _____

Name of Wonder: San Andreas Fault

State: _____

Distance from Home: _____ miles

_____ kms

Map Number _____

Name of Wonder: Devil's Tower

State: _____

Distance from Home: _____ miles

_____ kms

Map Number _____

Name of Wonder: La Brea Tar Pits

State: _____

Distance from Home: _____ miles

_____ kms

Map Number _____

Name of Wonder: Badlands

State: _____

Distance from Home: _____ miles

_____ kms

Map Number _____

Name of Wonder: Old Faithful

State: _____

Distance from Home: _____ miles

_____ kms

Map Number _____

Name of Wonder: Niagara Falls

State: _____

Distance from Home: _____ miles

_____ kms

Map Number _____

Name of Wonder: Great Salt Lake

State: _____

Distance from Home: _____ miles

_____ kms

GA1150

Trip Cards: Geological Wonders

Map Number _____

Name of Wonder: Lake Okeechobee

State: _____

Distance from Home: _____ miles

_____ kms

Map Number _____

Name of Wonder: Cape Cod

State: _____

Distance from Home: _____ miles

_____ kms

Map Number _____

Name of Wonder: Meteor Crater

State: _____

Distance from Home: _____ miles

_____ kms

Map Number _____

Name of Wonder: Cleopatra's Needle

State: _____

Distance from Home: _____ miles

_____ kms

Map Number _____

Name of Wonder: Mackinac Island

State: _____

Distance from Home: _____ miles

_____ kms

Map Number _____

Name of Wonder: Hot Springs

State: _____

Distance from Home: _____ miles

_____ kms

Map Number _____

Name of Wonder: Jackson Hole

State: _____

Distance from Home: _____ miles

_____ kms

Map Number _____

Name of Wonder: Mt. McKinley

State: _____

Distance from Home: _____ miles

_____ kms

Trip Cards: Geological Wonders

Map Number _____

Name of Wonder: Hawaii Volcano House

State: _____

Distance from Home: _____ miles

_____ kms

Map Number _____

Name of Wonder: Death Valley

State: _____

Distance from Home: _____ miles

_____ kms

Map Number _____

Name of Wonder: Mammoth Cave

State: _____

Distance from Home: _____ miles

_____ kms

Map Number _____

Name of Wonder: Wisconsin Dells

State: _____

Distance from Home: _____ miles

_____ kms

Map Number _____

Name of Wonder: Stone Mountain

State: _____

Distance from Home: _____ miles

_____ kms

Map Number _____

Name of Wonder: Painted Desert

State: _____

Distance from Home: _____ miles

_____ kms

Map Number _____

Name of Wonder: Craters of the Moon

State: _____

Distance from Home: _____ miles

_____ kms

Map Number _____

Name of Wonder: Black Canyon of Gunnison

State: _____

Distance from Home: _____ miles

_____ kms

GA1150

Trip Cards: Science Centers and Museums

Map Number _____

Name of Center: Experimental Aircraft
Association

State: _____

Distance from Home: _____ miles

_____ kms

Map Number _____

Name of Center: Fernbank Science
Center

State: _____

Distance from Home: _____ miles

_____ kms

Map Number _____

Name of Center: Des Moines Center
of Science

State: _____

Distance from Home: _____ miles

_____ kms

Map Number _____

Name of Center: Kitt Peak National
Observatory

State: _____

Distance from Home: _____ miles

_____ kms

Map Number _____

Name of Center: Kennedy Space Center

State: _____

Distance from Home: _____ miles

_____ kms

Map Number _____

Name of Center: Hall of Science of the
City of New York

State: _____

Distance from Home: _____ miles

_____ kms

Map Number _____

Name of Center: Cumberland Museum
and Science Center

State: _____

Distance from Home: _____ miles

_____ kms

Map Number _____

Name of Center: Bishop Museum

State: _____

Distance from Home: _____ miles

_____ kms

GA1150

Trip Cards: Science Centers and Museums

Map Number _____

Name of Center: The Science Museum
of Virginia

State: _____

Distance from Home: _____ miles

_____ kms

Map Number _____

Name of Center: Children's Museum of
Indianapolis

State: _____

Distance from Home: _____ miles

_____ kms

Map Number _____

Name of Center: Oregon Museum of
Science and Industry

State: _____

Distance from Home: _____ miles

_____ kms

Map Number _____

Name of Center: Maryland Science
Center

State: _____

Distance from Home: _____ miles

_____ kms

Map Number _____

Name of Center: Cranbook Institute of
Science

State: _____

Distance from Home: _____ miles

_____ kms

Map Number _____

Name of Center: Alabama Space and
Rocket Center

State: _____

Distance from Home: _____ miles

_____ kms

Map Number _____

Name of Center: Siouxland Heritage
Museum

State: _____

Distance from Home: _____ miles

_____ kms

Map Number _____

Name of Center: National Air and Space
Museum

State: _____

Distance from Home: _____ miles

_____ kms

Trip Cards: Science Centers and Museums

Map Number _____

Name of Center: Franklin Institute Science Museum

State: _____

Distance from Home: _____ miles

_____ kms

Map Number _____

Name of Center: Museum of Science and Industry

State: _____

Distance from Home: _____ miles

_____ kms

Map Number _____

Name of Center: The Science Place

State: _____

Distance from Home: _____ miles

_____ kms

Map Number _____

Name of Center: Discovery Place Charlotte Nature Museum

State: _____

Distance from Home: _____ miles

_____ kms

Map Number _____

Name of Center: The Exploratorium

State: _____

Distance from Home: _____ miles

_____ kms

Map Number _____

Name of Center: Center of Science and Industry

State: _____

Distance from Home: _____ miles

_____ kms

Map Number _____

Name of Center: Boston Children's Museum

State: _____

Distance from Home: _____ miles

_____ kms

Map Number _____

Name of Center: Pacific Science Center

State: _____

Distance from Home: _____ miles

_____ kms

GA1150

Student Activity Page: National Parks

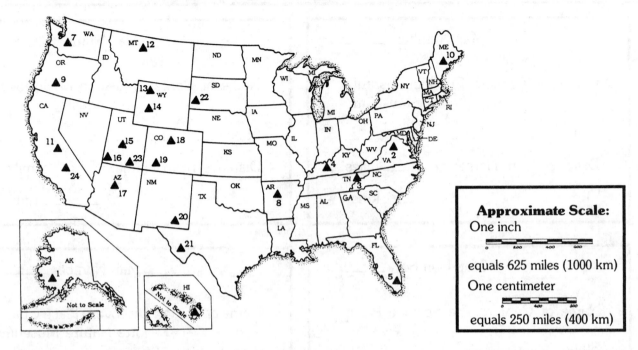

Approximate Scale:
One inch

equals 625 miles (1000 km)
One centimeter

equals 250 miles (400 km)

Map Number	Departure from (Your City & State)	Destination (State)	Distance in Miles (km)	National Park to Explore
		Alaska		Denali National Park
		Hawaii		Hawaii Volcanoes National Park
		Washington		Mt. Rainier National Park
		Oregon		Crater Lake National Park
		California		Yosemite National Park
		Montana		Glacier National Park
		Wyoming		Yellowstone National Park
		Wyoming		Grand Teton National Park
		Utah		Bryce Canyon National Park
		Utah		Zion National Park
		Arizona		Grand Canyon National Park
		Colorado		Rocky Mountain National Park
		Colorado		Mesa Verde National Park
		New Mexico		Carlsbad Caverns National Park
		Texas		Big Bend National Park
		South Dakota		Wind Cave National Park
		Arkansas		Hot Springs National Park
		Florida		Everglades National Park
		Tennessee		Great Smoky Mountains National Park
		Kentucky		Mammoth Cave National Park
		Maine		Acadia National Park
		Virginia		Shenandoah National Park
		Utah		Capitol Reef National Park
		California		Kings Canyon National Park

GA1150

Student Activity Page: Geological Wonders

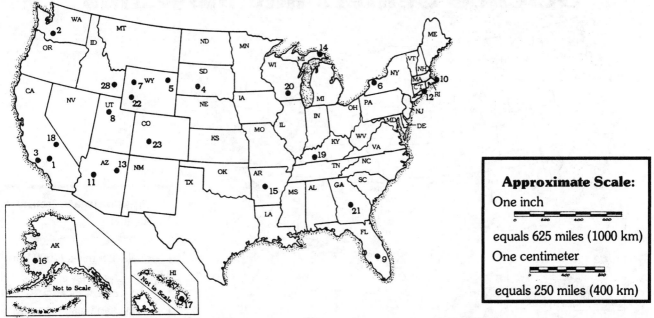

Approximate Scale:
One inch
equals 625 miles (1000 km)
One centimeter
equals 250 miles (400 km)

Map Number	Departure from (Your City & State)	Destination (State)	Distance in Miles (km)	Feature to Explore
		Washington		Mt. St. Helens
		California		San Andreas Fault
		Wyoming		Devil's Tower
		California		La Brea Tar Pits
		South Dakota		Badlands
		Wyoming		Old Faithful
		New York		Niagara Falls
		Utah		Great Salt Lake
		Florida		Lake Okeechobee
		Massachusetts		Cape Cod
		Arizona		Meteor Crater
		New York		Cleopatra's Needle
		Michigan		Mackinac Island
		Arkansas		Hot Springs
		Wyoming		Jackson Hole
		Alaska		Mt. McKinley
		Hawaii		Hawaii Volcano House
		California		Death Valley
		Kentucky		Mammoth Cave
		Wisconsin		Wisconsin Dells
		Georgia		Stone Mountain
		Arizona		Painted Desert
		Idaho		Craters of the Moon
		Colorado		Black Canyon of Gunnison

Student Activity Page:
Science Centers and Museums

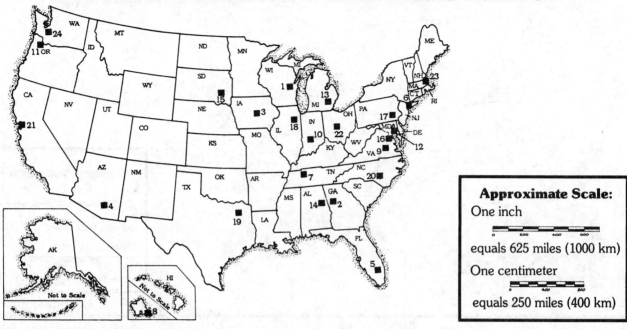

Approximate Scale:
One inch

equals 625 miles (1000 km)

One centimeter

equals 250 miles (400 km)

Map Number	Departure from (Your City & State)	Destination (State)	Distance in Miles (km)	Science Center or Museum to Explore
		Oshkosh, WI		Experimental Aircraft Association
		Atlanta, GA		Fernbank Science Center
		Des Moines, IA		Des Moines Center of Science
		Tucson, AZ		Kitt Peak National Observatory
		Cape Canaveral, FL		Kennedy Space Center
		New York, NY		Hall of Science of the City of New York
		Nashville, TN		Cumberland Museum and Science Center
		Honolulu, HI		Bishop Museum
		Richmond, VA		The Science Museum of Virginia
		Indianapolis, IN		Children's Museum of Indianapolis
		Portland, OR		Oregon Museum of Science and Industry
		Baltimore, MD		Maryland Science Center
		Bloomfield Hills, MI		Cranbook Institute of Science
		Huntsville, AL		Alabama Space and Rocket Center
		Sioux Falls, SD		Siouxland Heritage Museum
		Washington, D.C.		National Air and Space Museum
		Philadelphia, PA		Franklin Institute Science Museum
		Chicago, IL		Museum of Science and Industry
		Dallas, TX		The Science Place
		Charlotte, NC		Discovery Place Charlotte Nature Museum
		San Francisco, CA		The Exploratorium
		Columbus, OH		Center of Science and Industry
		Boston, MA		Boston Children's Museum
		Seattle, WA		Pacific Science Center

GA1150

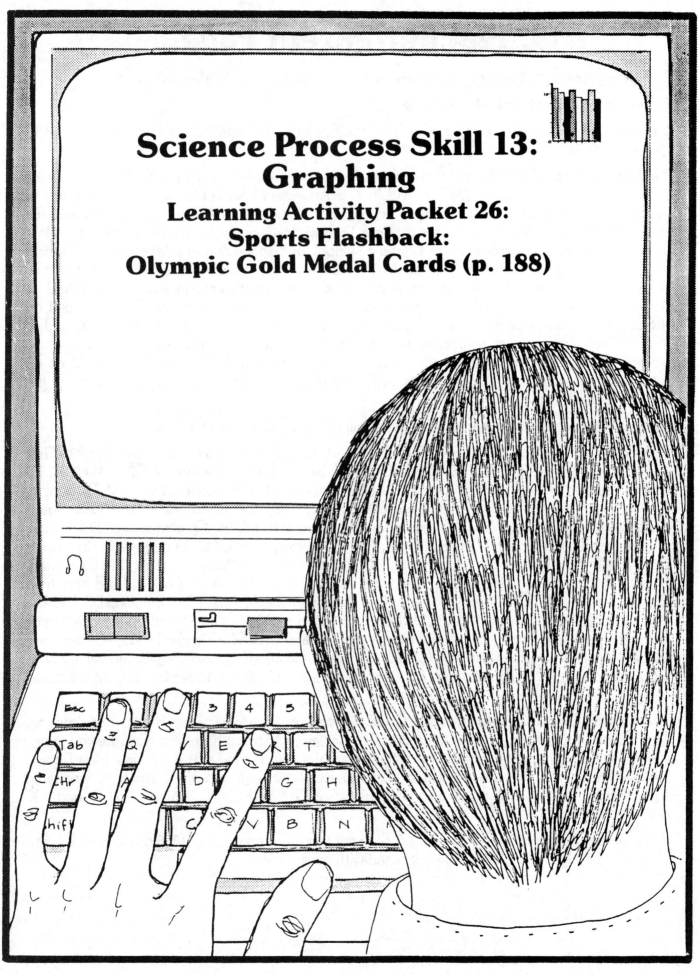

Science Process Skill 13: Graphing
Learning Activity Packet 26:
Sports Flashback:
Olympic Gold Medal Cards (p. 188)

187

Teacher/Parent Page

Learning Activity Packet 26: Sports Flashback: Olympic Gold Medal Cards

Science Process Skill 13: Graphing

Purpose: To introduce youngsters to the concept of a grid and how a grid can be used to gain information

Teaching Tips: The following three pages feature twenty-four Olympic Gold Medal Cards related to the 1984 Olympic Games held in Los Angeles. Make copies of the three pages of medals and two student activity pages on pages 192 and 193. Have youngsters cut out the twenty-four cards which have medals that can be won. Have youngsters observe medal 1. Note its three responses: identification of Olympic symbol, grid space and answer to activity. Inform youngsters that they can win a gold medal with three correct responses, silver medal with two correct responses and a bronze with one correct response. Direct youngsters' attention to Student Activity Page 2 on page 193. Observe medal 1 and how correct responses were recorded on the chart. Symbol is archery, grid space is G5 and answers to questions are 80-100 and 5-10. Because three correct responses were given, a gold medal worth 3 points was won. Have youngsters do Olympic Gold Medal Cards 2-24. Have them record answers on the chart on the second student activity page, page 193. Record total medals won and total points at the bottom of the chart.

Special Tip: Emphasize that all youngsters will earn medals in the exercise.

Sports Flashback: Olympic Gold Medal Card Answers: Question-Symbol-Grid Answers: (1) archery, G5, 80-100, 5-10; (2) baseball, D4, cheetah; (3) basketball, E3 and F3, salmon; (4) boxing, E3, Au; (5) canoeing, B1, 2.5 (about 1.1 kg); (6) cycling, F4, Olympiad; (7) equestrian, C6 and I10, Europe, Asia, Africa, Australia, North and South America; (8) fencing, G5, blue, yellow, black, green and red; (9) gymnastics, D2, Pacific; (10) handball (team), F7, 287 ft. (87 m); (11) hockey (field), D5, 73 degrees F. (23 degree C); (12) judo, D4 and D5, Archimedes; (13) modern pentathlon, H9, frog; (14) rowing, B1, On earth pole vault record is 5.78 m (19.1 ft.); on moon 34.7 m (115 ft.); (15) shooting, E9, hamstring; (16) soccer (football), C4, American Eagle; (17) swimming, D3 and E3, cycle; (18) water polo, D1, star; (19) tennis, C2 and D2, ZIP, mailing letters and packages; (20) track and field, E3, California Valley quail; (21) volleyball, G5, O positive; (22) weightlifting, E2, Bernoulli; (23) wrestling, G6 and G7, faster, higher, braver (swifter, higher, stronger); (24) yachting, H5, new moon (July 28), first quarter (August 3), full moon (August 11)

Wild Card Olympic Gold Medal Card Answers: (1) archery, Jay Barrs, (2) swimming, Janet Evans (800 freestyle and 400 individual medley), (3) track and field, Carl Lewis, men's 100 m dash, long jump, (4) freestyle wrestling, Ken Monday, 163 lbs., (5) swimming, Matt Biondi, 50 and 100 m freestyle, (6) track and field, Louise Ritter, high jump, (7) freestyle wrestling, John Smith, 137 lbs., (8) track and field, Florence Griffith-Joyner, women's 100 m and 200 m dash

Extending Source: Write to United States Olympic Committee, 1750 East Boulder St., Colorado Springs, CO 80909. Symbols used with permission.

GA1150

Sports Flashback:Olympic Gold Medal Cards

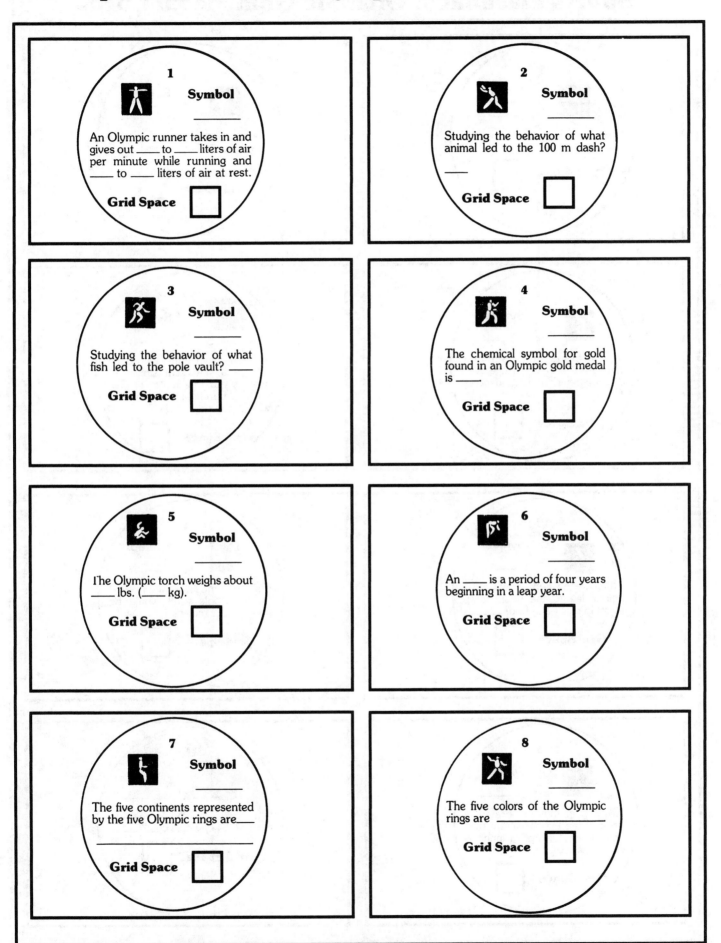

1

Symbol
_____

An Olympic runner takes in and gives out ____ to ____ liters of air per minute while running and ____ to ____ liters of air at rest.

Grid Space

2

Symbol
_____

Studying the behavior of what animal led to the 100 m dash?

____

Grid Space

3

Symbol
_____

Studying the behavior of what fish led to the pole vault? ____

Grid Space

4

Symbol
_____

The chemical symbol for gold found in an Olympic gold medal is ____

Grid Space

5

Symbol
_____

The Olympic torch weighs about ____ lbs. (____ kg).

Grid Space

6

Symbol
_____

An ____ is a period of four years beginning in a leap year.

Grid Space

7

Symbol
_____

The five continents represented by the five Olympic rings are ____
_____

Grid Space

8

Symbol
_____

The five colors of the Olympic rings are _____

Grid Space

GA1150

Sports Flashback: Olympic Gold Medal Cards

9

Symbol
_____

Los Angeles is located in the _____ time zone.

Grid Space ☐

10

Symbol
_____

The elevation above sea level of Los Angeles is _____ feet (_____ m).

Grid Space ☐

11

Symbol
_____

The average mean summer temperature in Los Angeles is _____ degrees F and _____ degrees C.

Grid Space ☐

12

Symbol
_____

The famous scientist who once uttered a statement similar to what is now the motto of California. "Eureka, I have found it" was _____.

Grid Space ☐

13

Symbol
_____

Studying the behavior of what animal led to the broad jump event in track and field? _____

Grid Space ☐

14

Symbol
_____

On the moon, the record Olympic pole vault would be about _____ meters (_____ feet).

Grid Space ☐

15

Symbol
_____

A group of muscles located in back of the upper leg that may tear in an Olympic runner is called the _____.

Grid Space ☐

16

Symbol
_____

What bird is located on one side of the 1984 Olympic coin? _____

Grid Space ☐

190

GA1150

Sports Flashback: Olympic Gold Medal Cards

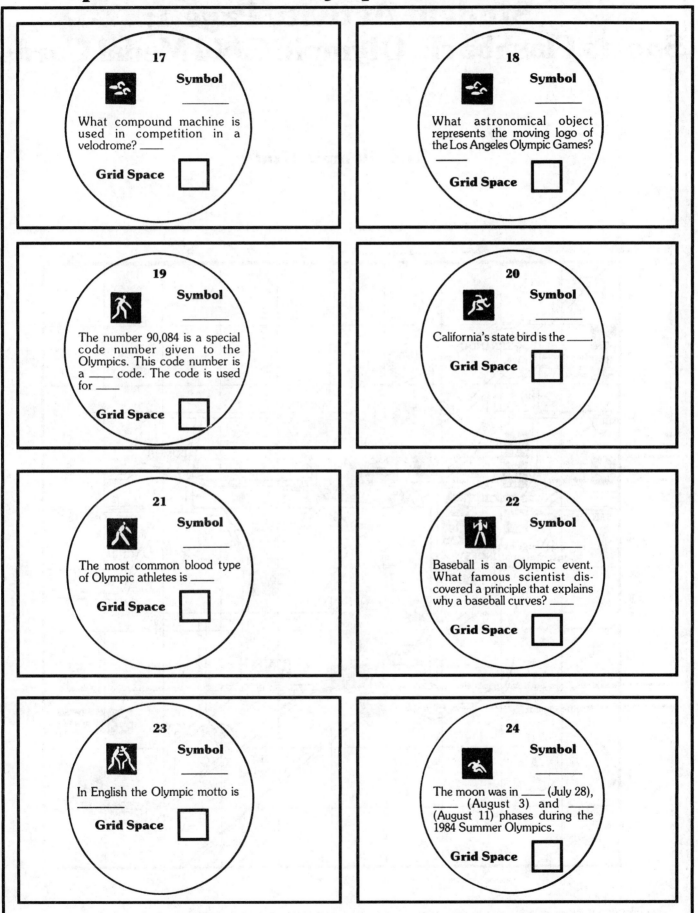

17

Symbol
_____

What compound machine is used in competition in a velodrome? _____

Grid Space ☐

18

Symbol
_____

What astronomical object represents the moving logo of the Los Angeles Olympic Games? _____

Grid Space ☐

19

Symbol
_____

The number 90,084 is a special code number given to the Olympics. This code number is a _____ code. The code is used for _____

Grid Space ☐

20

Symbol
_____

California's state bird is the _____.

Grid Space ☐

21

Symbol
_____

The most common blood type of Olympic athletes is _____

Grid Space ☐

22

Symbol
_____

Baseball is an Olympic event. What famous scientist discovered a principle that explains why a baseball curves? _____

Grid Space ☐

23

Symbol
_____

In English the Olympic motto is _____

Grid Space ☐

24

Symbol
_____

The moon was in _____ (July 28), _____ (August 3) and _____ (August 11) phases during the 1984 Summer Olympics.

Grid Space ☐

GA1150

Student Activity Page 1:
Sports Flashback: Olympic Gold Medal Cards

The Olympic Grid

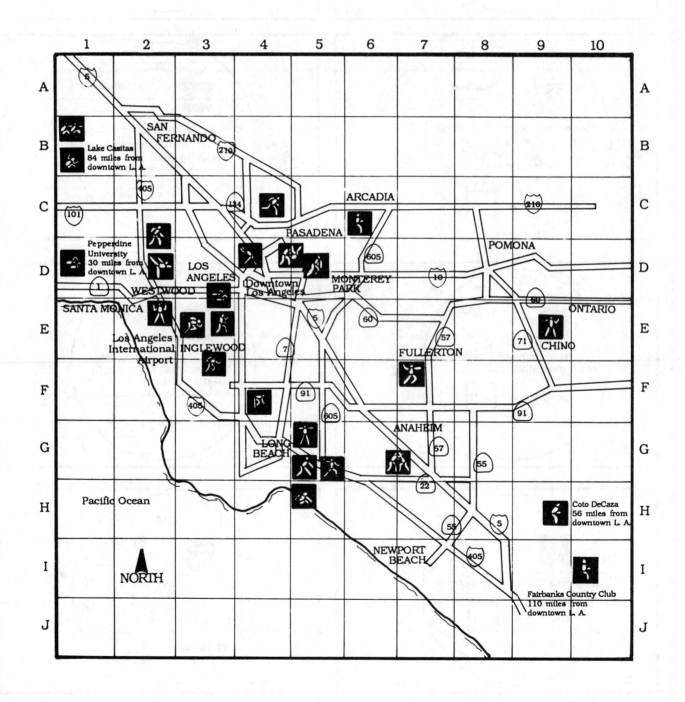

GA1150

Student Activity Page 2:
Sports Flashback: Olympic Gold Medal Cards

Fill in the chart below using information found on the grid on page 192. The type of medal that you earn (gold, silver, bronze) depends upon how many responses on the medal you get correct. The first one is done for you. Score three points for gold, two points for silver and one point for bronze.

Medal	Symbol	Grid Space	Answer	Medal Won	Points Earned
1	Archery	G5	80-100, 5-10	Gold	3
2					
3					
4					
5					
6					
7					
8					
9					
10					
11					
12					
13					
14					
15					
16					
17					
18					
19					
20					
21					
22					
23					
24					
Totals					

GA1150

Wild Card Olympic Gold Medal Cards

Name the event in which the following people won gold medals in the 1988 Summer Olympics in Seoul, Korea.

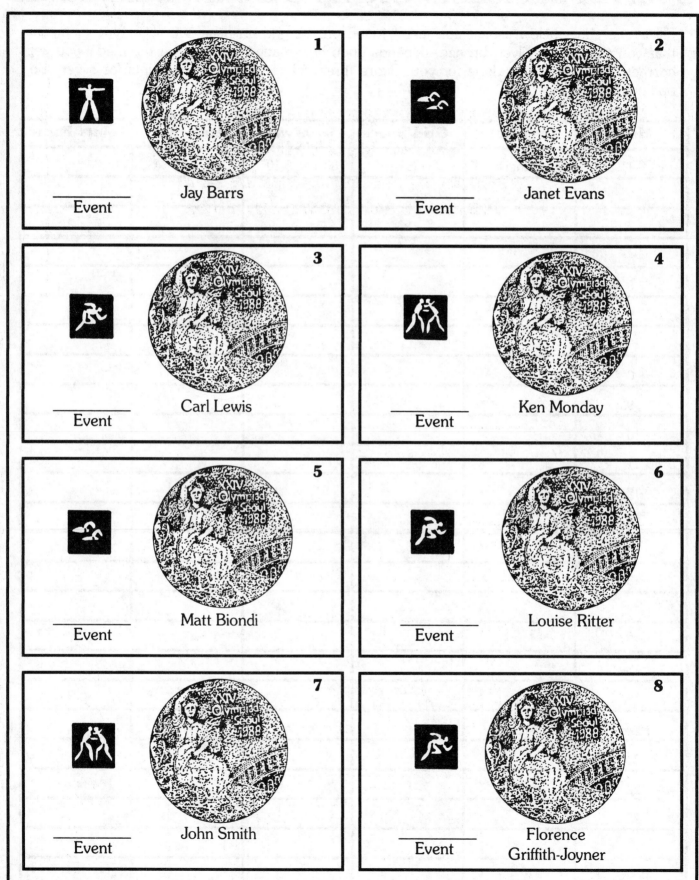

1

——— Event ——— Jay Barrs

2

——— Event ——— Janet Evans

3

——— Event ——— Carl Lewis

4

——— Event ——— Ken Monday

5

——— Event ——— Matt Biondi

6

——— Event ——— Louise Ritter

7

——— Event ——— John Smith

8

——— Event ——— Florence Griffith-Joyner

GA1150

Science Process Skill 14:
Classifying
Learning Activity Packet 27:
Track Them Down (p. 196)

Teacher/Parent Page

Learning Activity Packet 27: Track Them Down

Science Process Skill 14: Classifying

Purpose: To demonstrate a method of matching cards by properties such as characteristics of skeletons, tracks and adults

Teaching Tips: The development of classification skills permits youngsters to classify cards based on likenesses and differences and describe them as part of a larger whole. Track Them Down Cards enhance classification skills and make the study of animals come alive in your classroom. Follow these steps: (1) Make copies of the cards for each child or make a single copy for classroom use as an all-class project. (2) Give a copy to each child. Have each child cut out the thirty matching cards: ten skeleton cards, ten track cards and ten animal cards. (3) Have each youngster identify the picture on each card. (4) Encourage youngsters to match three cards in ten equal sets starting with the skeleton and track cards concluding with the picture of the adult. For example, a rabbit skeleton, rabbit track and picture of a rabbit make up a complete set of three cards. There are ten such sets in the activity. Laminate cards. Use cards often. Have youngsters play matching, sequencing and concentration games with the cards. Encourage youngsters to draw or cut out more cards to add to their collection as they learn more about skeletons, tracks and living things being integral parts of a larger system.

Special Tip: Morse code is used as a key for correct answers with no special message intended. Using the encyclopedia, however, youngsters could develop their own Morse code.

Card and Student Activity Page Answers:

Set I Frog
. __ Frog Skeleton
__ . . . Frog Track
__ . __ . Picture of Frog

Set II Human
__ . . Human Skeleton
. Human Footprint or Track
. . __ . Picture of Person

Set III Cat
__ __ . Cat Skeleton
. . . . Cat Track
. . Picture of a Cat

Set IV Rabbit
. __ __ __ Rabbit Skeleton
__ . __ Rabbit Track
. __ . . Picture of a Rabbit

Set V Hippopotamus
__ __ Hippopotamus Skeleton
__ . Hippopotamus Track
__ __ __ Picture of a Hippopotamus

Set VI Deer
. __ __ . Deer Skeleton
__ __ . __ Deer Track
. __ . Picture of a Deer

Set VII Horse
. . . Horse Skeleton
__ Horse Track
. . __ Picture of a Horse

Set VIII Chicken
. . . __ Chicken Skeleton
. __ __ Chicken Track
__ . . __ Picture of a Chicken

Set IX Giraffe
__ . __ __ Giraffe Skeleton
__ __ . . Giraffe Track
. __ __ __ __ Picture of a Giraffe

Set X Dog
. . __ __ __ Dog Skeleton
. . . __ __ Dog Track
. . . . __ Picture of a Dog

Wild Card Answers: (1) gray squirrel (front left), (2) raccoon (front left), (3) pigeon (left), (4) opossum (front right), (5) striped skunk (front left), (6) deer mouse (front left), (7) muskrat (front right), (8) great black-backed gull (left)

Extending Source: Jerry DeBruin, *Young Scientists Explore Animals* (Carthage, IL: Good Apple, Inc., 1982).

GA1150

Track Them Down Cards

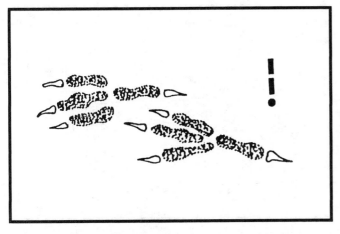

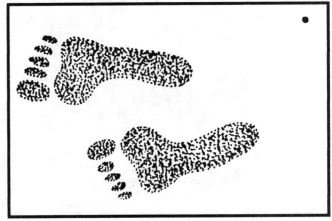

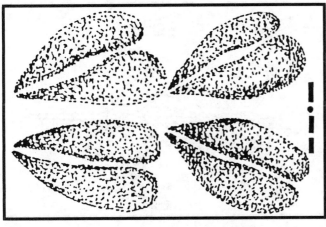

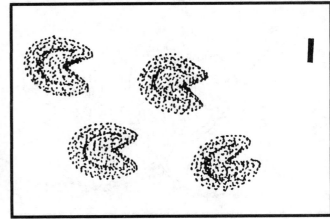

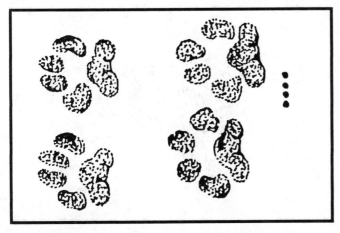

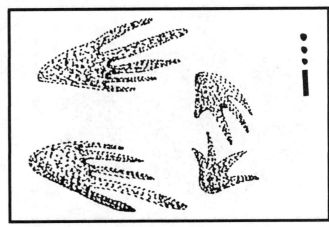

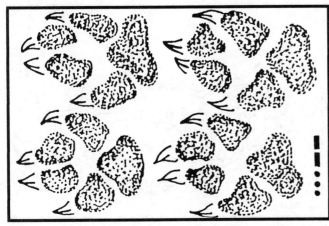

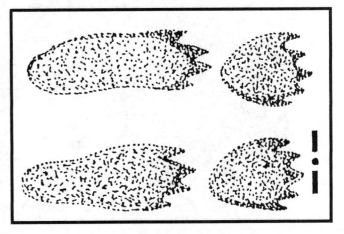

197

GA1150

Track Them Down Cards

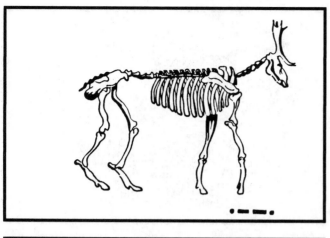

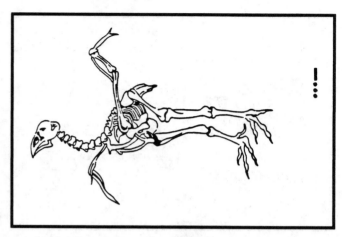

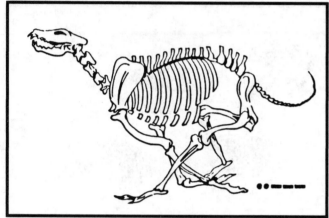

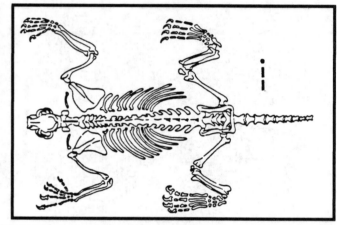

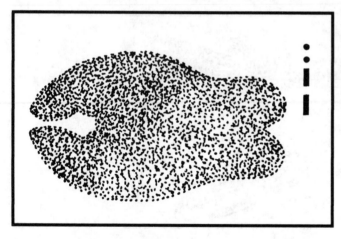

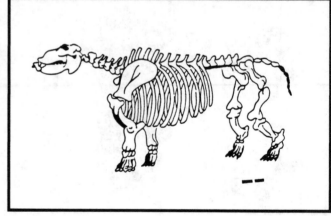

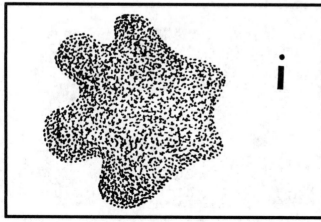

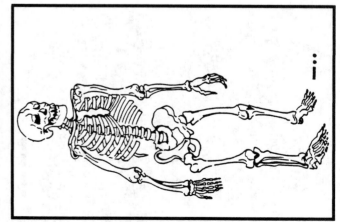

GA1150

Track Them Down Cards

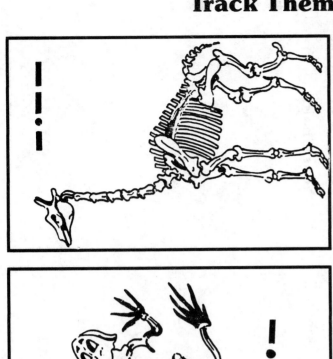

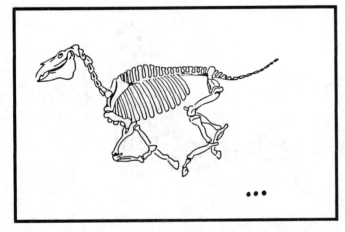
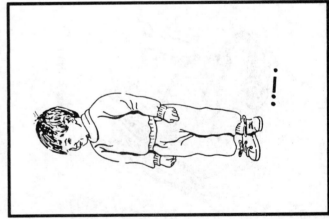

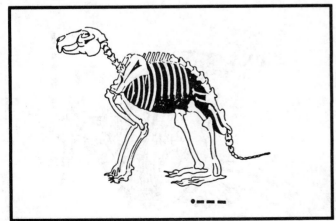

199

Track Them Down Cards

Your Choice

Your Choice

Student Activity Page: Track Them Down

In the blank, write the name of the object found on each card identified by the Morse code symbol. The first one is done for you.

Secret Code	**Name**	**Secret Code**	**Name**
1. . __	1. <u>Frog Skeleton</u>	16. . __ __ .	16. _____
2. __ . . .	2. _____	17. __ __ . __	17. _____
3. __ . __ .	3. _____	18. . __ .	18. _____
4. __ . .	4. _____	19. . . .	19. _____
5. .	5. _____	20. __	20. _____
6. . . __ .	6. _____	21. . . __	21. _____
7. __ __ .	7. _____	22. . . . __	22. _____
8.	8. _____	23. . __ __	23. _____
9. . .	9. _____	24. __ . . __	24. _____
10. . __ __ __	10. _____	25. __ . __ __	25. _____
11. __ . __	11. _____	26. __ __ . .	26. _____
12. . __ . .	12. _____	27. . __ __ __ __	27. _____
13. __ __	13. _____	28. . . __ __ __	28. _____
14. __ .	14. _____	29. . . . __ __	29. _____
15. __ __ __	15. _____	30. . . . . __	30. _____

Wild Cards: Track Them Down

Name these tracks.

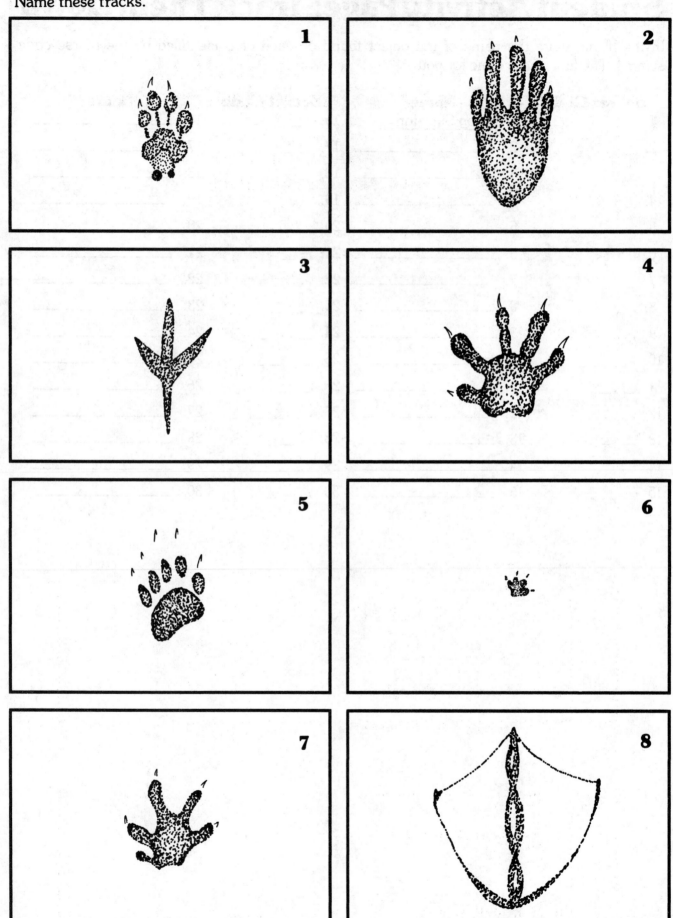

Science Process Skill 15:
Using Space/Time Relationships

Teacher/Parent Page

Learning Activity Packet 28: History of Science

Science Process Skill 15: Using Space/Time Relationships

Purpose: To help youngsters identify the major events in science and some of the famous scientists responsible for these events

Teaching Tips: These pages feature drawings of fifty-four 35 mm blank film frames with descriptions of matching scientific events. Make copies of the pages for your youngsters. Have youngsters cut out each event. Place events in chronological order. Glue each event to correct, matching film frame in order in which those events occurred. Magnetic tape also works well for this activity. When completed and done correctly, the resultant filmstrip represents a chronological history of science. Have youngsters glue or tape the first frame of Strip #2 to Tab A on Strip #1. Follow same procedure to assemble complete filmstrip. Laminate for lasting durability. To extend this study, have youngsters do the student activity page on page 211 in which they make a filmstrip viewer from a small box such as a crayon or cereal box. Cut hole the size of a filmstrip frame in front of box to view each individual frame. Cut slits in both sides of box through which the film can be pulled. Grasp filmstrip and pull through box to view each individual frame in the history of science. Small dowels or spools can be used as take-up reels for the completed filmstrip. Then have youngsters write a documentary film entitled *The History of Science* and show it to the class.

Special Tip: Can be done also as a class activity. Each youngster chooses one to two frames and investigates those events. After youngsters have completed their research, they come together as a group and complete a single group filmstrip.

Frame Answers: Frame Number-Answer Letter(s): 1. BBB, 2. AAA, 3. ZZ, 4. YY, 5. XX, 6. WW, 7. VV, 8. UU, 9. TT, 10. SS, 11. RR, 12. QQ, 13. PP, 14. OO, 15. NN, 16. MM, 17. LL, 18. KK, 19. JJ, 20. II, 21. HH, 22. GG, 23. FF, 24. EE, 25. DD, 26. CC, 27. BB, 28. AA, 29. Z, 30. Y, 31. X, 32. W, 33. V, 34. U, 35. T, 36. S, 37. R, 38. Q, 39. P, 40. O, 41. N, 42. M, 43. L, 44. K, 45. J, 46. I, 47. H, 48. G, 49. F, 50. E, 51. D, 52. C, 53. B, 54. A

Extending Source: Jerry DeBruin, *Scientists Around the World* (Carthage, IL: Good Apple, Inc., 1987).

GA1150

History of Science Filmstrip Frames

Charles Lyell becomes founder of modern geology.

GG

Theodor Schwann helps to prove that cells make up all organisms.

EE

Arab astronomers map the stars.

WW

Isaac Newton discovers laws of mechanics.

MM

Halley's Comet sighted for the first time since 1911.

I

Soviet Union launches first artificial satellite.

N

Neil Armstrong becomes first person to land on and step on the moon.

L

Robert Boyle applies scientific method to chemistry.

OO

James Watson and Francis Crick build ladder-like model of DNA.

O

Aristotle stresses careful observation in scientific studies.

AAA

Archaeologists find an untouched Maya tomb more than 1500 years old in Guatemala.

D

Archimedes discovers the laws of the lever and pulley.

ZZ

Descartes uses geometry to explain human vision.

RR

Yuri Gagarin becomes the first human being to travel in space.

M

William Harvey publishes his theory on how blood circulates.

QQ

Robert Koch discovers bacteria that cause tuberculosis.

Y

Dmitri Mendeleev develops periodic table of elements.

AA

Alexander Fleming discovers penicillin, the first antibiotic.

R

John Dalton announces his atomic theory.

HH

Paul Ehrlich treats diseases with chemicals.

U

Charles Darwin states theory of evolution of plants and animals.

DD

Marie and Pierre Curie discover the element radium.

W

Galen develops the first medical theory based on experiments.

XX

Sally Ride, aboard the space shuttle *Challenger*, becomes the first American woman in space.

E

Astronomers announce what appears to be the first sighting of another planet in another solar system.

B

Max Planck advances quantum theory.

V

Joseph Priestley and Carl Scheele independently discover oxygen.

KK

GA1150

History of Science Filmstrip Frames

Johannes Kepler establishes astronomy as an exact science.

SS

Robert Hooke uses microscope to discover cells.

NN

Surgeons transplant heart of a baboon into a baby girl who lives twenty days. First person to receive an animal heart.

C

Antoine Lavoisier discovers how combustion takes place.

JJ

Enrico Fermi discovers first controlled nuclear chain reaction.

Q

James Clerk Maxwell develops electromagnetic theory.

CC

Pioneer 10 crosses the orbit of Neptune, thus becoming the first spacecraft to travel beyond all known planets.

F

U.S. launches *Columbia*, the first reusable manned spacecraft.

J

Gregor Mendel discovers laws of heredity.

BB

Wilhelm Roentgen discovers X rays.

X

Carolus Linneaus classifies plants and animals.

LL

Ernest Rutherford sets forth his theory of atomic structure.

S

Hippocrates teaches that diseases have causes.

BBB

Edward Jenner discovers smallpox vaccine.

I

Guion S. Bluford, Jr., aboard the space shuttle *Challenger*, becomes the first black American in space.

G

Jonas Salk produces first effective polio vaccine.

P

Microbiologists do first successful recombinant DNA procedure as they take a gene from a toad and put it into a bacterium.

K

Galileo discovers pendulum clock.

PP

Louis Pasteur says microorganisms cause fermentation and disease.

Z

Michael Faraday induces electric current by moving a magnet.

FF

Albert Einstein presents his theory of relativity.

T

Galileo discovers many important physical laws.

TT

NASA spacecraft relays data from Comet Giacobini-Zinner in the first direct probe of a comet in history.

A

First permanent artificial heart put in a human being. This is the first such operation in history.

H

Leonardo da Vinci studies anatomy, botany, astronomy and geology.

VV

Ptolemy says the earth is the center of the universe.

YY

Vesalius writes first scientific book on human anatomy.

UU

GA1150

History of Science Blank Filmstrip Frames

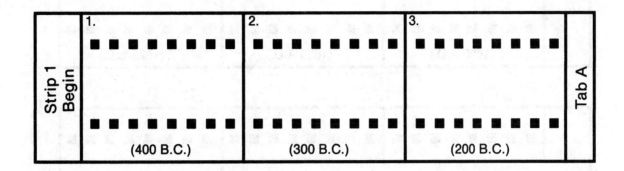

Strip 1 Begin

1. (400 B.C.) 2. (300 B.C.) 3. (200 B.C.) Tab A

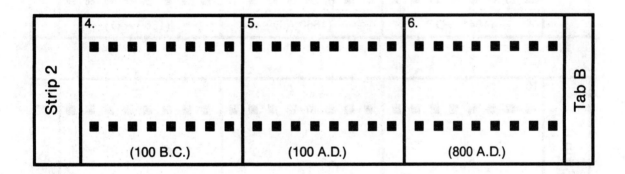

Strip 2

4. (100 B.C.) 5. (100 A.D.) 6. (800 A.D.) Tab B

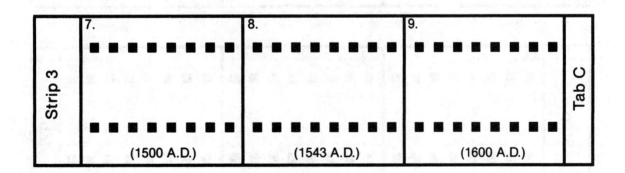

Strip 3

7. (1500 A.D.) 8. (1543 A.D.) 9. (1600 A.D.) Tab C

GA1150

History of Science Blank Filmstrip Frames

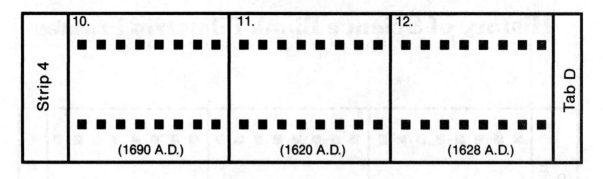

Strip 4 — Tab D

10. (1690 A.D.)   11. (1620 A.D.)   12. (1628 A.D.)

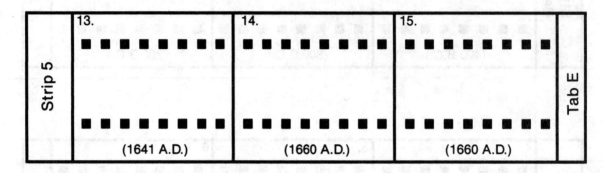

Strip 5 — Tab E

13. (1641 A.D.)   14. (1660 A.D.)   15. (1660 A.D.)

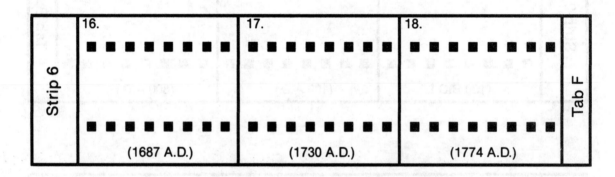

Strip 6 — Tab F

16. (1687 A.D.)   17. (1730 A.D.)   18. (1774 A.D.)

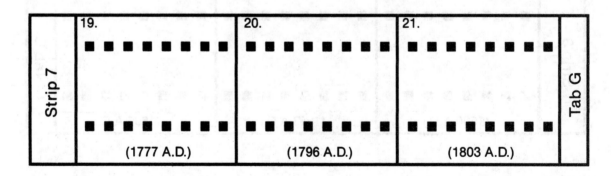

Strip 7 — Tab G

19. (1777 A.D.)   20. (1796 A.D.)   21. (1803 A.D.)

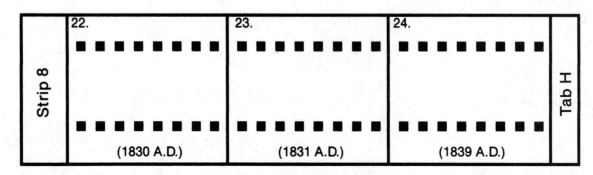

Strip 8 — Tab H

22. (1830 A.D.)   23. (1831 A.D.)   24. (1839 A.D.)

GA1150

History of Science Blank Filmstrip Frames

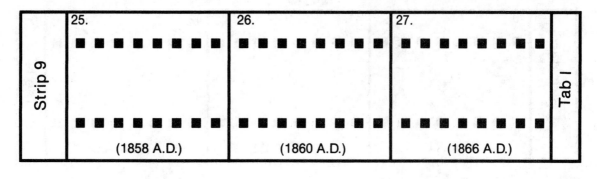

Strip 9 | Tab I

25. (1858 A.D.)
26. (1860 A.D.)
27. (1866 A.D.)

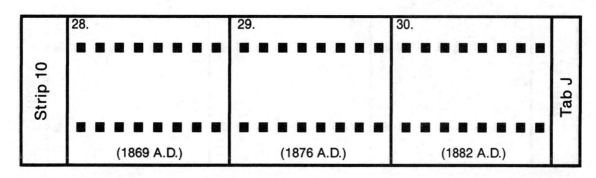

Strip 10 | Tab J

28. (1869 A.D.)
29. (1876 A.D.)
30. (1882 A.D.)

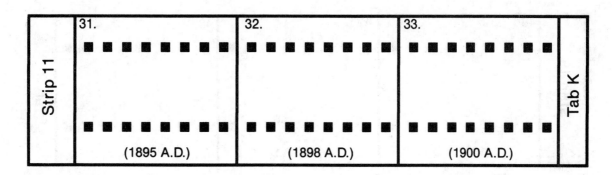

Strip 11 | Tab K

31. (1895 A.D.)
32. (1898 A.D.)
33. (1900 A.D.)

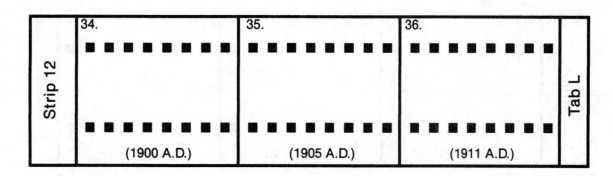

Strip 12 | Tab L

34. (1900 A.D.)
35. (1905 A.D.)
36. (1911 A.D.)

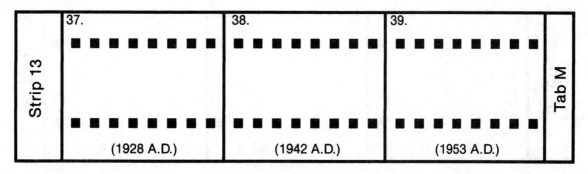

Strip 13 | Tab M

37. (1928 A.D.)
38. (1942 A.D.)
39. (1953 A.D.)

GA1150

History of Science Blank Filmstrip Frames

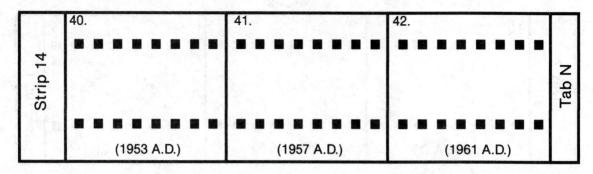

Strip 14 — **Tab N**

40. (1953 A.D.)
41. (1957 A.D.)
42. (1961 A.D.)

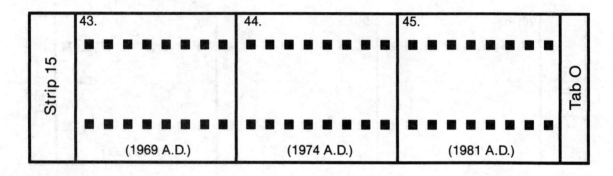

Strip 15 — **Tab O**

43. (1969 A.D.)
44. (1974 A.D.)
45. (1981 A.D.)

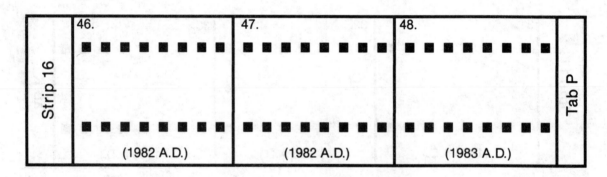

Strip 16 — **Tab P**

46. (1982 A.D.)
47. (1982 A.D.)
48. (1983 A.D.)

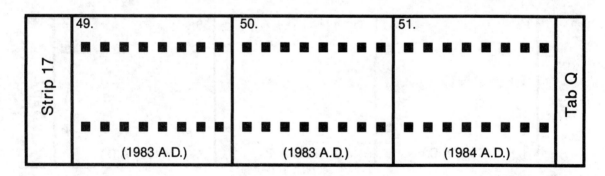

Strip 17 — **Tab Q**

49. (1983 A.D.)
50. (1983 A.D.)
51. (1984 A.D.)

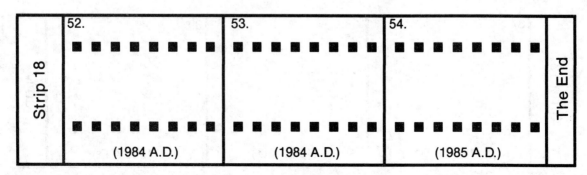

Strip 18 — **The End**

52. (1984 A.D.)
53. (1984 A.D.)
54. (1985 A.D.)

GA1150

Student Activity Page: History of Science

How to Make a Filmstrip Viewer

1. Obtain a cereal box or crayon box that looks like this:

2. Cut a hole the size of a filmstrip frame in the center of the box like this:

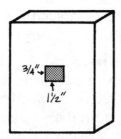

3. Cut slits the width of a filmstrip in each side of the box like this:

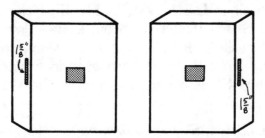

4. Thread filmstrip through slits. Pull filmstrip through box to view *The History of Science* like this:

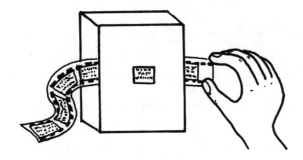

GA1150

Teacher/Parent Page

Learning Activity Packet 29: Tribute to Science

Science Process Skill 15: Using Space/Time Relationships

Purpose: To identify major scientific events that have occurred throughout space and time

Teaching Tips: This activity features twenty-six cards that represent some major scientific happenings that have occurred throughout time. Each card features a letter of the alphabet. Make copies of the cards for each youngster or one complete set for the classroom. Have youngsters cut out cards and find the ten cards that feature events that have occurred from 1972 to 1988. On the student activity page on page 220, have youngsters write the names of all twenty-six events, locations and years in which the events took place. Then on the two blank cards, have the youngsters draw and date a picture of their favorite major scientific event that occurred during their lifetime. Discuss how science has progressed over time based on major scientific discoveries. Then challenge the youngsters with this bonus question: "Can you arrange the letters of the ten correct events in such a way that will give you a ten-letter word that describes a feeling you have towards others?" *Neighborly* is one such word.

Card and Student Activity Page Answers: A. tab top cans invented—1963, C. Model T Ford car invented—1903, D. telephone invented—1876, F. Frisbee discovered—1957, J. television invented—1929, K. Band-Aid invented—1920, M. Lindbergh crosses Atlantic in *Spirit of St. Louis*—1927, P. film *Bambi* made—1954, Q. Wright Brothers fly first airplane—1903, S. Einstein discovers $E = MC^2$—1951, T. Galileo Galilei invents telescope—1609, U. *Sputnik* launched—1957, V. light bulb invented—1879, W. Popsicle discovered—1924, X. tyrannosaurus rex—65 million years ago, Z. New York—site of first pizza place—1895. Circled letters of ten events occurring from 1972 to 1988: N. King Tut's visit to U.S.—1981, E. Mt. St. Helens explosion—1980, I. Three Mile Island meltdown—1979, G. first test tube baby, Louise Joy Brown—1978, H. first *Star Wars* movie featuring Luke Skywalker, Ben Kenobi, Darth Vader, et al.—1977, B. Bicentennial—1976, O. *Apollo-Soyuz* linkup—1975, R. Lucy discovered in Ethiopia—1974, L. OPEC oil and gas crisis in U.S.—1973, Y. two Chinese pandas arrive at the Washington, D.C. Zoo (Hsing-Hsing and Ling-Ling)—1972

Extending Source: Jerry DeBruin, *Scientists Around the World* (Carthage, IL.: Good Apple, Inc., 1987).

Tribute to Science Cards

A

Lift, pull tab to open.

B

Color the square with the stars orange and the white stripes green. Then stare at me for 30 seconds. Look at white paper or a white wall. You will then see the true me.

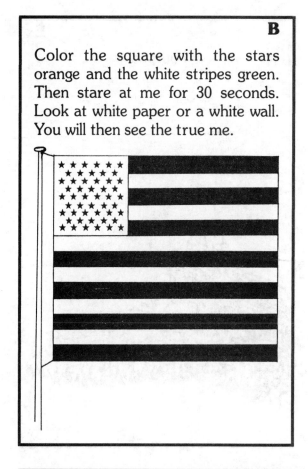

C

My model is *T*.

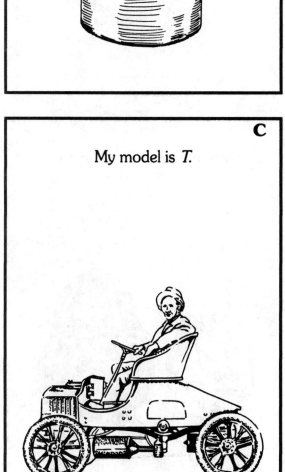

D

"Mr. Watson, come here. I want you."

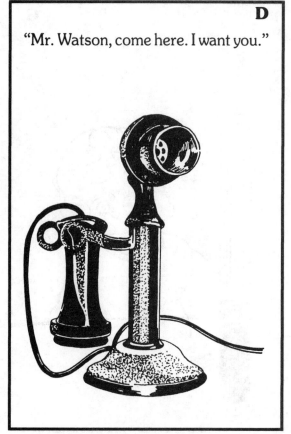

GA1150

Tribute to Science Cards

E

I burped.

F

Come fly me.

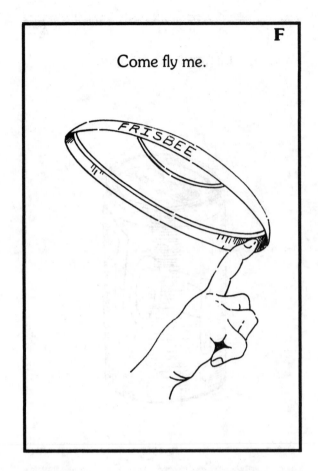

G

My life began in a test tube.

H

"May the force be with you."

214

GA1150

Tribute to Science Cards

I

Somebody goofed.

J

I bring you fascinating science happenings in living color.

K

Mom, I scraped my knee again.

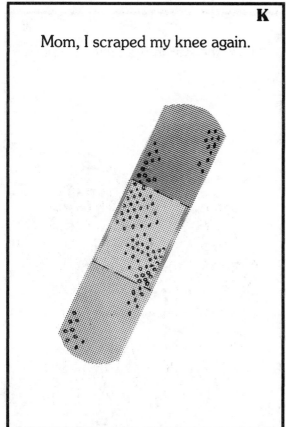

L

What a gas!

215

GA1150

Tribute to Science Cards

M

They call me Lucky Lindy or Lone Eagle.

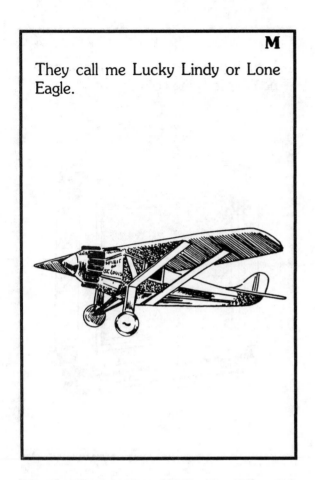

N

I visit the U.S.

O

Glad to meet you.

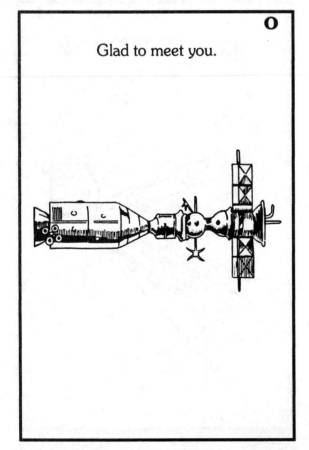

P

I am the star in the movie *Bambi*.

216

GA1150

Tribute to Science Cards

Q

I am the first airplane to fly. I flew 120 feet (36 m) in 12 seconds at Kitty Hawk.

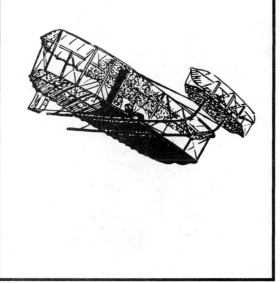

R

Here's Lucy.

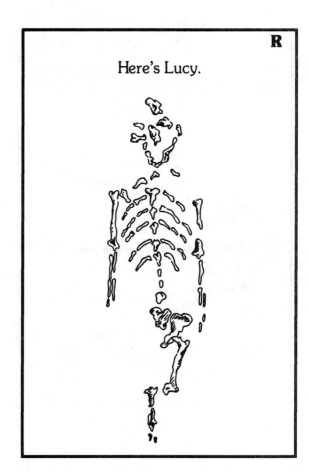

S

Faster than light?

$$E = MC^2$$

T

I see far-out heavenly bodies.

GA1150

Tribute to Science Cards

U

In Russian, my name means "traveler." I was the first ship into space.

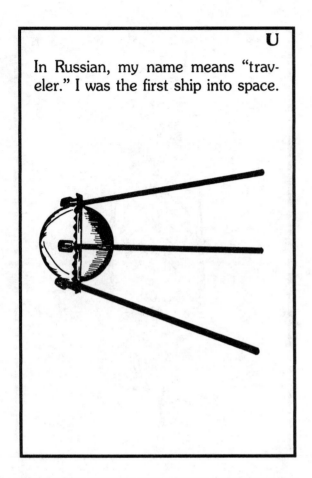

V

I see the light.

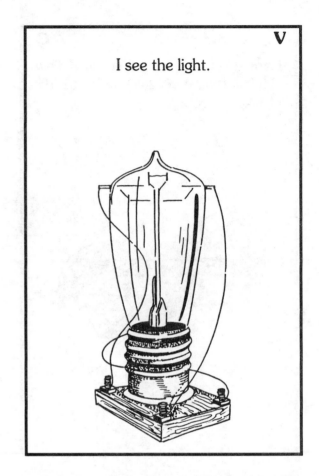

W

Cold but a good lick in the chops.

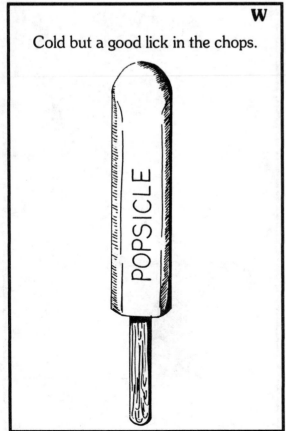

POPSICLE

X

I might be old, but I'm still lovable.

GA1150

Tribute to Science Cards

Y

We are Siamese—no, excuse me,—Chinese.

Z

Please, come in for pizza.

Your Choice

Your Choice

GA1150

Student Activity Page: Tribute to Science

Using the cards, write the name and year of the event in the blanks below. Circle the *letter* of those events that have occurred from 1972 to 1988. Then ask your teacher for the bonus question.

	Name of Event	**Year**
A		
B		
C		
D		
E		
F		
G		
H		
I		
J		
K		
L		
M		
N		
O		
P		
Q		
R		
S		
T		
U		
V		
W		
X		
Y		
Z		

Teacher/Parent Page

Learning Activity Packet 30: Tickets to Science Museums

Science Process Skill 15: Using Space/Time Relationships

Purpose: To identify major science museums in the United States; to name various characteristics about the states in which these science museums are located

Teaching Tips: This activity can be used at any time during the year but is most appropriate in late spring shortly before youngsters are dismissed for summer vacation. It is during the summer that some youngsters, with family members, will travel. Other youngsters can "travel" vicariously to science-related points of interest. All youngsters can "travel" by using these activities. Discuss with youngsters several science sites such as the Lyndon B. Johnson Space Center in Houston, Texas, and The Exploratorium in San Francisco, California. Locate these sites on a map. Make copies of the twenty-four tickets and twenty-four matching ticket stubs. Discuss with youngsters how each ticket features information about the state in which the science-related point of interest is located. Each matching ticket stub has a picture of the state in which the site is found. Have youngsters cut out tickets and stubs. Have them match, then tape, the correct stub to the matching ticket. On the ticket stub, locate the city in the state where that site is found. Discuss what one may see at each site. Complete student activity page on page 226. Then play science quiz games using state's nickname, flower and bird. Finally, have youngsters plan a trip to the next stop on the ticket or to one of their own favorite sites. Compute number of miles (km), costs for gas, food, lodging and incidental expenses. Happy traveling.

Special Tip: Encourage youngsters to extend their study further by making their own tickets and ticket stubs to include all fifty states.

Ticket and Ticket Stub Card Answers: 1X, 2W, 3V, 4U, 5T, 6S, 7R, 8Q, 9P, 10O, 11N, 12M, 13L, 14K, 15J, 16I, 17H, 18G, 19F, 20E, 21D, 22C, 23B, 24A

Extending Source: Joanne Cleaver, *Doing Children's Museums: A Guide to 225 Hands-On Museums* (Charlotte, VT: Williamson Publishing, 1988).

Science Museum Ticket Cards

TICKET

1 Admit One

Name of State:
Washington

Nickname of State:
Evergreen State

State Bird:
Willow Goldfinch

State Flower:
Coast Rhododendron

Next Stop:
Mt. St. Helens

TICKET

2 Admit One

Name of State:
Massachusetts

Nickname of State:
Bay State, Old Colony

State Bird:
Chickadee

State Flower:
Arbutus

Next Stop:
Boston Museum
of Science

TICKET

3 Admit One

Name of State:
Ohio

Nickname of State:
Buckeye State

State Bird:
Cardinal

State Flower:
Scarlet Carnation

Next Stop:
Neil Armstrong Air
and Space Museum

TICKET

4 Admit One

Name of State:
California

Nickname of State:
Golden State

State Bird:
California Valley Quail

State Flower:
Golden Poppy

Next Stop:
Lawrence Hall of
Science

TICKET

5 Admit One

Name of State:
North Carolina

Nickname of State:
Tar Heel State

State Bird:
Cardinal

State Flower:
Flowering Dogwood

Next Stop:
Morehead Planetarium

TICKET

6 Admit One

Name of State:
Texas

Nickname of State:
Lone Star State

State Bird:
Mockingbird

State Flower:
Bluebonnet

Next Stop:
Lyndon B. Johnson
Space Center

TICKET

7 Admit One

Name of State:
Illinois

Nickname of State:
Prairie State

State Bird:
Cardinal

State Flower:
Native Violet

Next Stop:
Field Museum of
Natural History

TICKET

8 Admit One

Name of State:
Pennsylvania

Nickname of State:
Keystone State

State Bird:
Ruffed Grouse

State Flower:
Mountain Laurel

Next Stop:
Buhl Science Center

GA1150

Science Museum Ticket Cards

★★★★★★★★★★★★★★★★★
TICKET
★★★★★★★★★★★★★★★★★

9 Admit One

Name of District:
District of Columbia

Nickname of District:
Washington, D.C.

District Bird:
Wood Thrush

District Flower:
American Beauty Rose

Next Stop:
Capitol Children's
Museum

★★★★★★★★★★★★★★★★★
TICKET
★★★★★★★★★★★★★★★★★

10 Admit One

Name of State:
South Dakota

Nickname of State:
Coyote State
Sunshine State

State Bird:
Ring-Necked Pheasant

State Flower:
American Pasqueflower

Next Stop:
Mount Rushmore

★★★★★★★★★★★★★★★★★
TICKET
★★★★★★★★★★★★★★★★★

11 Admit One

Name of State:
Alabama

Nickname of State:
Heart of Dixie
Yellowhammer State

State Bird:
Yellowhammer

State Flower:
Camellia

Next Stop:
George Washington
Carver Museum

★★★★★★★★★★★★★★★★★
TICKET
★★★★★★★★★★★★★★★★★

12 Admit One

Name of State:
Michigan

Nickname of State:
Wolverine State

State Bird:
Robin

State Flower:
Apple Blossom

Next Stop:
Detroit's Children's
Museum

★★★★★★★★★★★★★★★★★
TICKET
★★★★★★★★★★★★★★★★★

13 Admit One

Name of State:
Maryland

Nickname of State:
Old Line State

State Bird:
Baltimore Oriole

State Flower:
Black-Eyed Susan

Next Stop:
Chesapeake Maritime
Bay Museum

★★★★★★★★★★★★★★★★★
TICKET
★★★★★★★★★★★★★★★★★

14 Admit One

Name of State:
Oregon

Nickname of State:
Beaver State

State Bird:
Western Meadowlark

State Flower:
Oregon Grape

Next Stop:
Columbia River
Maritime Museum

★★★★★★★★★★★★★★★★★
TICKET
★★★★★★★★★★★★★★★★★

15 Admit One

Name of State:
Indiana

Nickname of State:
Hoosier State

State Bird:
Cardinal

State Flower:
Peony

Next Stop:
Sand Dunes of Indiana

★★★★★★★★★★★★★★★★★
TICKET
★★★★★★★★★★★★★★★★★

16 Admit One

Name of State:
Virginia

Nickname of State:
Old Dominion

State Bird:
Cardinal

State Flower:
Dogwood

Next Stop:
Roanoke Valley
Science Museum

Science Museum Ticket Cards

TICKET

17 Admit One

Name of State:
Hawaii

Nickname of State:
Aloha State

State Bird:
Hawaiian Goose

State Flower:
Hibiscus

Next Stop:
Diamond Head

TICKET

18 Admit One

Name of State:
Tennessee

Nickname of State:
Volunteer State

State Bird:
Mockingbird

State Flower:
Iris

Next Stop:
Great Smoky
Mountains National
Park

TICKET

19 Admit One

Name of State:
New York

Nickname of State:
Empire State

State Bird:
Bluebird

State Flower:
Rose

Next Stop:
Niagara Falls

TICKET

20 Admit One

Name of State:
Florida

Nickname of State:
Sunshine State

State Bird:
Mockingbird

State Flower:
Orange Blossom

Next Stop:
Walt Disney World

TICKET

21 Admit One

Name of State:
Arizona

Nickname of State:
Grand Canyon State

State Bird:
Cactus Wren

State Flower:
Blossom of Saguaro
Cactus

Next Stop:
Meteorcrater Museum
of Astrogeology

TICKET

22 Admit One

Name of State:
Iowa

Nickname of State:
Hawkeye State

State Bird:
Eastern Goldfinch

State Flower:
Wild Rose

Next Stop:
Effigy Mounds
National Monument

TICKET

23 Admit One

Name of State:
Georgia

Nickname of State:
Peach State, Empire
State of the South

State Bird:
Brown Thrasher

State Flower:
Cherokee Rose

Next Stop:
Six Flags over Georgia

TICKET

24 Admit One

Name of State:
Wisconsin

Nickname of State:
Badger State

State Bird:
Robin

State Flower:
Wood Violet

Next Stop:
Old World Wisconsin

GA1150

Ticket Stubs for Science Museum Ticket Cards

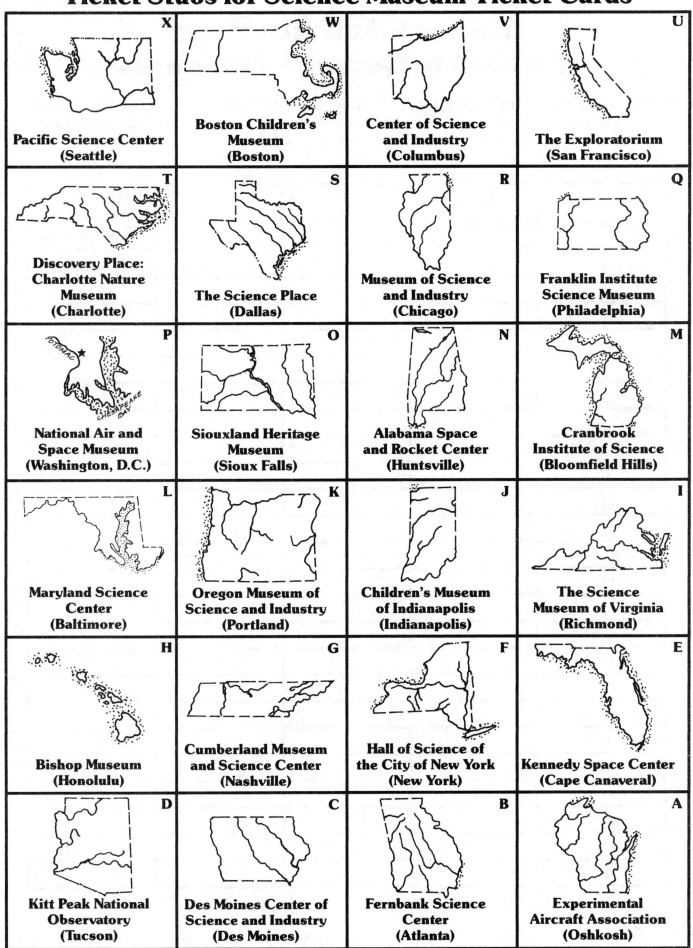

X **Pacific Science Center** **(Seattle)**	**W** **Boston Children's** **Museum** **(Boston)**	**V** **Center of Science** **and Industry** **(Columbus)**	**U** **The Exploratorium** **(San Francisco)**
T **Discovery Place:** **Charlotte Nature** **Museum** **(Charlotte)**	**S** **The Science Place** **(Dallas)**	**R** **Museum of Science** **and Industry** **(Chicago)**	**Q** **Franklin Institute** **Science Museum** **(Philadelphia)**
P **National Air and** **Space Museum** **(Washington, D.C.)**	**O** **Siouxland Heritage** **Museum** **(Sioux Falls)**	**N** **Alabama Space** **and Rocket Center** **(Huntsville)**	**M** **Cranbrook** **Institute of Science** **(Bloomfield Hills)**
L **Maryland Science** **Center** **(Baltimore)**	**K** **Oregon Museum of** **Science and Industry** **(Portland)**	**J** **Children's Museum** **of Indianapolis** **(Indianapolis)**	**I** **The Science** **Museum of Virginia** **(Richmond)**
H **Bishop Museum** **(Honolulu)**	**G** **Cumberland Museum** **and Science Center** **(Nashville)**	**F** **Hall of Science of** **the City of New York** **(New York)**	**E** **Kennedy Space Center** **(Cape Canaveral)**
D **Kitt Peak National** **Observatory** **(Tucson)**	**C** **Des Moines Center of** **Science and Industry** **(Des Moines)**	**B** **Fernbank Science** **Center** **(Atlanta)**	**A** **Experimental** **Aircraft Association** **(Oshkosh)**

GA1150

Student Activity Page:
Tickets to Science Museums

In the boxes below, write the letter of the ticket stub that best matches the ticket number. Then print the city and state in which that science point of interest is found. Compute round-trip distance from your home to site. The first one is done for you.

Ticket Number	Stub Letter	City	State	Miles/Kms from Home Round-Trip
1	X	Seattle	Washington	To Be Determined
2				
3				
4				
5				
6				
7				
8				
9				
10				
11				
12				
13				
14				
15				
16				
17				
18				
19				
20				
21				
22				
23				
24				

GA1150

Teacher/Parent Page

Learning Activity Packet 31: License Plate Science

Science Process Skill 15: Using Space/Time Relationships

Purpose: To identify the locations of major science points of interest and to compute the time required to travel to each site

Teaching Tips: This activity features twenty-four license plate activity cards of various national parks, science museums and geological sites. An outline of an unidentified state is found on each card. Make a copy of each page for each youngster. Have youngsters cut out cards. After studying a U.S. map and the student activity page on page 231, have youngsters identify each state by writing its name *above* the outline of the state on the license plate card. Using the names of the science features listed on the student activity page, have youngsters print the name of the science feature on the matching license plate card. After the names of the states and science features are written on the license plate cards, have the youngsters find out the number of hours driving time at 60 mph (100 km/h) it would take to reach each destination from their homes. With a ruler or measuring tape, have youngsters measure the distance between their homes and the destination on a U.S. map. Using the map, have youngsters divide the total miles (km) driven by 60 (100). This will give them the approximate number of hours driving time. Some youngsters may also choose to travel by air. On a blank sheet of paper, have youngsters design their own license plates which feature a drawing of their state with state name and the name of at least one science site found in their state.

Special Tip: Correlate this activity with Learning Activity Packet 30: Tickets to Science Museums, on pages 221-226.

Card and Student Activity Page Answers: 1. Washington—Pacific Science Center, 2. Oregon—Crater Lake National Park, 3. South Dakota—Badlands National Park, 4. Florida—Kennedy Space Center, 5. Montana—Glacier National Park, 6. Alaska—Mt. McKinley, 7. Wisconsin—Experimental Aircraft Association, 8. Wyoming—Yellowstone National Park, 9. Arizona—Meteor Crater, 10. New York—Hall of Science of the City of New York, 11. Texas—Big Bend National Park, 12. Idaho—Craters of the Moon, 13. Virginia—The Science Museum of Virginia, 14. Utah—Bryce Canyon National Park, 15. Arkansas—Hot Springs, 16. Illinois—Museum of Science and Industry, 17. Kentucky—Mammoth Cave National Park, 18. Colorado—Black Canyon of Gunnison, 19. Washington, D.C.—National Air and Space Museum, 20. Maine—Acadia National Park, 21. California—San Andreas Fault, 22. Massachusetts—Boston Children's Museum, 23. Tennessee—Great Smoky Mountains National Park, 24. Hawaii—Hawaii Volcano House

Wild Card Mystery "Park" Tour Answers: 1. Kansas, 2. Illinois, 3. Wisconsin, 4. Georgia, 5. Missouri, 6. Alabama, 7. Maryland, 8. Kansas

Extending Source: Irol W. Balsley, *Where on Earth?* (Carthage, IL: Good Apple, Inc., 1986).

GA1150

License Plate Science Cards

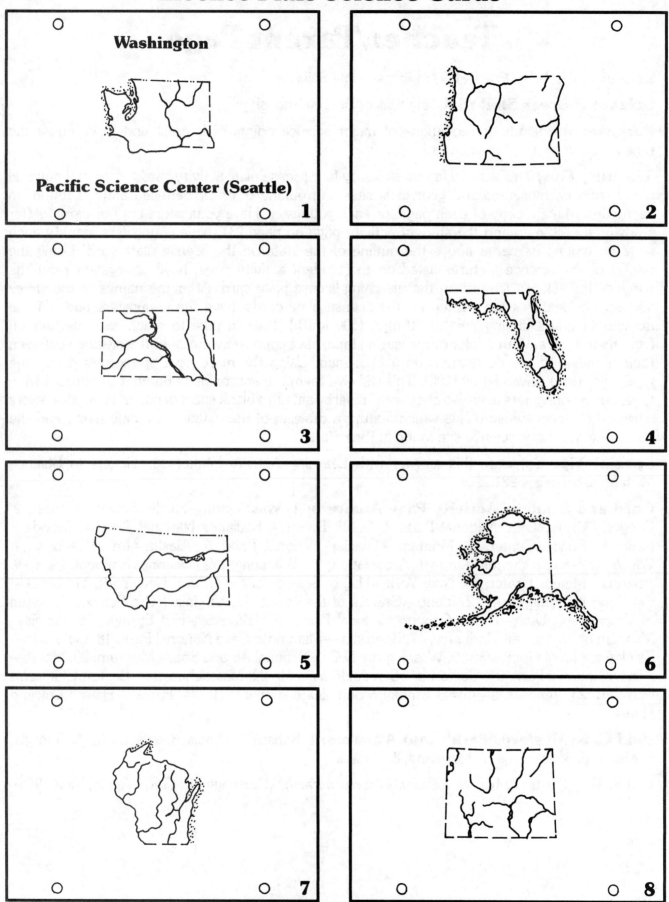

Washington

Pacific Science Center (Seattle)

1

2

3

4

5

6

7

8

228

GA1150

License Plate Science Cards

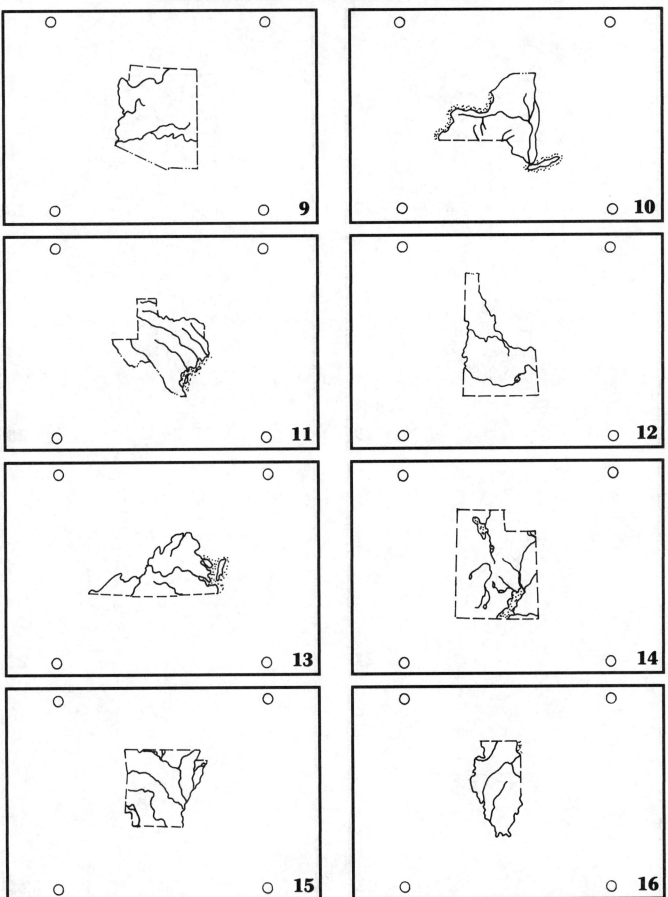

229

GA1150

License Plate Science Cards

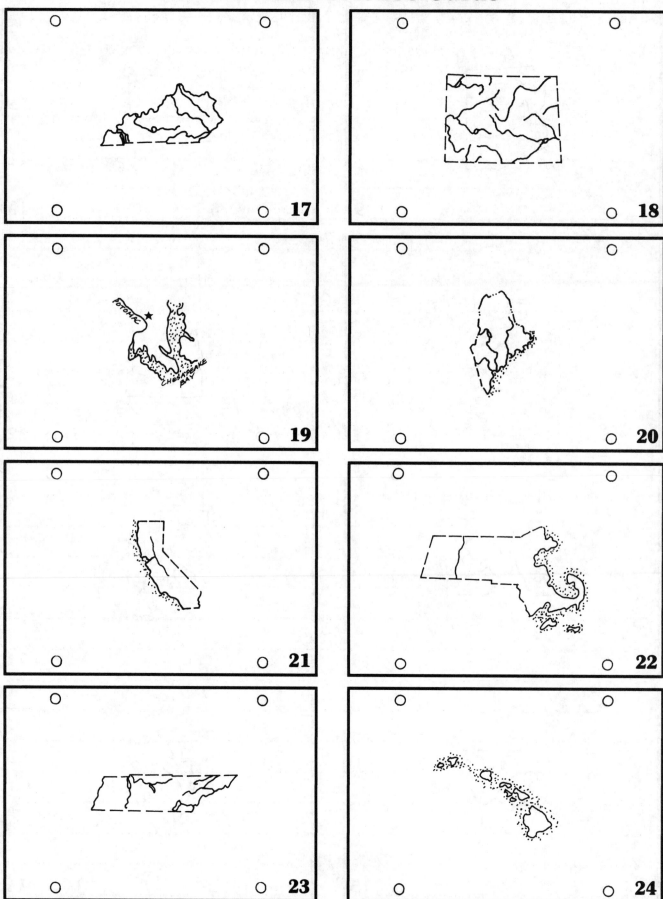

17

18

19

20

21

22

23

24

230

Student Activity Page: License Plate Science

Using an atlas, print the name of the matching state on the top of the license plate card. Record the names of the states in the chart below. Then using the names of the science features below, print the name of the matching science feature on the bottom of the correct license plate. The first one is done for you. Complete your trips by finding out how many hours driving time at 60 mph (100 km/hr) it would take you to reach your destination. Divide the number of miles by 60 or number of km by 100 to find your answer.

License Plate #	State	Science Feature	Driving Time
1	Washington	Pacific Science Center—Seattle	
2		Crater Lake National Park	
3		Badlands National Parks	
4		Kennedy Space Center	
5		Glacier National Park	
6		Mt. McKinley	
7		Experimental Aircraft Association	
8		Yellowstone National Park	
9		Meteor Crater	
10		Hall of Science of the City of New York	
11		Big Bend National Park	
12		Craters of the Moon	
13		The Science Museum of Virginia	
14		Bryce Canyon National Park	
15		Hot Springs	
16		Museum of Science and Industry	
17		Mammoth Cave National Park	
18		Black Canyon of Gunnison	
19		National Air and Space Museum	
20		Acadia National Park	
21		San Andreas Fault	
22		Boston Children's Museum	
23		Great Smoky Mountains National Park	
24		Hawaii Volcano House	

GA1150

Wild Card Mystery "Park" Tours

Name the state in which the word *park* is found.

1

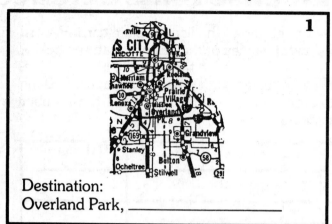

Destination:
Overland Park, _____

2

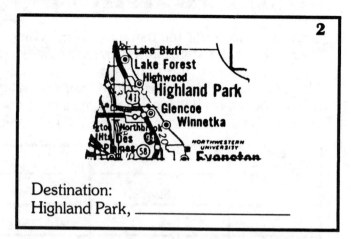

Destination:
Highland Park, _____

3

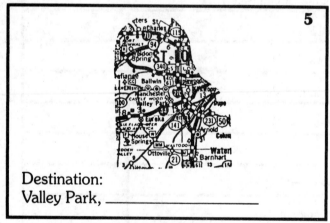

Destination:
Park Falls, _____

4

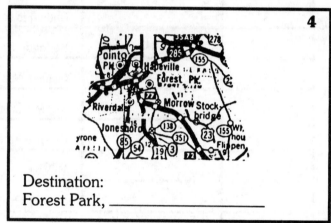

Destination:
Forest Park, _____

5

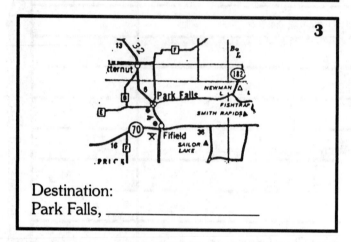

Destination:
Valley Park, _____

6

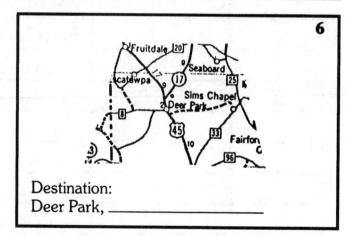

Destination:
Deer Park, _____

7

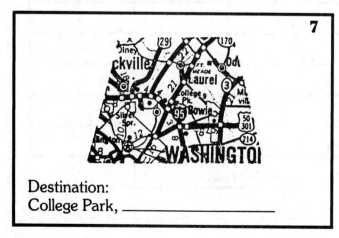

Destination:
College Park, _____

8

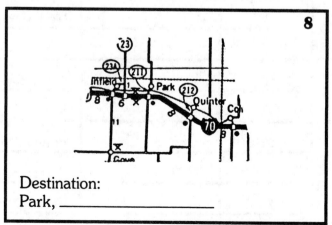

Destination:
Park, _____

GA1150

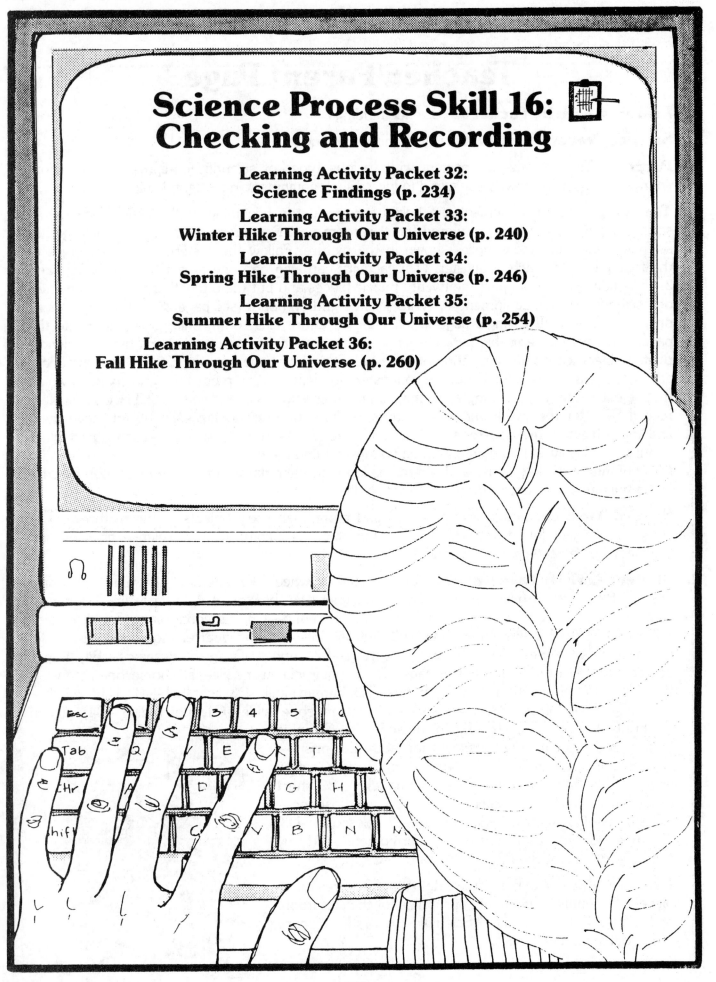

Science Process Skill 16: Checking and Recording

GA1150

Teacher/Parent Page

Learning Activity Packet 32: Science Findings

Science Process Skill 16: Checking and Recording

Purpose: To familiarize youngsters with various types of scientific equipment. In addition, youngsters will learn how to use a grid to locate such equipment in a scientific picture.

Teaching Tips: This activity can best be done at the beginning of the school year when science equipment is being gathered for classroom use. Encourage youngsters to help gather science equipment and supplies shown in the picture. Follow these steps: 1. Make copies of the four pages for each youngster. (This activity can also be done as a whole class activity.) 2. Have youngsters cut apart the twenty puzzle pieces and put them together to make a picture of a scientist and his equipment. 3. Write science grid on board (see page 238). 4. Mount pieces on poster board. (If a single page is used for an entire classroom, enlarge and laminate the page. Then with an erasable pen, challenge youngsters to find and circle each hidden science-related object whose name is found on the student activity page on page 239. 5. On the student activity page on page 239, encourage youngsters to identify, then record the grid space in which that object is found. For example, the magnifying glass is found in grid space B2. Have youngsters record B2 after the words *magnifying glass*. 6. As youngsters locate each object, have them find that object in the classroom, school or home. 7. Discuss the role that each object plays in our everyday lives. For example, when youngsters find the first aid kit (A4), have them identify the contents of the kit, its use and where it is found in their classroom, home or school. Discuss the importance of science safety in all facets of life.

Special Tips: Encourage youngsters to find more than sixty objects in the picture and to color each object found. Include bonus object such as infinity symbol (science goes on and on) made by tied shoelaces in A1 and A2.

Student Activity Page Answers: animal exercise wheel—E1, ant farm—E4, ants—E4, apple poster—B3, atomizer (plant mister)—B4, bar magnet—B3, beaker—C4, bird poster—B3, candle flame—D3, cane—B3, clamp—D3, cricket—C3, diamond—C3, dissecting pan—B4, dry cell—E2, eyedropper—B1, fire extingusher—E2, first aid kit—A4, first quarter moon—A2, fish—C1, fish filter—C1, fishnet—D1, fish tank—C1, frog—E2, funnel—E4, giant tweezers—B4, grapes poster—B3, hamster—A3, hamster cage—E1, hanging planet mobile—E2, horseshoe magnet—B1, human footprint—A1, human leg bones—A3, human skull—D3, light bulb—B3, light switch—C3, magnifying glass—B2, meterstick—E3, microscope slide—C1, petri dish—B4, pigeon footprint—E3, planet Earth—B2, plant and pot—C4, plug outlet—B3, pop can—A1, poster of tornado—B4, prism—B3, recycling symbol—E4, rubber stopper—C3, safety goggles—D4, Saturn model—C3, scissor handles—B2, short broom—A4, snail—C4, space shuttle—D4, stethoscope—C2, stones—C1, syringe—A3, tadpole—E2, telescope—D3, test tube—C4, test tube brush—A2, thermometer—D1, toy car—D4, tuning forks—B3 and B4, watch—C2

Extending Source: For a free catalog that features many pieces of scientific equipment appropriate for the classroom and home, write to Edmund Scientific Co., 7789 Edscorp Bldg., Barrington, NJ 08007.

Science Findings Cards

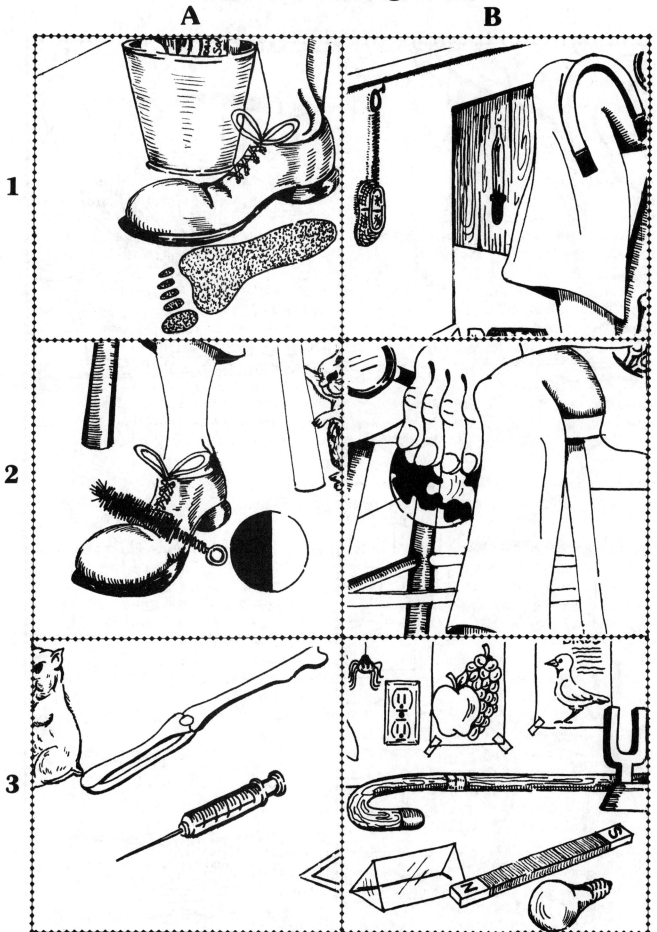

GA1150

Science Findings Cards

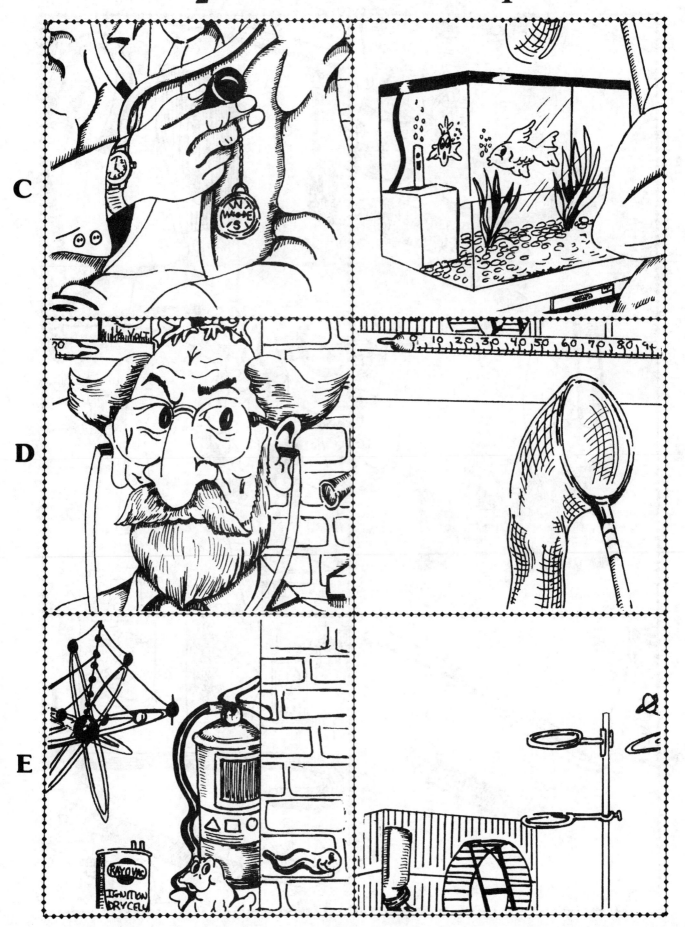

236

Science Findings Cards

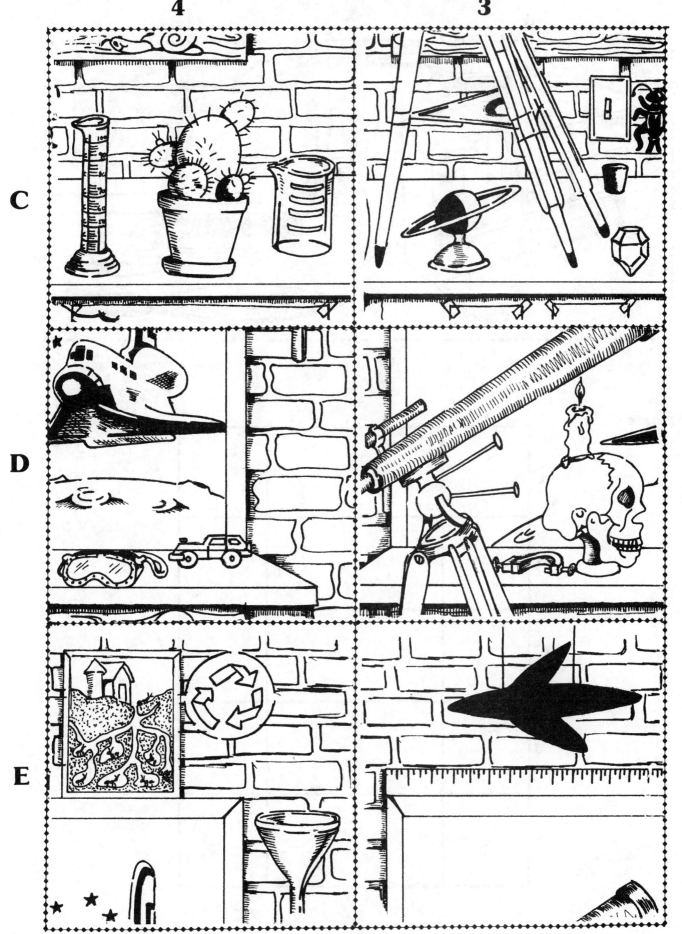

Science Findings Cards and Sample Grid

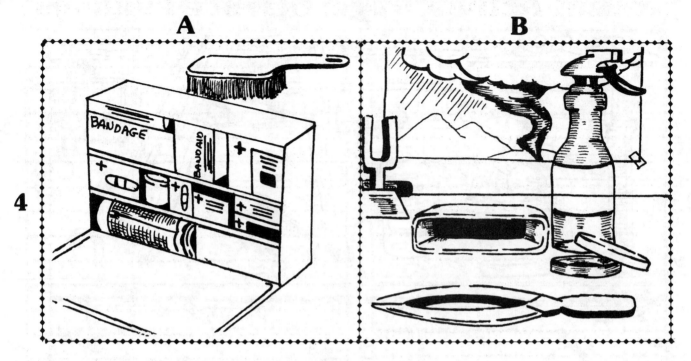

Sample Grid

	1	2	3	4
E				
D				
C				
B				
A				

GA1150

Student Activity Page: Science Findings

In the boxes below, print the names of the grid spaces in which each object is found.

Object	Grid Space
Animal exercise wheel	
Ant farm	
Ants	
Apple poster	
Atomizer (plant mister)	
Bar magnet	
Beaker	
Bird poster	
Candle flame	
Cane	
Clamp	
Cricket	
Diamond	
Dissecting pan	
Dry cell	
Eyedropper	
Fire extinguisher	
First aid kit	
First quarter moon	
Fish	
Fish filter	
Fishnet	
Fish tank	
Frog	
Funnel	
Giant tweezers	
Grapes poster	
Hamster	
Hamster cage	
Hanging planet mobile	
Horseshoe magnet	
Human footprint	
Human leg bones	
Human skull	

Object	Grid Space
Light bulb	
Light switch	
Magnifying glass	
Meterstick	
Microscope slide	
Petri dish	
Pigeon footprint	
Planet Earth	
Plant and pot	
Plug outlet	
Pop can	
Poster of tornado	
Prism	
Recycling symbol	
Rubber stopper	
Safety goggles	
Saturn model	
Scissor handles	
Short broom	
Snail	
Space shuttle	
Stethoscope	
Stones	
Syringe	
Tadpole	
Telescope	
Test tube	
Test tube brush	
Thermometer	
Toy car	
Tuning forks	
Watch	
Bonus: symbol for infinity	

239

Teacher/Parent Page

Learning Activity Packet 33: Winter Hike Through Our Universe

Science Process Skill 16: Checking and Recording

Purpose: To develop in youngsters an appreciation for nature and describe the seasonal changes in nature

Teaching Tips: The following four pages feature sixteen reduced cards that make up a booklet of winter activities that help youngsters develop an appreciation for nature during winter. Make copies of the pages. Have youngsters cut out the small pages. With a hole punch, make a hole in the upper left corner of each page. Add extra pages as needed. Cut a similar sized piece of single-layered cardboard. Punch a hole in corner to match the holes in the pages. Put a 20″ (51 cm) length of string through the holes and tie securely. (Ring fasteners or staples can also be used to attach pages to cardboard.) Attach a pencil to the other end of the string to complete the mini book sketch pad. After giving proper safety precautions, especially those related to weather (page 8), inform the youngsters that they can slide their sketch pads into their pockets. Then take the youngsters on a winter nature hike. Using their sketch pads, youngsters record what they see, hear, touch and smell. After the hike is completed, have youngsters complete the student activity page on page 245 to extend their learning.

Special Tip(s): (1) Have students go on the hike in groups of two so periodic temperature checks of skin can be done. (2) Small pages can be enlarged if additional writing space is needed.

Winter Hike Sketch Pad Answers: Page 7: Cold Winter—hot chocolate, nuts, raisins, carob, sunflower seeds, pumpkin seeds, granola, chocolate bars, fruit. Warm Winter—lemonade, water, ice, fruit, snacks, chocolate bars. Page 14: fox (W), pheasant (W), mouse (J), deer (W), gray squirrel (J), rabbit (J), dog (W), weasel or mink (J), sparrow (J), cat (W). Page 16: 1. long underwear, 2. I'm under water.

Extending Source: Jerry DeBruin, *Young Scientists Explore Nature* (Carthage, IL: Good Apple, Inc., 1986).

GA1150

Winter Hike Through Our Universe Sketch Pad Pages

1

Winter Hike Through Our Universe

by

Name _____

Paste a picture
of yourself here.

2

Color

My
(Red)

Winter
(Yellow)

Hike
(Green)

WALK

By

3

Fill in the Blanks

My Winter Log

Name _____
Street _____
City _____
State _____
Zip _____
Phone _____
Birthday _____

Draw in the hands.

Start Hike
Time

End Hike
Time

Total Hike Time _____ minutes
_____ seconds

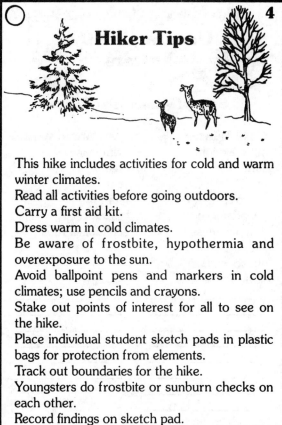

4

Hiker Tips

This hike includes activities for cold and warm winter climates.
Read all activities before going outdoors.
Carry a first aid kit.
Dress warm in cold climates.
Be aware of frostbite, hypothermia and overexposure to the sun.
Avoid ballpoint pens and markers in cold climates; use pencils and crayons.
Stake out points of interest for all to see on the hike.
Place individual student sketch pads in plastic bags for protection from elements.
Track out boundaries for the hike.
Youngsters do frostbite or sunburn checks on each other.
Record findings on sketch pad.

GA1150

Winter Hike Through Our Universe Sketch Pad Pages

Fill in the Blanks

5

A winter story. . .

Today, _____ , 19 ____ , I went on a hike to _____. I went with _____. I felt _____. I thought those who went with me were _____. I built a snowman. It was _____ inches (_____ cm) tall.

Mark the Items

6

Put an *X* next to the items appropriate for a cold winter hike. Put an *O* next to the items appropriate for a warm winter hike.

long underwear	snowsuit
rain gear	coat with hood
warm socks	swimsuit
thin socks	loose shirt
boots	scarf
tennis shoes	beach towel
sled	toy wagon
ice skates	roller skates
snow skis	water skis
warm shelter	sleeping bag
crayons	ballpoint pen
first aid kit	sunglasses
shorts	sweatshirt
T-shirt	hat
sun cap	layered clothes
blanket	mittens

Unscramble the Letters

7

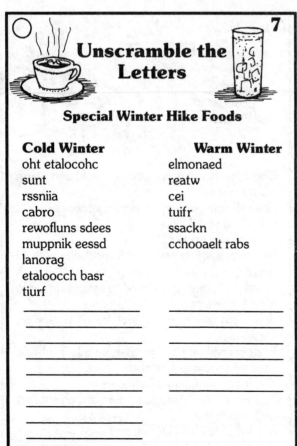

Special Winter Hike Foods

Cold Winter	Warm Winter
oht etalocohc	elmonaed
sunt	reatw
rssniia	cei
cabro	tuifr
rewofluns sdees	ssackn
muppnik eessd	cchooaelt rabs
lanorag	
etaloocch basr	
tiurf	

_____ _____

_____ _____

_____ _____

_____ _____

_____ _____

_____ _____

Circle the Hazard

8

Circle each of the hazards that you encounter on your hike.

Cold Winter	Warm Winter
thin ice on ponds	hot sun
overhanging ice	mud slides
icy sidewalks	stinging nettle
snowdrift tunnels	quicksand
breaking tree branches	falling branches
frostbite	mosquitos
wet clothes	strange animals
strange animals	spider bites
private property	bee stings
	ticks
	private property

GA1150

Winter Hike Through Our Universe Sketch Pad Pages

9

Check the Box

The day was:

Cold Winter	Warm Winter
☐ **Sunny**	☐ **Sunny**
☐ **Partly Cloudy**	☐ **Partly Cloudy**
☐ **Cloudy**	☐ **Cloudy**
☐ **Snowy**	☐ **Rainy**

10

Shade In

The temperature was: The wind was:

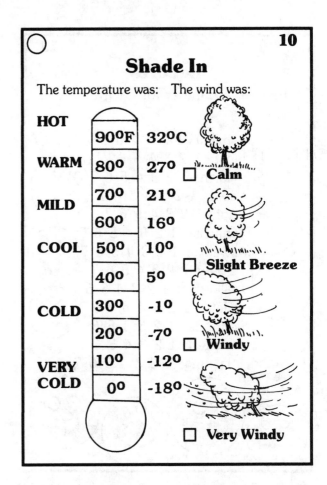

	°F	°C	
HOT	90°F	32°C	
WARM	80°	27°	☐ **Calm**
MILD	70°	21°	
	60°	16°	
COOL	50°	10°	
	40°	5°	☐ **Slight Breeze**
COLD	30°	-1°	
	20°	-7°	☐ **Windy**
VERY COLD	10°	-12°	
	0°	-18°	

☐ **Very Windy**

11

Color In

I saw these winter colors:

Cold Winter   **Warm Winter**

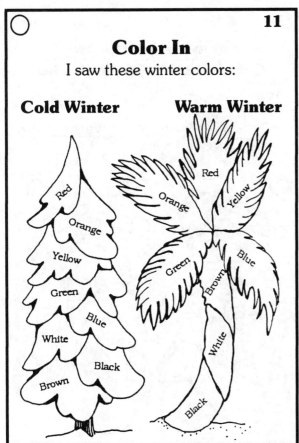

12

List

The names of things that had these shapes are

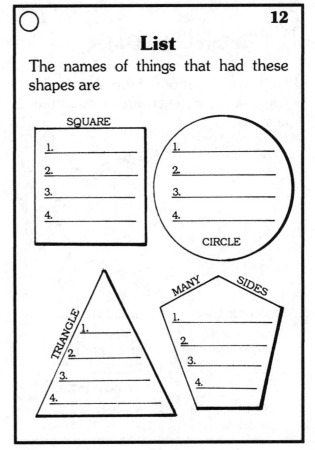

SQUARE

1. _____
2. _____
3. _____
4. _____

CIRCLE

1. _____
2. _____
3. _____
4. _____

TRIANGLE

1. _____
2. _____
3. _____
4. _____

MANY   SIDES

1. _____
2. _____
3. _____
4. _____

GA1150

Winter Hike Through Our Universe Sketch Pad Pages

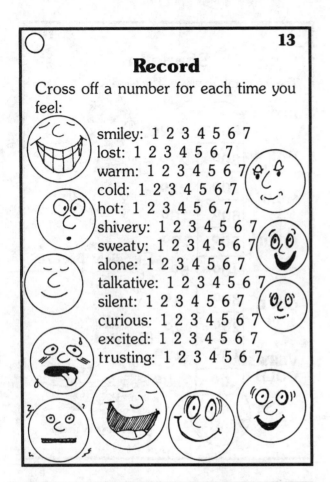

13

Record

Cross off a number for each time you feel:

smiley: 1 2 3 4 5 6 7
lost: 1 2 3 4 5 6 7
warm: 1 2 3 4 5 6 7
cold: 1 2 3 4 5 6 7
hot: 1 2 3 4 5 6 7
shivery: 1 2 3 4 5 6 7
sweaty: 1 2 3 4 5 6 7
alone: 1 2 3 4 5 6 7
talkative: 1 2 3 4 5 6 7
silent: 1 2 3 4 5 6 7
curious: 1 2 3 4 5 6 7
excited: 1 2 3 4 5 6 7
trusting: 1 2 3 4 5 6 7

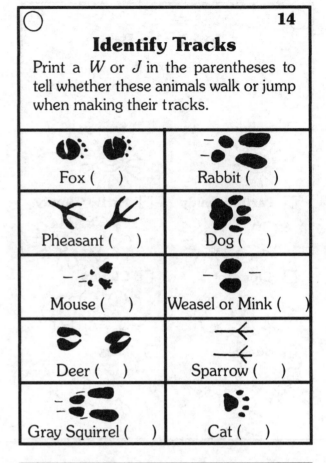

14

Identify Tracks

Print a *W* or *J* in the parentheses to tell whether these animals walk or jump when making their tracks.

Fox ( )	Rabbit ( )
Pheasant ( )	Dog ( )
Mouse ( )	Weasel or Mink ( )
Deer ( )	Sparrow ( )
Gray Squirrel ( )	Cat ( )

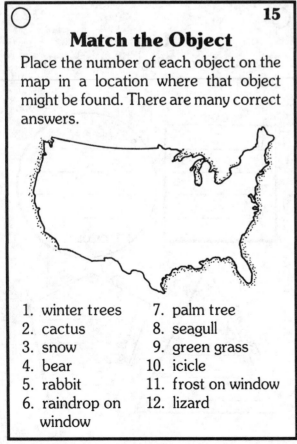

15

Match the Object

Place the number of each object on the map in a location where that object might be found. There are many correct answers.

1. winter trees
2. cactus
3. snow
4. bear
5. rabbit
6. raindrop on window
7. palm tree
8. seagull
9. green grass
10. icicle
11. frost on window
12. lizard

16

Winter Thinkers

Cold Winter   **Warm Winter**

1.
$$\frac{\text{wear}}{\text{LONG}}$$

2.
$$\frac{\text{water}}{\text{I'm}}$$

244

GA1150

Student Activity Page: Winter Hike Through Our Universe

After you finish your hike and have completed your answers, use the space below to record any further observations and feelings. Try your hand at drawing your favorite scene, cartoon, doodle, mind bender, bumper sticker, T-shirt saying or postage stamp. You may also want to write a poem, letter or limerick or compose a story about your fantasies, dreams, insights or other creative ideas.

Science Diary and Log

NAME _____

DATE _____

_____

_____

_____

_____

_____

_____

_____

_____

_____

_____

_____

_____

_____

_____

_____

_____

_____

_____

_____

_____

_____

_____

GA1150

Teacher/Parent Page

Learning Activity Packet 34: Spring Hike Through Our Universe

Science Process Skill 16: Checking and Recording

Purpose: To develop in youngsters an appreciation for nature and describe seasonal changes in nature

Teaching Tips: The following six pages feature twenty-four reduced cards that make up a booklet of spring activities that help youngsters develop an appreciation for nature during spring. Make copies of the pages. Have youngsters cut out the small pages. With a hole punch, make a hole in the upper left corner of each page. Add extra pages as needed. Cut a similarly sized piece of single-layered cardboard. Punch a hole in the corner to match the holes in the pages. Put a 20" (51 cm) length of string through the holes and tie securely. (Ring fasteners or staples can also be used to attach pages to cardboard.) Attach a pencil to the other end of the string to complete the mini book sketch pad. After giving proper safety precautions, inform the youngsters that they can insert their sketch pads into their pockets. Then take the youngsters on a spring nature hike. Using their sketch pads, youngsters record what they see, hear, touch and smell. On the student activity page on page 253 have youngsters, upon their return from the nature walk, do the suggested activities to extend their learning.

Special Tip: Design a bulletin board entitled "Spring Has Sprung" that features the twenty-four reduced sketch pad pages.

Spring Hike Sketch Pad Answers: Page 5: The day spring begins is March 20; spring ends June 20; spring is about ninety days long. Page 9: calm, light breeze, gentle breeze, blowing gale. Page 10: nuclear, nuclear power plant; coal, charcoal grill; water, waterfall; solar, sun; oil, oil truck; gasoline, gas station; food, snack bar. Page 12: acorn, oak tree; larva, honeybee; caterpillar, butterfly; seed, flower; tadpole, frog; fry, salmon; chick, swan; kit, beaver; fawn, deer; cub, bear; joey, kangaroo; gosling, goose; pup, seal or dog. Page 13: larva 2, pupa 3, adult 4, eggs 1. Page 14: f, h, a, b, c, k, i, j, e, g, d. Page 15: maple seed, helicopter; fish, breaststroke; frog, broad jump; seal, water ballet; flea, rocket propulsion; water spider, water skiing; penguin, modern dance; salmon, pole vault; cheetah, 100-meter dash; whale, submarine. Page 16: spiders, bird, squirrel, kite, tree, vine, wind vane. Page 21: waterfall, upstream, spring has sprung

Extending Source: Jerry DeBruin, *Young Scientists Explore Nature* (Carthage, IL: Good Apple, Inc., 1986).

GA1150

1

Spring Hike Through Our Universe

Name _____
(Write your name in pencil.)

Initials _____
(Use something from nature to write your initials here.)

2

Bicycle Checklist

I check my bike before I use it. The items I circle are in need of repair, and the ones I crossed out are safe.

chain
brakes
reflector
wheels
saddle (seat)
handle grips
horn
handlebars
light
spokes
tires
tire valve
crank and pedals
registration sticker

lock and chain
name on bike
picture of bike at
   home
recorded serial
   number
other _____

3

Fill in the Blanks

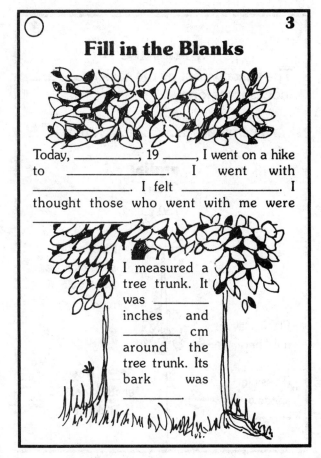

Today, _____, 19 _____, I went on a hike to _____. I went with _____. I felt _____. I thought those who went with me were _____

I measured a tree trunk. It was _____ inches and _____ cm around the tree trunk. Its bark was _____

4

Rub Pencil on Page over Bark

Here is my favorite bark rubbing.

GA1150

Spring Hike Through Our Universe Sketch Pad Pages

5

Write the Days

Write the days when spring begins and ends. _____ _____

Write the day when ice left the river or pond. _____

Write the day when the first seed was planted. _____

The spring season has _____ days.

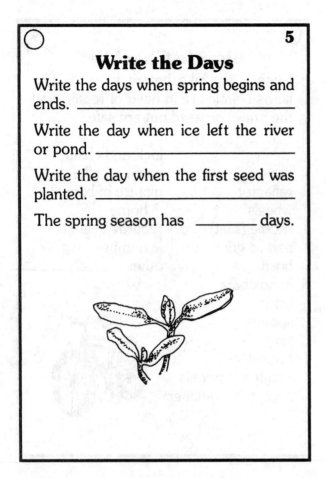

6

Check the Box
The day was:

☐ **Sunny**

☐ **Partly Cloudy**

☐ **Cloudy**

☐ **Windy**

7

Color In
The sun was:

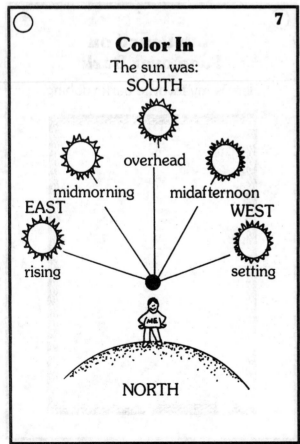

8

Measure

The shadow cast by the stick is _____ inches (cm) long.

The time is _____ (a.m.) (p.m.)

Sundial
Sun

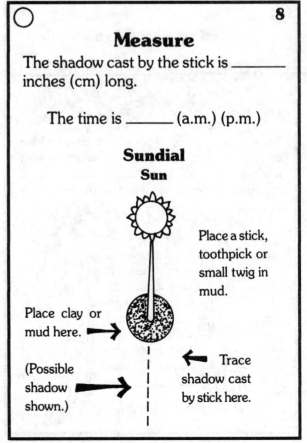

Place a stick, toothpick or small twig in mud.

Place clay or mud here. ➡

(Possible shadow shown.) ➡

⬅ Trace shadow cast by stick here.

248

GA1150

Spring Hike Through Our Universe Sketch Pad Pages

Fill in the Blanks

9

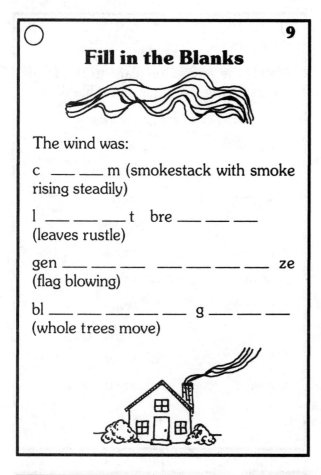

The wind was:

c ___ ___ m (smokestack with smoke rising steadily)

l ___ ___ ___ t bre ___ ___ ___ (leaves rustle)

gen ___ ___ ___ ___ ___ ___ ___ ___ ze (flag blowing)

bl ___ ___ ___ ___ ___ g ___ ___ ___ (whole trees move)

Match

10

I saw these forms of energy:

nuclear   charcoal grill

coal   sun

water   oil truck

solar   waterfall

oil   snack bar

gasoline   gas station

food   nuclear power plant

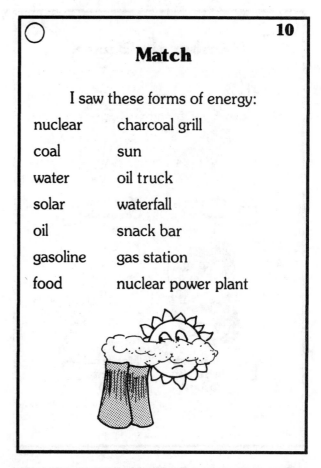

Record

11

Cross off a number for each time you talk to a person.

1 2 3 4 5 6 7
8 9 10 11 12 13
14 15 16 17 18 19 20

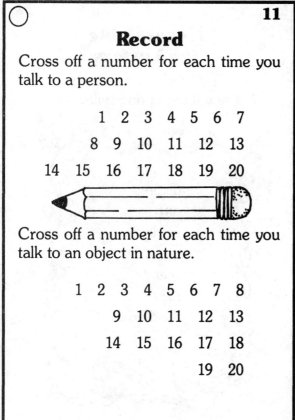

Cross off a number for each time you talk to an object in nature.

1 2 3 4 5 6 7 8
9 10 11 12 13
14 15 16 17 18
19 20

Predict

12

Write the name of each adult for the things listed below.

acorn _____

larva _____

caterpillar _____

seed _____

tadpole _____

fry _____

chick _____

kit _____

fawn _____

cub _____

joey _____

gosling _____

pup _____

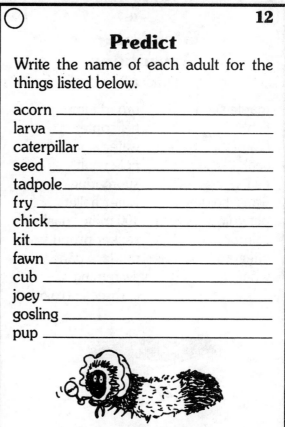

GA1150

Spring Hike Through Our Universe Sketch Pad Pages

13
Number the Boxes

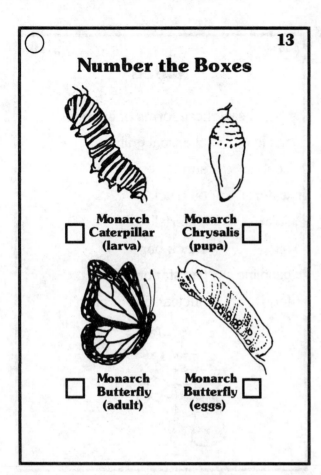

Monarch Caterpillar (larva) ☐

Monarch Chrysalis (pupa) ☐

Monarch Butterfly (adult) ☐

Monarch Butterfly (eggs) ☐

14
Diet

Match the animal or plant to the food it eats. Write the letter in the blank.

a. monarch butterfly   ___ sunlight

b. honeybee   ___ air

c. frog   ___ milkweed

d. salmon   ___ nectar

e. beaver   ___ insects

f. oak tree   ___ mouse

g. grass   ___ grass

h. dandelion   ___ worm

i. rabbit   ___ twigs

j. bird   ___ water

k. hawk   ___ sea creatures

15
Match Nature's Inventions
Draw a line.

maple seed	broad jump
fish	helicopter
frog	water skiing
seal	pole vault
flea	submarine
water spider	water ballet
penguin	100-meter dash
salmon	rocket propulsion
cheetah	modern dance
whale	swimming (breaststroke)

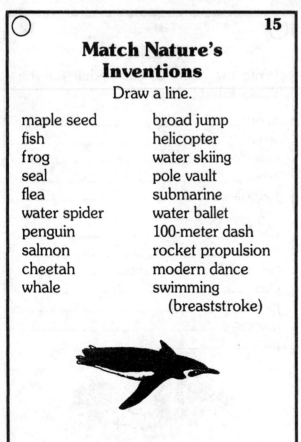

16
Unscramble the Letters

I saw these spring swingers:

dispres

dirb

qsirlreu

iket

reet

neiv

iwnd vnea

GA1150

Spring Hike Through Our Universe Sketch Pad Pages

17

Put a Check in the Blank

I saw the following plants and animals:

___ spider
___ hawk
___ daddy longlegs
___ crow
___ chipmunk
___ mole
___ fox
___ lichen
___ mushroom
___ squirrel
___ skunk
___ deer
___ goldenrod
___ daisy
___ frog
___ moss
___ butterfly
___ sow bug
___ tadpole
___ rabbit

___ worm
___ tulip tree
___ oak tree
___ pine tree
___ raccoon
___ woodchuck
___ owl
___ duck
___ pheasant
___ ladybug
___ snake
___ snail
___ millipede
___ sumac
___ toad
others:

_____
_____
_____
_____

18

Check the Box —Bird Travelers—

I saw these birds from the South:

☐ blackbirds
☐ robins
☐ bluebirds
☐ morning doves
☐ song sparrows
☐ warblers
☐ cooper hawks
☐ thrushers
☐ snow geese
☐ purple martins
☐ swallows
☐ cedar waxwings
☐ starlings
☐ bobolinks
☐ tanagers
☐ orioles
☐ finches
☐ eagles
☐ painted buntings

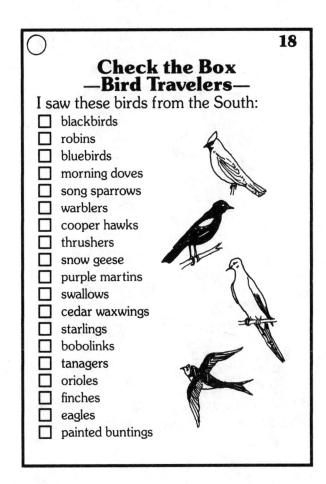

19

Write the Name

I found these things that begin with the following letters:

S_____

P_____

R_____

I_____

N_____

G_____

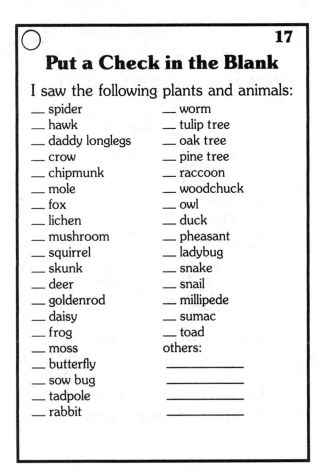

20

Connect the Dots

I saw these spring constellations on a night hike:

North
Star

Little Dipper

Big Dipper

Draco

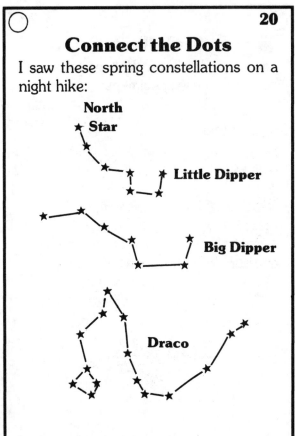

251

GA1150

Spring Hike Through Our Universe Sketch Pad Pages

21
Spring Thinkers

Use these spring words as examples and make up your own "spring thinkers."

22
Draw

Design your own bumper sticker for spring.

My Spring Bumper Sticker

23
Collect

Tape samples here. With permission, I collected these specimens:

bird feather

small rock

soil sample

twig

air (bubble under tape)

seed

leaf

sap

24
Circle the Objects

Every piece of litter picked up is a help. I found and picked up this litter.

GA1150

Student Activity Page:
Spring Hike Through Our Universe

After you finish your hike and have completed your answers, use the space below to record any further observations and feelings. Try your hand at drawing your favorite scene, cartoon, doodle, mind bender, bumper sticker, T-shirt saying or postage stamp. You may also want to write a poem, letter or limerick or compose a story about your fantasies, dreams, insights or other creative ideas.

Science Diary and Log

NAME _____

DATE _____

_____

_____

_____

_____

_____

_____

_____

_____

_____

_____

_____

_____

_____

_____

_____

_____

_____

GA1150

Teacher/Parent Page

Learning Activity Packet 35: Summer Hike Through Our Universe

Science Process Skill 16: Checking and Recording

Purpose: To develop in youngsters an appreciation for nature and describe how nature changes with each change in season

Teaching Tips: The following five pages feature eighteen reduced pages that make up a booklet of summer activities that when given to youngsters, help them develop an appreciation for nature during the summer. Make copies of the pages. Have youngsters cut out the smaller pages. With a hole punch, make a hole in the upper left corner of each page. Add extra pages as needed. Cut a similarly sized piece of single-layered cardboard. Punch a hole in corner to match pages. Put a 20″ (51 cm) length of string through the holes and tie securely. (Ring fasteners or staples can also be used.) Attach a pencil to the other end of the string to complete this mini book sketch pad. After giving proper safety precautions (page 4), inform the youngsters that the mini book sketch pad is a gift to them from you to be used in the summer. Go over each page with the youngsters. Tell youngsters that the sketch pad fits into their pocket and can be used as a recording device for things seen, heard, touched or smelled while on a nature hike during the summer.

Special Tip(s): 1. Make additional copies of the envelope on page 259. With permission, have youngsters collect various objects and place in the envelopes. Label each for further study. 2. Correlate this activity with the "Student Diploma for Summer Science" found on pages 314-320.

Summer Hike Sketch Pad Answers: Page 7: cirrus, cumulus, nimbus, stratus. Page 16: woodpecker, crawdad, butterfly, squirrel, chipmunk, beaver

Extending Source: Jerry DeBruin, *Young Scientists Explore Nature* (Carthage, IL: Good Apple, Inc., 1986).

Summer Hike Through Our Universe Sketch Pad Pages

1

Summer Hike Through Our Universe

Name _____

Address _____

Phone _____

2

Fill in the Blanks

Today, _____, 19 _____, I went on a hike
to _____ I went with _____
I felt _____ I thought those who went
with me were _____

I measured a
tree trunk. It
was _____
inches and
_____ cm
around the
tree trunk. Its
bark was
_____

3

Rub Pencil on Page over Bark

Here is my favorite bark rubbing.

4

I Stayed Away From . . .

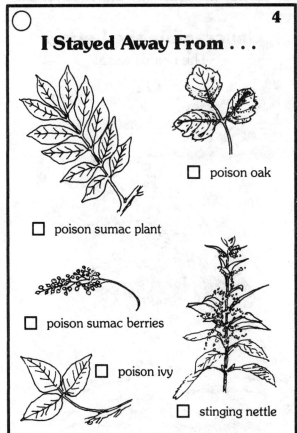

☐ poison oak

☐ poison sumac plant

☐ poison sumac berries

☐ poison ivy

☐ stinging nettle

GA1150

Summer Hike Through Our Universe Sketch Pad Pages

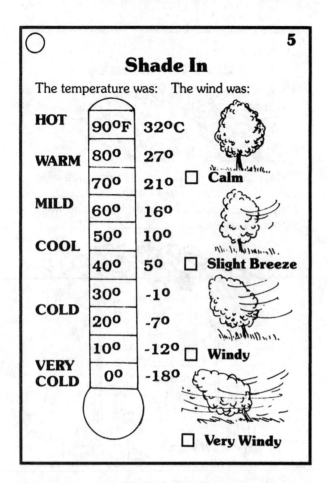

5

Shade In

The temperature was: The wind was:

HOT	90°F	32°C
WARM	80°	27°
	70°	21°
MILD	60°	16°
	50°	10°
COOL	40°	5°
	30°	-1°
COLD	20°	-7°
	10°	-12°
VERY COLD	0°	-18°

☐ **Calm**

☐ **Slight Breeze**

☐ **Windy**

☐ **Very Windy**

6

Check the Box

The day was:

☐ **Sunny**

☐ **Partly Cloudy**

☐ **Cloudy**

☐ **Rainy**

7

Unscramble the Letters

The clouds were:

ricsur

mucusul

minubs

rastuts

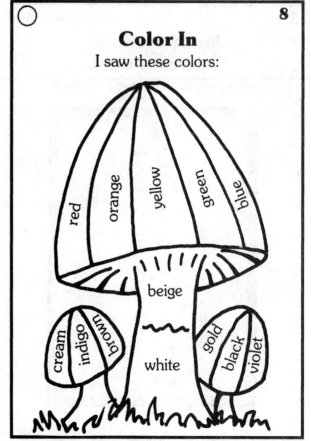

8

Color In

I saw these colors:

red

orange

yellow

green

blue

beige

cream   indigo   brown

white

gold   black   violet

GA1150

Summer Hike Through Our Universe Sketch Pad Pages

9

Put a Check in the Blank

I saw the following plants and animals:

- _ spider
- _ hawk
- _ daddy longlegs
- _ crow
- _ chipmunk
- _ mole
- _ fox
- _ lichen
- _ mushroom
- _ squirrel
- _ skunk
- _ deer
- _ goldenrod
- _ daisy
- _ frog
- _ moss
- _ butterfly
- _ sow bug
- _ tadpole
- _ rabbit

- _ worm
- _ tulip tree
- _ oak tree
- _ pine tree
- _ raccoon
- _ woodchuck
- _ owl
- _ duck
- _ pheasant
- _ ladybug
- _ snake
- _ snail
- _ millipede
- _ sumac
- _ toad

others:

_____
_____
_____
_____

10

Color In

Here are things that change color during different seasons.

Spring   Summer

Winter   Fall

11

Box-Number Sequence

I saw some things that change what they look like as they grow. Number one is the youngest; number four is the oldest.

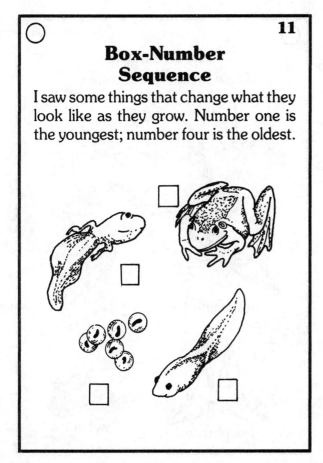

12

Draw in Empty Circle

I saw some things that eat other things. An animal that might eat the bird below is. . .

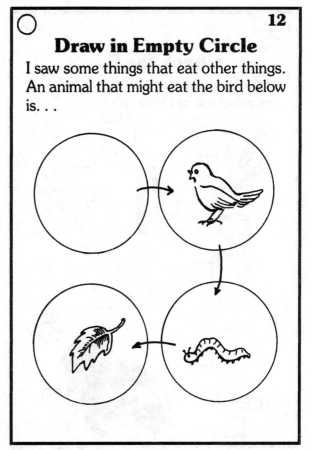

GA1150

Summer Hike Through Our Universe Sketch Pad Pages

13

List

The names of things that had these shapes are

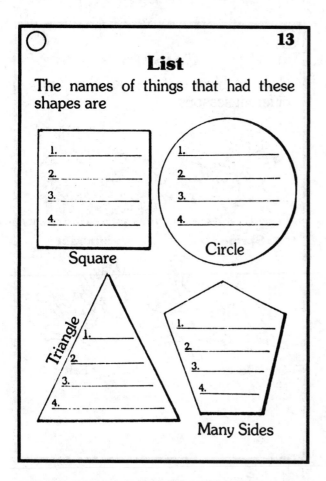

Square

Circle

Triangle

1. _____
2. _____
3. _____
4. _____

Many Sides

1. _____
2. _____
3. _____
4. _____

14

Match

I saw these animal tracks and will draw a line to the animal that made the track.

15

Check the Box

I smelled things on the hike that reminded me of these smells:

16

Unscramble

I saw these animal homes:

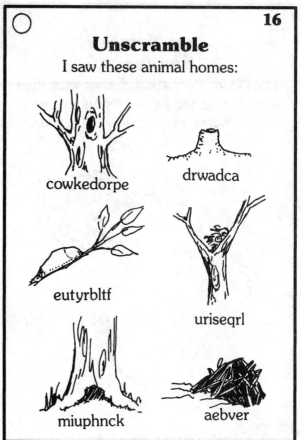

cowkedorpe

drwadca

eutyrbltf

uriseqrl

miuphnck

aebver

GA1150

Summer Hike Through Our Universe Sketch Pad Pages

17

Attach Specimens

The park ranger gave me permission to take some things off the ground and to tape them here. They are. . .

18

Write

We told some stories about our universe. My story tells about my thoughts and feelings. It reads . . .

Cut on solid lines. Fold flap on dotted line. Slide edge of envelope under flap. Tape flap to side. Tape end of envelope shut. Place specimens in envelope.

GA1150

Teacher/Parent Page

Learning Activity Packet 36: Fall Hike Through Our Universe

Science Process Skill 16: Checking and Recording

Purpose: To develop in youngsters the power of observation and an appreciation for seasonal changes in nature

Teaching Tips: The following four pages feature sixteen reduced pages that make up a booklet of fall activities for student use. Make copies of the pages. Have youngsters cut out the small pages. With a hole punch, make a hole in the upper left corner of each page. Add extra pages as needed. Cut a similar sized piece of single-layered cardboard. Punch a hole in the corner to match the holes in the pages. Put a 20" (51 cm) length of string through the holes and tie securely. (Ring fasteners or staples can also be used to attach pages to the cardboard.) Attach a pencil to the other end of the string to complete the mini book sketch pad. After giving proper safety precautions, tell the youngsters that they can easily insert their sketch pads into their pockets. Have the youngsters go on a hike around school and home and record what they see, hear, touch and smell. On the student activity page on page 265, have the youngsters, upon their return from the hike, do the suggested activities to further extend their learning.

Special Tip: Using the wild cards as a springboard into further study, have youngsters develop a complete deck of cards of the deaf alphabet.

Fall Hike Sketch Pad Answers: Page 7: 4, 7, 2, 1, 3, 5, 9, 6, 8. Page 13: Michael Faraday— 22 September 1851, Walter Reed— 13 September 1851, John Dalton—6 September 1766, Chen Ning Yang—22 September 1922, Enrico Fermi—29 September 1901. Page 14: Jonas Salk, Alfred Nobel, Marie Curie, Robert Goddard, Benjamin Banneker. Pages 15-16: (1) geese flying south in *V* pattern, (2) pumpkin for Halloween, (3) leaves falling from tree, (4) squirrel burying acorns in soil, (5) squirrel's nest in a tree, (6) boy wearing sweater, (7) smoke coming from chimney, (8) rake with pile of leaves, (9) shocks of corn, (10) clock—fall back from daylight savings time to standard time

Wild but Silent Card Answers: I Love You.

Extending Source: Jerry DeBruin, *Creative, Hands-On Science Experiences* (rev. ed., Carthage, IL: Good Apple, Inc., 1986).

Fall Hike Through Our Universe Sketch Pad Pages

1

Fall Hike Through Our Universe

Name _____

Address _____

_____

School _____

2

Fill in the Blanks

Today, _____, 19____,

I went on a hike to _____.

I went with _____.

I thought those who went with me were

_____

_____

_____

3

Draw

Draw the face of a kind, loving person below.

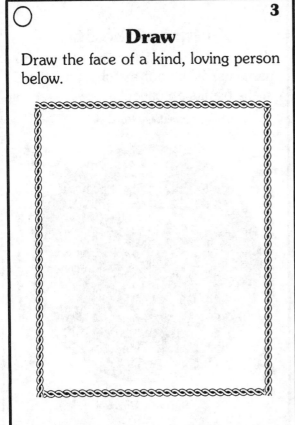

4

Write the Name

Make a list of things that *fall* in autumn.

1. _____

2. _____

3. _____

4. _____

5. _____

GA1150

Fall Hike Through Our Universe Sketch Pad Pages

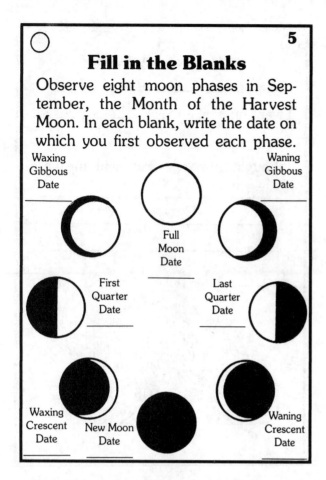

5

Fill in the Blanks

Observe eight moon phases in September, the Month of the Harvest Moon. In each blank, write the date on which you first observed each phase.

Waxing Gibbous Date

Waning Gibbous Date

Full Moon Date

First Quarter Date

Last Quarter Date

Waxing Crescent Date

New Moon Date

Waning Crescent Date

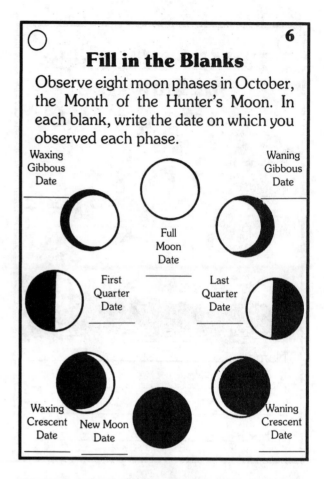

6

Fill in the Blanks

Observe eight moon phases in October, the Month of the Hunter's Moon. In each blank, write the date on which you observed each phase.

Waxing Gibbous Date

Waning Gibbous Date

Full Moon Date

First Quarter Date

Last Quarter Date

Waxing Crescent Date

New Moon Date

Waning Crescent Date

7

Number the Blanks

Below are the names of nine fall constellations. Using the diagram on page 8, write the matching number of each constellation in each blank.

_____ Cepheus

_____ Cygnus

_____ Ursa Major

_____ Ursa Minor

_____ Cassiopeia

_____ Draco

_____ Sagittarius

_____ Andromeda

_____ Capricorn

8

Picture of the Star

We are fall constellations. Can you name us? Write our matching numbers in the blanks on page 7.

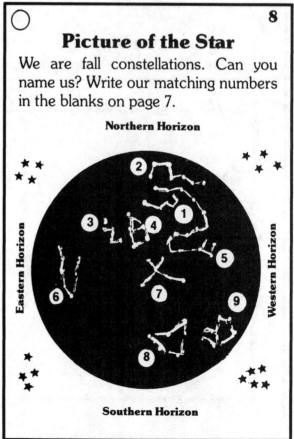

Northern Horizon

Eastern Horizon

Western Horizon

Southern Horizon

262

GA1150

Fall Hike Through Our Universe Sketch Pad Pages

9
Write the Name

I found these things that begin with the following letters:

F _____

A _____

L _____

L _____

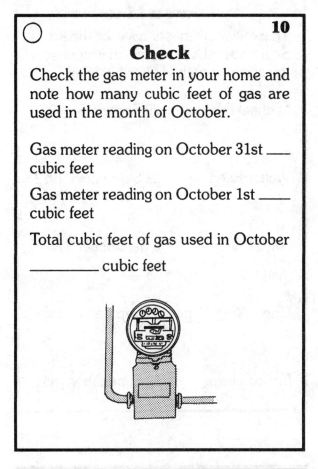

10
Check

Check the gas meter in your home and note how many cubic feet of gas are used in the month of October.

Gas meter reading on October 31st ___ cubic feet

Gas meter reading on October 1st ___ cubic feet

Total cubic feet of gas used in October

_____ cubic feet

11
Fill in the Blanks

Investigate the amount of insulation in your home. Find out what R value means. In the blank below, write the number of R value insulation in your home _____.

The R value insulation number in my home is _____

12
Write the Name

Write the names and percentages of chemicals used in lawn fertilizer in the fall.

_____ ___%

_____ ___%

_____ ___%

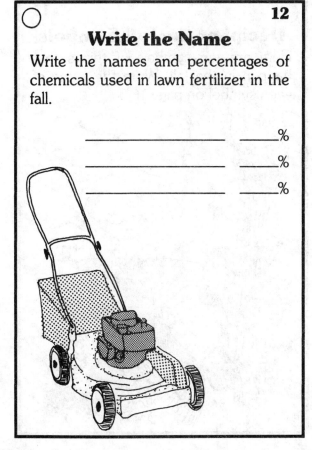

Fall Hike Through Our Universe Sketch Pad Pages

13
Draw a Line
These five scientists have birthdays in September. Draw a line that connects the scientist with his/her birthday.

Michael Faraday   29 September 1901

Walter Reed   22 September 1922

John Dalton   6 September 1766

Chen Ning Yang   13 September 1851

Enrico Fermi   22 September 1851

14
Unscramble the Letters
These five scientists have birthdays in October and November. Unscramble the letters to name each scientist.

28 October 1914   SAONJ KALS

_____

21 October 1833   DREFLA ONLEB

_____

7 November 1867   ERIAM ECRUI

_____

5 October 1882   TERROB GARDODD

_____

9 November 1731   BNAINEJM NNABEREK

_____

15
Decipher the Fall Symbols
Here are ten symbols of things that happen in the fall. Write the name of each symbol on page 16.

16
Write the Name
1. _____
2. _____
3. _____
4. _____
5. _____
6. _____
7. _____
8. _____
9. _____
10. _____

GA1150

Student Activity Page: Fall Hike Through Our Universe

After you finish your hike and have completed your answers, use the space below to record any further observations and feelings. Try your hand at drawing your favorite scene, cartoon, doodle, mind bender, bumper sticker, T-shirt saying or postage stamp. You may also want to write a poem, letter or limerick or compose a story about your fantasies, dreams, insights or other creative ideas.

Science Diary and Log

NAME _____

DATE _____

_____

_____

_____

_____

_____

_____

_____

_____

_____

_____

_____

_____

_____

_____

_____

_____

_____

_____

_____

_____

_____

_____

GA1150

Wild but Silent Cards That Speak on the Hike of Life

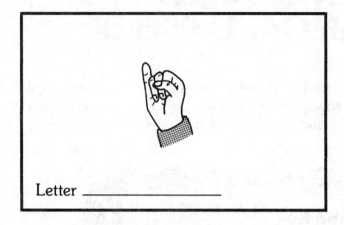

Letter _____

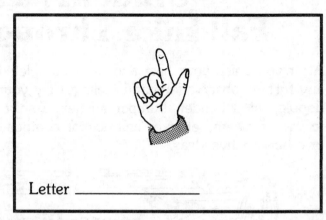

Letter _____

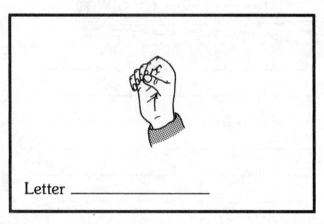

Letter _____

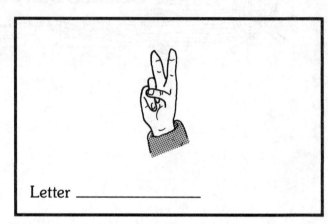

Letter _____

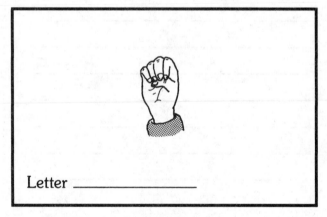

Letter _____

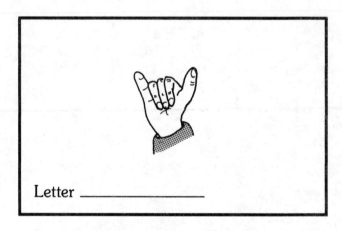

Letter _____

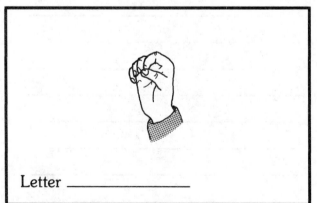

Letter _____

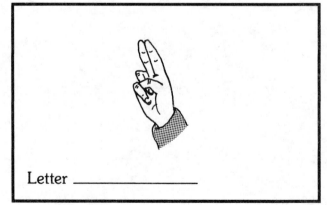

Letter _____

GA1150

Science Process Skill 17: Inferring

**Learning Activity Packet 37:
Scientific Relationships (p. 268)**

**Learning Activity Packet 38:
Fact or Myth (p. 274)**

Teacher/Parent Page

Learning Activity Packet 37: Scientific Relationships

Science Process Skill 17: Inferring

Purpose: Inferences are ideas that have been refined through observation and testing. Youngsters will learn that the more observations that they do, the more valid their inferences will be.

Teaching Tips: Inferences are the result of making observations about various phenomena in our galaxy. Inferences involve the use of logic and logic statements such as, "If this happens, then this will happen." By making inferences, youngsters are able to see the type of relationship that exists between various physical and biological phenomena. The type of relationship is coded on each of the cards: WP = whole-part, PU = purpose, OA = object to action, D = degree, PW = part-whole, AO = action to object, A = antonym, SY = synonym, S = sequence and PL = place. Follow these steps: (1) Make copies of the sixteen cards for each youngster. (2) Mount on cardboard. (3) Have youngsters first *observe* the figures on each card; then use logic to determine the correct response. Stress that youngsters should record their initial response (pre) and their final response (post) as a result of further observation and study. Have youngsters make a simple pre-post record of their responses and note how the correct number of responses increases as the more observations and study are done. Record answers on student activity page on page 273.

Special Tip: This activity may be used as a lesson in reading. Encourage youngsters to develop their own relationship cards.

Scientific Relationships Card Answers: 1. 3, 2. 1, 3. 2, 4. 2, 5. 3, 6. 2, 7. 2, 8. 1, 9. 1, 10. 3, 11. 1, 12. 4, 13. 2, 14. 2, 15. 2, 16. 2

Extending Source: For ideas on analogies and their types, see *MAT: Miller Analogies Test* by William Bader (New York: Prentice-Hall Publishers, 1988).

GA1150

Scientific Relationships Cards

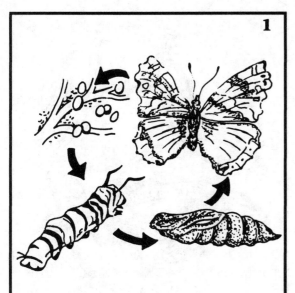

Eggs relate to caterpillar as chrysalis relates to:

1. cocoon
2. antennae
3. adult butterfly
4. larva

S

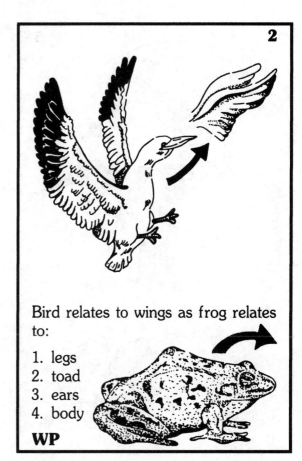

Bird relates to wings as frog relates to:

1. legs
2. toad
3. ears
4. body

WP

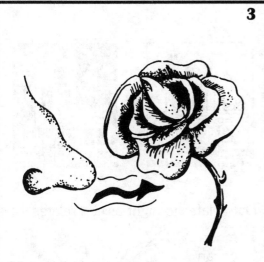

Nose relates to smell as teeth relate to:

1. candy bar
2. chew
3. gum
4. white

PU

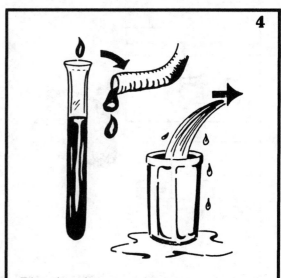

Blood relates to artery as water relates to:

1. body
2. pipe
3. rabbit
4. mouse

OA

GA1150

Scientific Relationships Cards

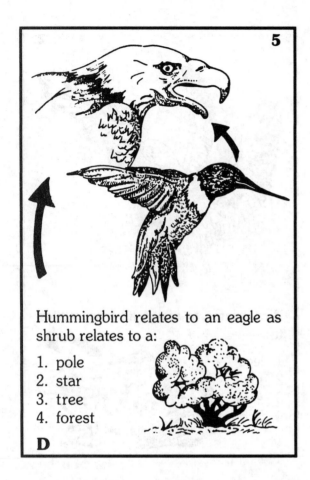

Hummingbird relates to an eagle as shrub relates to a:

1. pole
2. star
3. tree
4. forest

D

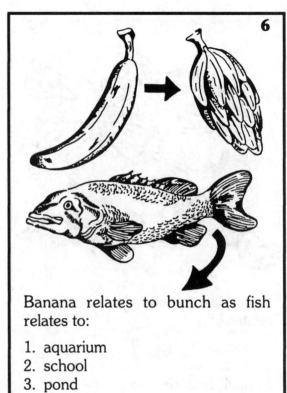

Banana relates to bunch as fish relates to:

1. aquarium
2. school
3. pond
4. shark

PW

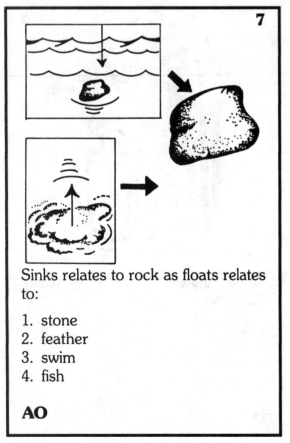

Sinks relates to rock as floats relates to:

1. stone
2. feather
3. swim
4. fish

AO

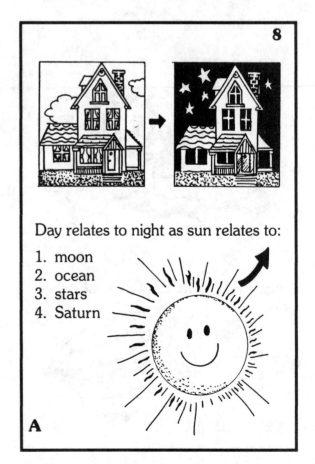

Day relates to night as sun relates to:

1. moon
2. ocean
3. stars
4. Saturn

A

GA1150

Scientific Relationships Cards

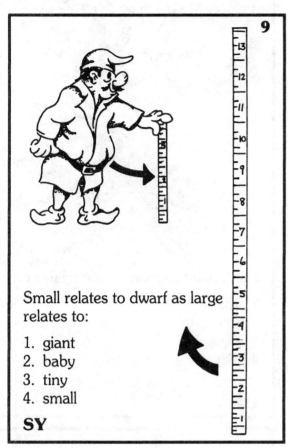

9

Small relates to dwarf as large relates to:

1. giant
2. baby
3. tiny
4. small

SY

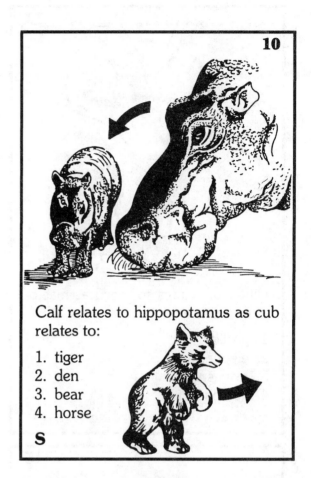

10

Calf relates to hippopotamus as cub relates to:

1. tiger
2. den
3. bear
4. horse

S

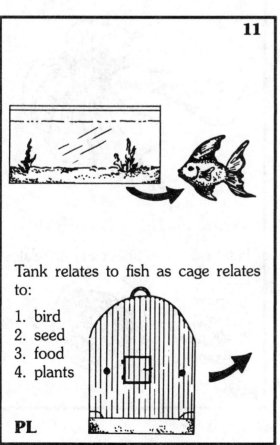

11

Tank relates to fish as cage relates to:

1. bird
2. seed
3. food
4. plants

PL

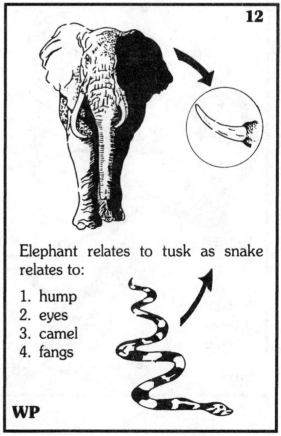

12

Elephant relates to tusk as snake relates to:

1. hump
2. eyes
3. camel
4. fangs

WP

GA1150

Scientific Relationships Cards

13

Dinosaur relates to lizard as mastodon relates to:

1. gorilla
2. elephant
3. rattlesnake
4. apatosaurus

S

14

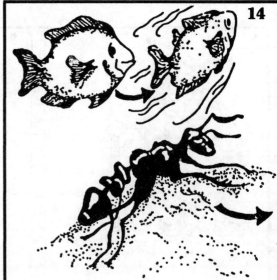

Fish relates to swim as ant relates to:

1. roar
2. crawl
3. squeak
4. alligator

OA

15

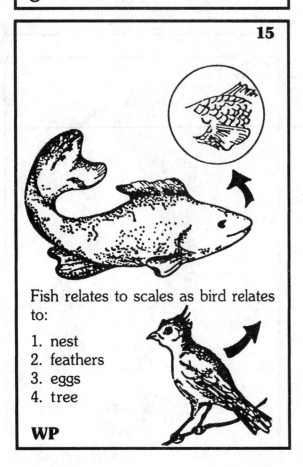

Fish relates to scales as bird relates to:

1. nest
2. feathers
3. eggs
4. tree

WP

16

Petal relates to flower as fur relates to:

1. snake
2. rabbit
3. alligator
4. women

PW

GA1150

Student Activity Page:
Scientific Relationships

Card #	Answer	Card #	Answer
1		9	
2		10	
3		11	
4		12	
5		13	
6		14	
7		15	
8		16	

My Scientific Relationship Card

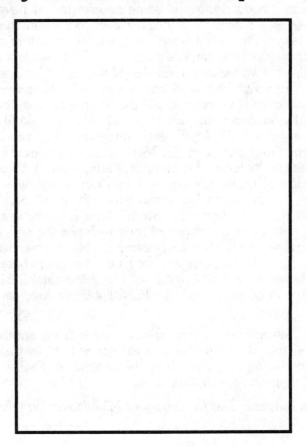

GA1150

Teacher/Parent Page

Learning Activity Packet 38: Fact or Myth

Science Process Skill 17: Inferring

Purpose: To identify inferences as beliefs scientists hold that are refined through observation, acquiring information and testing. Youngsters will learn that the more observations done and the more information acquired by valid testing, the more valid their inferences will be.

Teaching Tips: Inferences are the result of observations and the gathering of information through testing various phenomena. By gathering information, youngsters become involved in the process of making valid inferences. Included in this activity are thirty-two science statements on cards. Make copies for each youngster or a single set for the classroom. Have youngsters cut apart cards. Read each card carefully to determine whether the statement is a fact or myth. On the student activity page on page 279, have youngsters shade in or color the corresponding circle *F* for fact, *M* for myth. The numbers in the circles are point values arbitrarily assigned to each statement. On the student activity page have youngsters add up the total number correct and total the points. 100 points represents a perfect score.

Special Tip: Emphasize that some of today's myths may actually evolve into facts as more observations and tests are conducted on such phenomena.

Fact or Myth Card Answers: 1. Myth, but there is a great deal of speculation about this topic. 2. Myth, but attempts are being made via *Pioneer 10* which left our solar system in June, 1983. 3. Myth, there is no scientific evidence to support this belief. 4. Fact, "shooting stars" are actually meteorites. 5. Myth, no organic material turns to stone, although minerals from water replace wood cells giving stone-like appearance. 6. Myth, dynamite needs a spark or percussion to be exploded. 7. Myth, lightning is more likely to strike the same place twice. 8. Myth, there is no scientific evidence to support this belief. 9. Fact, owls can see and hunt during the daytime. 10. Myth, like most gases, steam is invisible. When steam condenses, water vapor is formed and thus can be seen. 11. Myth, warts are caused by a virus. 12. Myth, there is no scientific evidence to support this belief. 13. Myth, daddy longlegs are not true spiders. They do have eight legs, but their legs are thinner and longer than true spiders and they lack a two-segmented body. 14. Myth, some people do not have the enzyme to digest milk and may experience diarrhea as a result. 15. Myth, however, hot water that has been heated or boiled before cooling may freeze faster; thus a hot water pipe may burst before a cold water pipe. 16. Myth, there are no separate water tanks in a camel's hump. 17. Fact, welders fill gas tanks with water to drive out gasoline-air mixture before welding tank. 18. Myth, water boils at 212 degrees Fahrenheit at sea level and its temperature cannot be raised any higher as long as the egg and water are kept in an open pan. 19. Myth, crocodiles have no tear glands. Therefore, they cannot shed tears. 20. Myth, but there is a great deal of speculation on this topic. 21. Myth, a skunk can tighten its muscles to spray whether on or off the ground. 22. Myth, each rattle does not represent a year as snakes may shed their skin three to four times per year. 23. Myth, recent research indicates this to be true but further research needs to be conducted in this area. 24. Myth, there is no scientific evidence to support this belief. 25. Myth, fish do not drink. Oxygen is taken out of the water as water passes over the gills. Very little water enters the stomach when a fish is breathing. 26. Myth, bees collect nectar which is changed to honey within the bee's body. 27. Myth, there is no difference in nutritional values of the two lunches. 28. Myth, bats react to echoes of their high-pitched squeaks, thus they have a sonar (sound) system rather than a radar (electronic) system. 29. Myth, scientists actually do not know the reasons for tooth decay. 30. Myth, black bears are not true hibernators because their body temperature, heart rate and breathing do not drop to the levels of true hibernators. 31. Fact, there is no cure for the common cold but colds can be prevented. 32. Fact, lightning does cause more fires than careless campers or tourists.

Wild Card Answers: 1. Myth, bulls cannot tell one color from another. 2. Myth, but there is a great deal of speculation on this. 3. Myth, the deepest gorge is Hells Canyon of the Snake River. 4. Fact. 5. Fact, although many wiring diagrams show the reverse. 6. Fact, weight reduction depends on limiting caloric intake. 7. Myth, larvae eat clothes. 8. Myth

Extending Source: Tom Burnam, *The Dictionary of Misinformation* (New York: Thomas Y. Crowell Company, 1975).

GA1150

Fact or Myth Cards

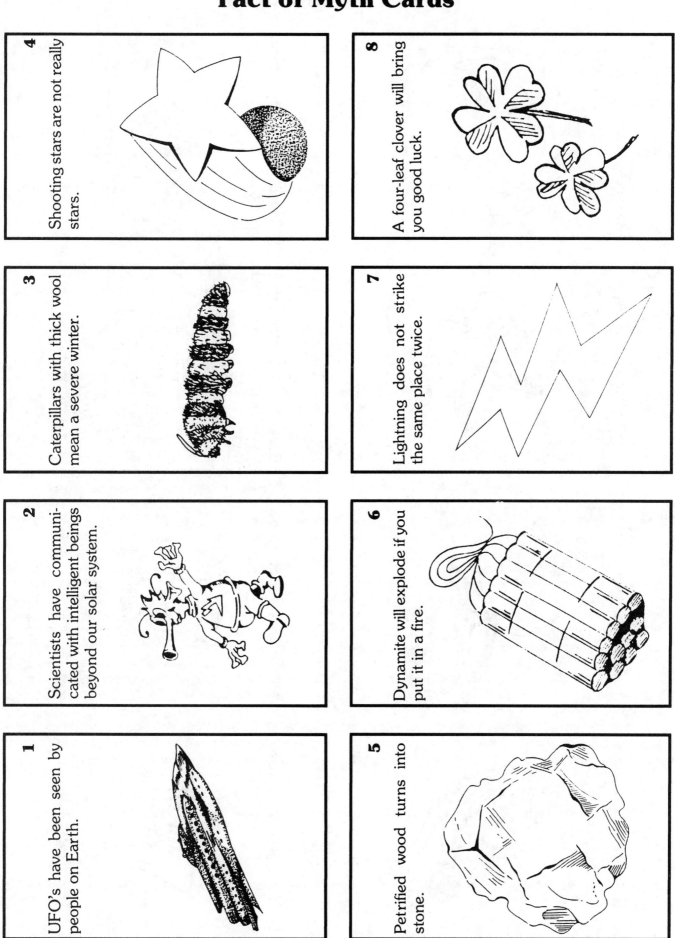

4 Shooting stars are not really stars.

8 A four-leaf clover will bring you good luck.

3 Caterpillars with thick wool mean a severe winter.

7 Lightning does not strike the same place twice.

2 Scientists have communicated with intelligent beings beyond our solar system.

6 Dynamite will explode if you put it in a fire.

1 UFO's have been seen by people on Earth.

5 Petrified wood turns into stone.

GA1150

Fact or Myth Cards

12 A comet is a sign of war.

11 Handling toads causes warts.

10 You can see steam.

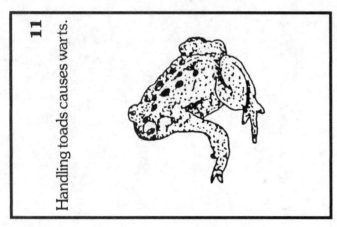

9 Owls can see in the daytime.

16 Camels store water in their humps.

15 Buckets of hot water freeze faster than buckets of cold water.

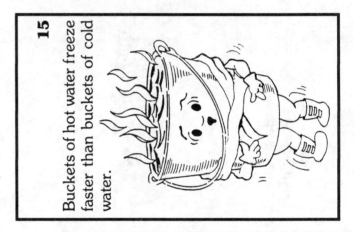

14 Milk is good for everyone.

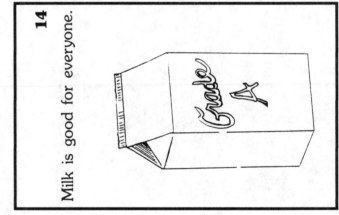

13 Daddy longlegs are spiders.

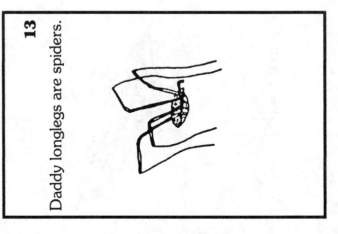

276

Fact or Myth Cards

20 Scientists believe that there was a lost continent called Atlantis.

24 A cat has nine lives.

19 Crocodiles shed crocodile tears.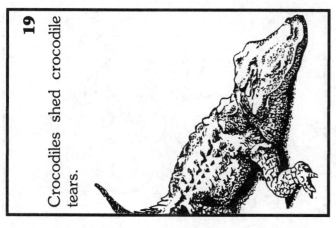

23 Plants are affected by your talking to them.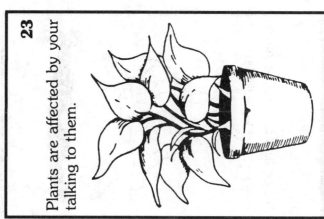

18 Hot boiling water cooks an egg faster than mildly boiling water.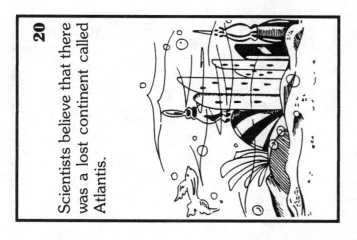

22 You can tell the age of a rattlesnake by the number of rattles.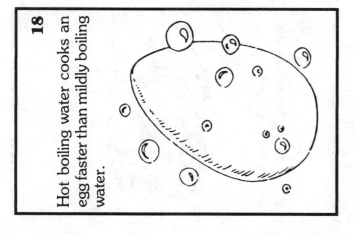

17 An empty gas can is more dangerous than a full one.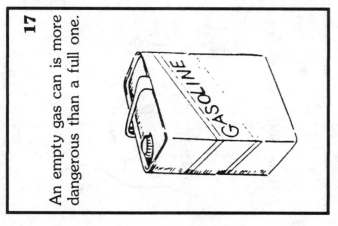

21 A skunk cannot spray if held by its tail off the ground.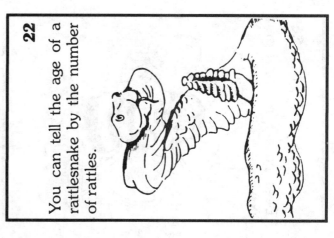

GA1150

Fact or Myth Cards

28 Bats can fly in the dark because they have a built-in radar system.

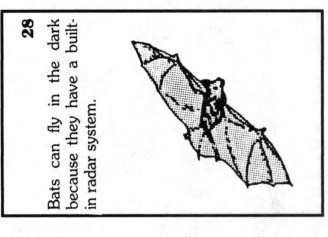

32 Lightning causes more fires than campers or tourists.

27 A hot lunch is more nutritious than a cold lunch.

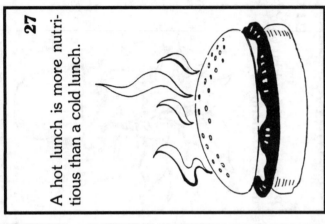

31 There is no cure for the common cold.

26 Bees collect honey from flowers.

30 Black bears hibernate during the winter.

25 Fish drink like people.

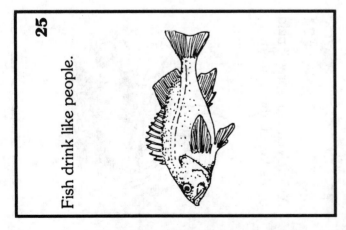

29 A clean tooth never decays.

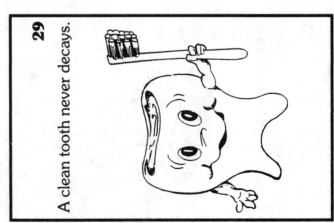

GA1150

Student Activity Page: Fact or Myth

Shade in or color the circle *F* for fact, *M* for myth. Write a *C* in the box if your response was correct. Record the points earned in the box. Fill in the blanks at the bottom of the page with the total number correct and total points earned. The first one is done for you.

Question	Response	Correct	Points	Question	Response	Correct	Points
1	Ⓕ ● ④	C	4	17	Ⓕ Ⓜ ③		
2	Ⓕ Ⓜ ④			18	Ⓕ Ⓜ ③		
3	Ⓕ Ⓜ ②			19	Ⓕ Ⓜ ②		
4	Ⓕ Ⓜ ②			20	Ⓕ Ⓜ ④		
5	Ⓕ Ⓜ ②			21	Ⓕ Ⓜ ③		
6	Ⓕ Ⓜ ③			22	Ⓕ Ⓜ ③		
7	Ⓕ Ⓜ ④			23	Ⓕ Ⓜ ④		
8	Ⓕ Ⓜ ②			24	Ⓕ Ⓜ ②		
9	Ⓕ Ⓜ ③			25	Ⓕ Ⓜ ③		
10	Ⓕ Ⓜ ③			26	Ⓕ Ⓜ ③		
11	Ⓕ Ⓜ ②			27	Ⓕ Ⓜ ④		
12	Ⓕ Ⓜ ②			28	Ⓕ Ⓜ ③		
13	Ⓕ Ⓜ ④			29	Ⓕ Ⓜ ④		
14	Ⓕ Ⓜ ④			30	Ⓕ Ⓜ ④		
15	Ⓕ Ⓜ ④			31	Ⓕ Ⓜ ④		
16	Ⓕ Ⓜ ③			32	Ⓕ Ⓜ ③		

Total Number Correct _____

Total Points Earned _____

GA1150

Wild Cards: Fact or Myth

Choose, then circle *fact* or *myth* with the correct response.

1
Fact   Myth
A bull can see red.

2
Fact   Myth
Copper bracelets help cure arthritis.

3
Fact   Myth
The Grand Canyon is the deepest gorge in the United States.

4
Fact   Myth
Your dreams can be in both black and white and in color.

5
Fact   Myth
Electrons flow from negative to positive.

6
Fact   Myth
There is no pill or medicine that will help a person lose weight.

7
Fact   Myth
Moths eat clothes.

8
Fact   Myth
Hair grows on a corpse.

GA1150

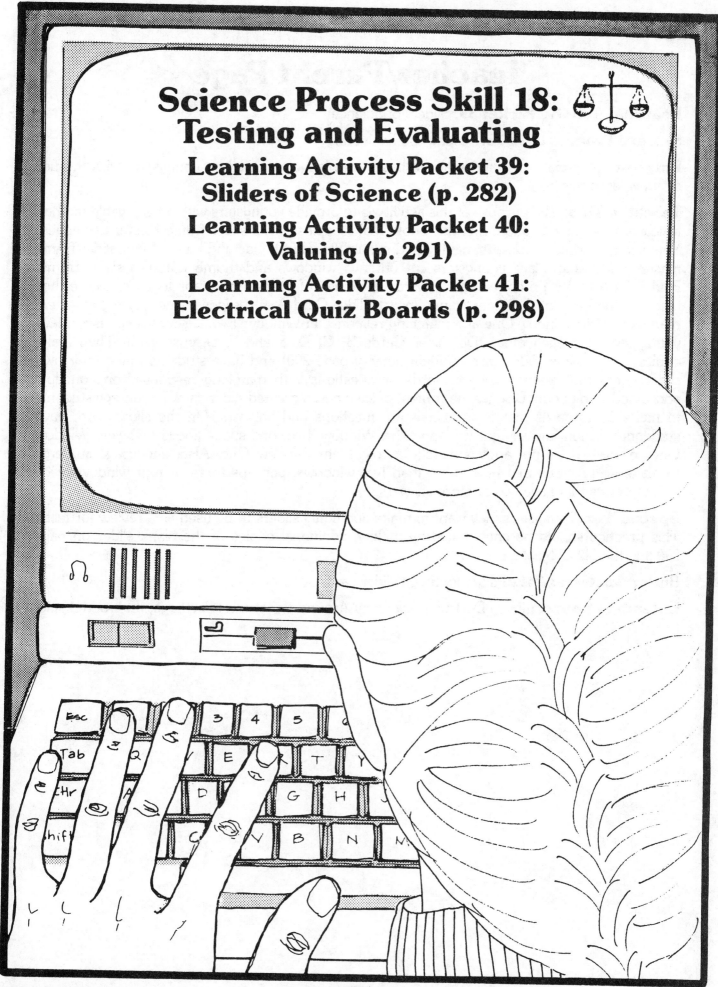

Science Process Skill 18: Testing and Evaluating

281

Teacher/Parent Page

Learning Activity Packet 39: Sliders of Science

Science Process Skill 18: Testing and Evaluating

Purpose: To review, test and evaluate basic knowledge acquired by youngsters with the use of activities in this book

Teaching Tips: The purpose of this activity is to provide youngsters with an enjoyable method to learn basic concepts found in this book. Make copies of the slider frame master as needed. Youngsters also need scissors, oaktag (old manila file folder), glue and tape. Mount slider frame master on oaktag. Have youngsters cut out two windows and thumb notch in slider frame. Fold Tabs A and B on dotted lines towards back side of frame. Tape tabs together where they meet on the back of the slider frame. Insert Slider Card A into slider frame. Have youngsters read word(s) in Window One and matching response in Window Two. Discuss responses. Have youngsters quiz each other. Do Slider Cards B, C, D, E and F. Discuss each. Then make copies of the blank slider card (student activity page 290) and have students make their own slider cards that feature science words or questions with matching responses on concepts addressed in the book. Discuss the content of each newly created slider card. Encourage students to make slider cards that feature in-depth questions and answers. On the slider card, have students position answer that will appear in Window Two, one space above or below Window One so answer will not appear directly across from Window One. Also, encourage students to make slider cards that have more than two windows, perhaps three or four windows wide for responses that have two or more answers.

Special Tip: Youngsters may want to make additional sliders to be used as a review for tests. This practice should be encouraged by making additional copies of the blank slider on page 290 and the Slider Master on page 283.

Slider Answers: Answers are found on slider cards.

Extending Source: Jerry DeBruin, *Scientists Around the World* (Carthage, IL: Good Apple, Inc., 1987).

Slider Frame Master
for Sliders of Science

Tab A

Fold Here

Fold Here

Tab B

Window One

Window Two

Slider Science Card A

SCIENCE	AREAS
16. Seismology	16. Science of earthquakes
15. Meteorology	15. Science of weather
14. Paleontology	14. Science of fossils
13. Nutrition	13. Science of planning for, taking in and digesting food
12. Physiology	12. Science of what goes on inside living things
11. Physics	11. Science of matter and energy
10. Oceanography	10. Science of the oceans
9. Geology	9. Science of the earth and rocks
8. Genetics	8. Science of heredity
7. Entomology	7. Science of insects
6. Engineering	6. Science of the design, construction and uses of machines
5. Chemistry	5. Science of what things are made of and their reactions
4. Biology	4. Science of living things
3. Astronomy	3. Science of the stars and other bodies in space
2. Anthropology	2. Science of humans and their works
1. Anatomy	1. Science of the structure of animals, and plants, especially humans

PULL

GA1150

Slider Science Card B

SCIENCE	HIGHLIGHTS
16. 1985 A.D. Comet Halley	16. Visible for the first time in 76 years
15. 1983 A.D. Sally Ride	15. First American woman in space
14. 1983 A.D. *Pioneer 10*	14. First spacecraft to travel beyond all known planets
13. 1983 A.D. Barbara McClintock	13. 1983 Nobel prize for working with "jumping genes"
12. 1969 A.D. Neil Armstrong	12. First person to land on and step on the moon
11. 1967 A.D. Christiaan Barnard	11. Did first human heart transplant
10. 1961 A.D. Yuri Gagarin	10. Becomes first human to travel in space
9. 1953 A.D. James Watson and Francis Crick	9. Discover ladder-like model of DNA.
8. 1953 A.D. Jonas Salk	8. Produces first effective polio vaccine
7. 1905 A.D. Albert Einstein	7. Tells about his Theory of Relativity
6. 1898 A.D. Marie and Pierre Curie	6. Discover element radium
5. 1858 A.D. Charles Darwin	5. Tells about his Theory of Evolution
4. 1687 A.D. Isaac Newton	4. Discovers laws of mechanics
3. 1641 A.D. Galileo (Galilei)	3. Discovers pendulum clock
2. 200 B.C. Archimedes	2. Discovers law of lever and pulley
1. 400 B.C. Hippocrates	1. Teaches that diseases have causes

PULL

GA1150

Slider Science Card C

SCIENCE	SYMBOLS
16. Hg	16. Mercury
15. Ag	15. Silver
14. Au	14. Gold
13. Pb	13. Lead
12. Cu	12. Copper
11. Ni	11. Nickel
10. Fe	10. Iron
9. Ca	9. Calcium
8. K	8. Potassium
7. Al	7. Aluminum
6. Na	6. Sodium
5. O	5. Oxygen
4. N	4. Nitrogen
3. C	3. Carbon
2. He	2. Helium
1. H	1. Hydrogen

PULL

GA1150

Slider Science Card D

SCIENCE	RECORDS
16. Largest and heaviest animal	16. Blue whale
15. Longest animal	15. Ribbon or bootlace worm
14. Fastest flying animal	14. Spine-tailed swift
13. Largest egg	13. Whale shark
12. Animal with heaviest brain	12. Sperm whale
11. Best animal at smelling	11. Male emperor moth
10. Fastest land animal	10. Cheetah
9. Longest lived mammal	9. Man
8. Oldest dog	8. Queensland Heeler named Bluey
7. Highest known shade temperature in the world	7. (136^0 F, 58^0 C) Al Aziziyah, Libya
6. Lowest recorded world temperature	6. (-127^0 F, -88^0 C) Vostok, Antarctica
5. Highest waterspout	5. (5014 ft., 1519 m) Eden, Australia
4. Greatest length of time without rainfall	4. (14 years) Arica, Chile
3. Greatest yearly snowfall	3. (1255 in., 3115.5 cm) Paradise Mt. Rainier, Washington, USA)
2. Fastest speed of a tornado	2. (280 mph, 448 kph) Coffeyville, Kansas, USA
1. Largest hailstone	1. (1.67 lb., .75 kg) Saipan, Mariana Islands

PULL

GA1150

Slider Science Card E

SCIENCE	ASTRONOMY
16. Light year	16. The distance that light travels in one year in a vacuum
15. A.U.	15. Astronomical unit: the distance (93 million miles) from the earth to the sun
14. First day of summer in the United States	14. When the Northern Hemisphere is tilted toward the sun, usually June 21st
13. Earth's period of revolution around the sun	13. 365¼ days
12. Earth's period of rotation on its axis	12. One day
11. Moon's period of revolution around the earth	11. One month
10. Comet	10. Large, dirty ice ball or iceberg
9. Falling star	9. Rock burning up as it enters the earth's atmosphere
8. Smallest planet	8. Pluto
7. Planet most like the sun	7. Jupiter
6. Planet most like the earth	6. Mars
5. Number of stars in the Milky Way Galaxy	5. 100 billion (100,000,000,000)
4. Planet closest to the sun	4. Mercury
3. Brightest star in the night sky	3. Sirius
2. Astrology	2. The study of how things on Earth are related to the stars in the sky
1. Astronomy	1. The study of laws that govern the movements of all the stars

PULL

GA1150

Slider Science Card F

SCIENCE	CYCLES
The reuse of things found in wastes	Recycle
Life cycle of a white blood cell	12 days
Life cycle of a red blood cell	120 days
Life cycle of a liver cell	540 days
Life cycle of a nerve cell	100 years
A plant that has more than a two-year cycle	Perennial
Number of hours in a circadian rhythm	24 hours
Number of tons of soil an earthworm digests in one year	36 tons
Number of years to form 1″ (2.5 cm) of soil	500 years
Number of days for *Voyager* to orbit the earth	9 days
Number of minutes for space shuttle to orbit the earth	75 minutes
Number of days to travel around an analemma	365 ¼ days (One year)
Moon's period of revolution around the earth	One month (30 days)
Earth's period of rotation on its axis	One day (24 hours)
Earth's period of revolution around the sun	One year (365 ¼ days)
Mars' period of revolution around the sun	687 days
Times during which certain events repeat themselves	Cycle

GA1150

Student Activity Page: Sliders of Science

Slider Master

16.	16.
15.	15.
14.	14.
13.	13.
12.	12.
11.	11.
10.	10.
9.	9.
8.	8.
7.	7.
6.	6.
5.	5.
4.	4.
3.	3.
2.	2.
1.	1.

PULL

Directions:

Design your own Sliders of Science by using this Slider Master. Print name or question in box on left side. Provide matching name or answer to question in box on right. Slide completed slider in assembled slider frame on page 283. Use as a review for tests or just use for pure enjoyment.

GA1150

Teacher/Parent Page

Learning Activity Packet 40: Valuing

Science Process Skill 18: Testing and Evaluating

Purpose: To involve youngsters in the clarification of their values related to contemporary issues in science

Teaching Tips: This activity involves youngsters in thinking about contemporary issues in science and asks them to circle their responses to the issues. Answers should remain confidential and teachers should be careful not to impose their value systems on youngsters. Bumper stickers, T-shirt sayings and postage stamps with related statements facilitate class discussion about contemporary issues. Make copies of the pages for youngsters so each youngster has a deck of value cards to be used in school and at home. Have youngsters cut out the cards. Mount on cardboard. The thirty-six cards are equally divided into four sets: self-concept, biological, physical and earth and space science issues. Select one bumper sticker, T-shirt saying or postage stamp and related statement to discuss. Have youngsters read the issue; then circle the number on the 1-10 scale that represents their feelings about the issue. Discuss issue raised by the statement. Assume neutral position. After discussion, inform youngsters that sometimes people change their original response because of information gained during the discussion. Explain that scientists, too, often change the way they look at and test a problem because of new information that has been acquired. Encourage youngsters to take cards home and discuss the issues with their family members. Cards can be laminated and erasable pens used so previous responses can be erased easily by using a damp cloth or towel.

Special Tip: This activity should be done by having youngsters form small groups with five to six members in each group to discuss each issue.

Value Card Answers: All responses are accepted.

Extending Source: Sidney Simon, *Values Clarification* (New York: Dodd, Mead and Company, 1985).

GA1150

Value Cards: Bumper Stickers

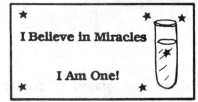

I Believe in Miracles

I Am One!

Couples who are unable to have babies should be allowed to have test tube babies.

Against 1 2 3 4 5 6 7 8 9 10 For

It Shouldn't Hurt to Be a Child

Parents should be permitted to spank their children if their children misbehave.

Against 1 2 3 4 5 6 7 8 9 10 For

Kids Don't Go with Strangers

Youngsters should be fingerprinted; if they are lost, they can be found more easily.

Against 1 2 3 4 5 6 7 8 9 10 For

Roaming Pets Cause Regrets

Youngsters who allow their pets to roam should allow other youngsters to keep their pets.

Against 1 2 3 4 5 6 7 8 9 10 For

Tired of TV?

Watch an Aquarium

Youngsters should spend more time watching aquariums than watching TV or playing video games.

Against 1 2 3 4 5 6 7 8 9 10 For

Recycle Yourself

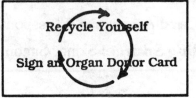

Sign an Organ Donor Card

People should donate their bodies to science when they die so others may live.

Against 1 2 3 4 5 6 7 8 9 10 For

Split Wood, Not Atoms

Natural resources should be used to create energy rather than splitting the atom for energy.

Against 1 2 3 4 5 6 7 8 9 10 For

---

55 M.P.H.

It's a Law We Can Live With

The 55 m.p.h. speed limit encourages conservation of energy and should be strictly enforced.

Against 1 2 3 4 5 6 7 8 9 10 For

GA1150

Value Cards: Bumper Stickers

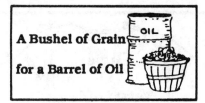

A Bushel of Grain for a Barrel of Oil

Scientists should help farmers grow surplus grain which could be traded for oil.

Against 1 2 3 4 5 6 7 8 9 10 For

Astronomy Is Looking Up

People should give money to scientists to find out if life exists elsewhere in the universe.

Against 1 2 3 4 5 6 7 8 9 10 For

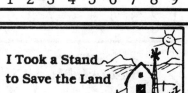

I Took a Stand to Save the Land

Scientists should encourage farmers to prevent real estate people from using farmland on which to build houses and factories.

Against 1 2 3 4 5 6 7 8 9 10 For

Archaeologists Dig It!

Scientists should dig up the remains of people to find out how these people lived.

Against 1 2 3 4 5 6 7 8 9 10 For

Value Cards: T-Shirt Sayings

#1 I Am Great— That Is True

I feel good about myself and what I do.

Against 1 2 3 4 5 6 7 8 9 10 For

I'm Black and Proud of It

There is a need for more Blacks and other minority scientists in science today.

Against 1 2 3 4 5 6 7 8 9 10 For

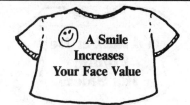

A Smile Increases Your Face Value

One should always smile even though things may not be going so well.

Against 1 2 3 4 5 6 7 8 9 10 For

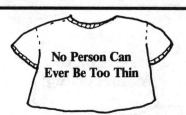

No Person Can Ever Be Too Thin

Youngsters should strive to be as thin as possible because being thin is the "in" thing to do.

Against 1 2 3 4 5 6 7 8 9 10 For

GA1150

Value Cards: T-Shirt Sayings

No Smoking

Smoking is bad for your health and should be prohibited.

Against 1 2 3 4 5 6 7 8 9 10 For

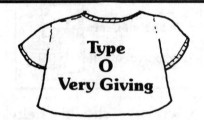

Type O Very Giving

People should give blood. There is little risk and blood saves lives.

Against 1 2 3 4 5 6 7 8 9 10 For

Better Active Today Than Radioactive Tomorrow

Scientists should help people understand that there is no danger in using a microwave oven and eating food cooked by a microwave.

Against 1 2 3 4 5 6 7 8 9 10 For

Recyclable Glass Recycles

Scientists should help the states pass bottle deposit laws.

Against 1 2 3 4 5 6 7 8 9 10 For

When You've Seen One Nuclear War, You've Seen Them All

Scientists should band together and pressure nations to ban all nuclear weapons.

Against 1 2 3 4 5 6 7 8 9 10 For

We Drove the Alaskan Highway

Engineers should build more four-lane highways so people can travel faster, farther and thus see more places.

Against 1 2 3 4 5 6 7 8 9 10 For

Hats on to Motorcycling!

Riding a motorcycle without wearing a helmet is dangerous and should be illegal.

Against 1 2 3 4 5 6 7 8 9 10 For

I'd Rather Be Flying; It's Safer

Scientists should help make more supersonic airplanes because they are safer and less noisy than automobiles.

Against 1 2 3 4 5 6 7 8 9 10 For

GA1150

Value Cards: Postage Stamps

Scientists need to be more concerned about what effects new scientific discoveries have on people's feelings.

Against 1 2 3 4 5 6 7 8 9 10 For

Scientists should discover more things that would relieve the pain and suffering of youngsters throughout the world, regardless of race, color, creed or nationality.

Against 1 2 3 4 5 6 7 8 9 10 For

Youngsters should heed the advice of an old scientist: "The more one learns, the less he/she knows."

Against 1 2 3 4 5 6 7 8 9 10 For

Scientists should encourage the government to pay farmers not to grow food in order to reduce surplus food supplies.

Against 1 2 3 4 5 6 7 8 9 10 For

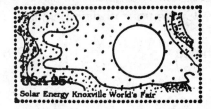

Scientists should protect the bald eagle at all costs because it is our nation's symbol.

Against 1 2 3 4 5 6 7 8 9 10 For

Seals should be allowed to be killed and their fur used for jackets and coats.

Against 1 2 3 4 5 6 7 8 9 10 For

Solar energy is the safest and least expensive of all types of energy.

Against 1 2 3 4 5 6 7 8 9 10 For

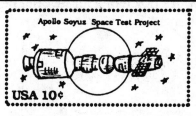

Scientists from the United States and Russia should work together on the exploration of space.

Against 1 2 3 4 5 6 7 8 9 10 For

GA1150

Value Cards: Postage Stamps and Free Choice Cards

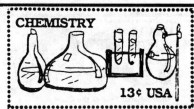

Scientists should be allowed to develop new chemicals even though these chemicals may hurt the environment.

Against   1   2   3   4   5   6   7   8   9   10   For

Scientists should continue to improve computers and other electronic devices (like video games) because they are good for youngsters.

Against   1   2   3   4   5   6   7   8   9   10   For

Scientists should put satellites into space to promote world communication even though this may lead to spying on some countries.

Against   1   2   3   4   5   6   7   8   9   10   For

Scientists should encourage farmers to spread fertilizer on their soil to make the soil richer for growing crops.

Against   1   2   3   4   5   6   7   8   9   10   For

Write your choice of your favorite T-shirt saying here.

Write your choice of your favorite bumper sticker here.

Paste your choice of your favorite postage stamp here.

Circle your choice below.

Pro Choice   Pro Life

Student Activity Page: Valuing

Search for your favorite bumper sticker, T-shirt saying and postage stamp. Write the messages for each in boxes A1, A2 and A3 below. In boxes B1, B2 and B3, write a value statement for each. Circle the numbers in boxes C1, C2 and C3 that represent your feelings about the statements. Below, design your very own of each.

A1 Write a mini bumper sticker saying here.	**B1** Write bumper sticker statement here.	**C1** How do you stand? Circle the number. Against For 1 2 3 4 5 6 7 8 9 10
A2 Write mini T-shirt saying here.	**B2** Write T-shirt statement here.	**C2** How do you stand? Circle the number. Against For 1 2 3 4 5 6 7 8 9 10
A3 Paste postage stamp here.	**B3** Write postage stamp statement here.	**C3** How do you stand? Circle the number. Against For 1 2 3 4 5 6 7 8 9 10

**My Bumper Sticker
(Design Your Own Here)**

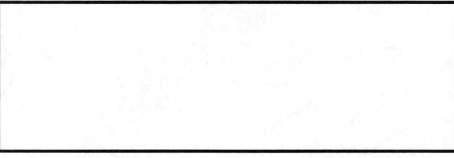

**My T-Shirt
(Design Your Own Here)**

**My Postage Stamp
(Design Your Own Here)**

GA1150

Teacher/Parent Page

Learning Activity Packet 41: Electrical Quiz Boards

Science Process Skill 18: Testing and Evaluating

Purpose: To review, test and evaluate basic scientific knowledge acquired by youngsters

Teaching Tips: The purpose of this activity is to provide youngsters with an enjoyable way to learn basic science concepts. In addition, youngsters will learn basic concepts of electricity. You will need an 8½" x 11" (22 cm x 28 cm) piece of tagboard (backs of writing tablets work well), aluminum foil, scissors, glue, ¾" clear tape, paper punch, 1.5 volt dry cell, bulb, bulb holder, dry cell holder, several wires and a copy of Quiz Board Card 1, Famous Scientists. Tape or glue Quiz Board Card 1 to tagboard. Fold on dotted line. Punch holes A-E through both edges of folded page. Unfold page and lay flat. Punch holes 1-5 through *single* thick page near edge. With scissors, cut five 12" x 1" (30 cm x 2.5 cm) strips of aluminum foil for wires. Fold each wire in half lengthwise to make 12" x ½" (30 cm x 1.3 cm) wires. Connect holes A and 4 with aluminum foil. (See Figure 1.) Cover aluminum foil with ¾" (2 cm) clear tape. Proceed to connect holes B to 3, C to 5, D to 1 and E to 2. *Be sure to cover each wire with ¾" (2 cm) clear tape to avoid a short circuit.* Set up quiz board tester so it looks like the one below. (See Figure 2.)

Touch probes to matching holes to correctly match A-E with 1-5. If the light goes on, you have the correct match. Set up other quiz boards in the same manner, using the answers given below to connect points accordingly.

Tip: Tape fold-over ends of paper fastener to ends of wires on probes. (See Figure 3.) This prevents sharp-ended wires from penetrating the aluminum foil within each matching hole. By doing this, your electrical constellation quiz board will last longer.

Figure 1. Back Side A

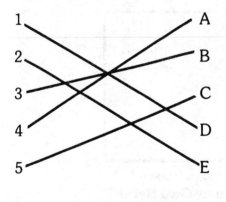

Figure 2. Tester

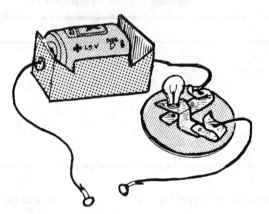

Figure 3. Tip

Special Tip: Be certain that each wire is covered with clear tape to avoid short circuit.

Quiz Board Card Answers: Card 1: A4, B3, C5, D1, E2; Card 2: A2, B5, C3, D4, E1; Card 3: A3, B2, C5, D4, E1; Card 4: A3, B5, C4, D2, E1

Extending Source: Jerry DeBruin, *Young Scientists Explore Electricity & Magnetism* (Carthage, IL: Good Apple, Inc., 1985).

GA1150

Quiz Board Card 1: Famous Scientists

1. ◯   Walter Reed

2. ◯   Marie Curie

3. ◯   Robert Goddard

4. ◯   Maria Mitchell

5. ◯   Benjamin Banneker

A. ◯

B. ◯

C. ◯

D. ◯

E. ◯

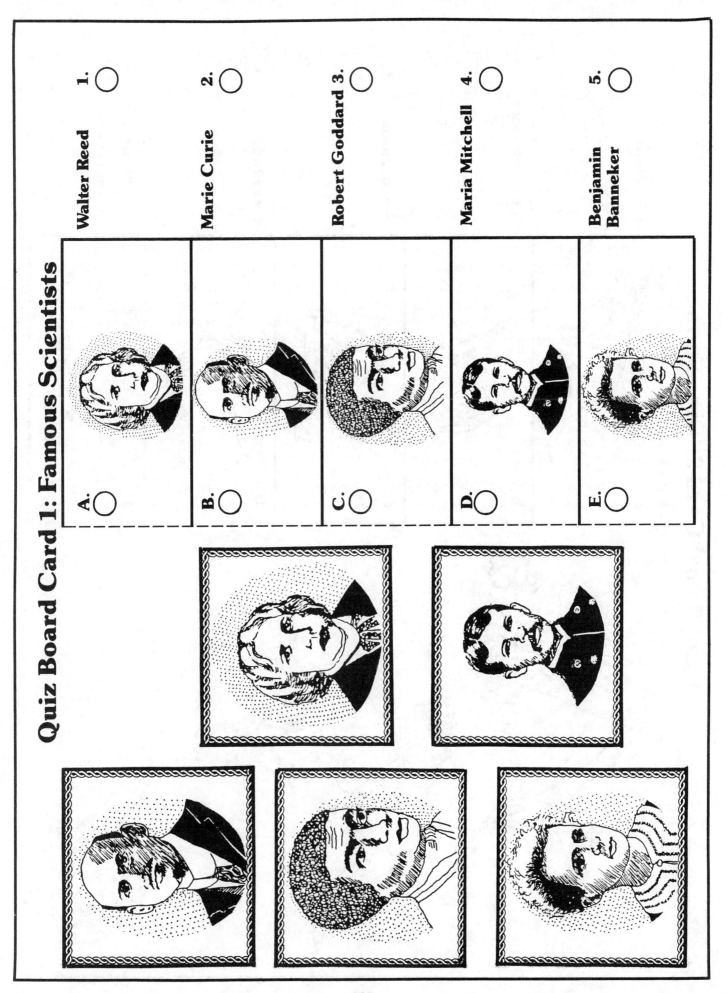

GA1150

Quiz Board Card 2: Dinosaurs

1. ○ **Triceratops**

2. ○ **Tyrannosaurus**

3. ○ **Stegosaurus**

4. ○ **Pteranodon**

5. ○ **Apatosaurus (Brontosaurus)**

A. ○

B. ○

C. ○

D. ○

E. ○

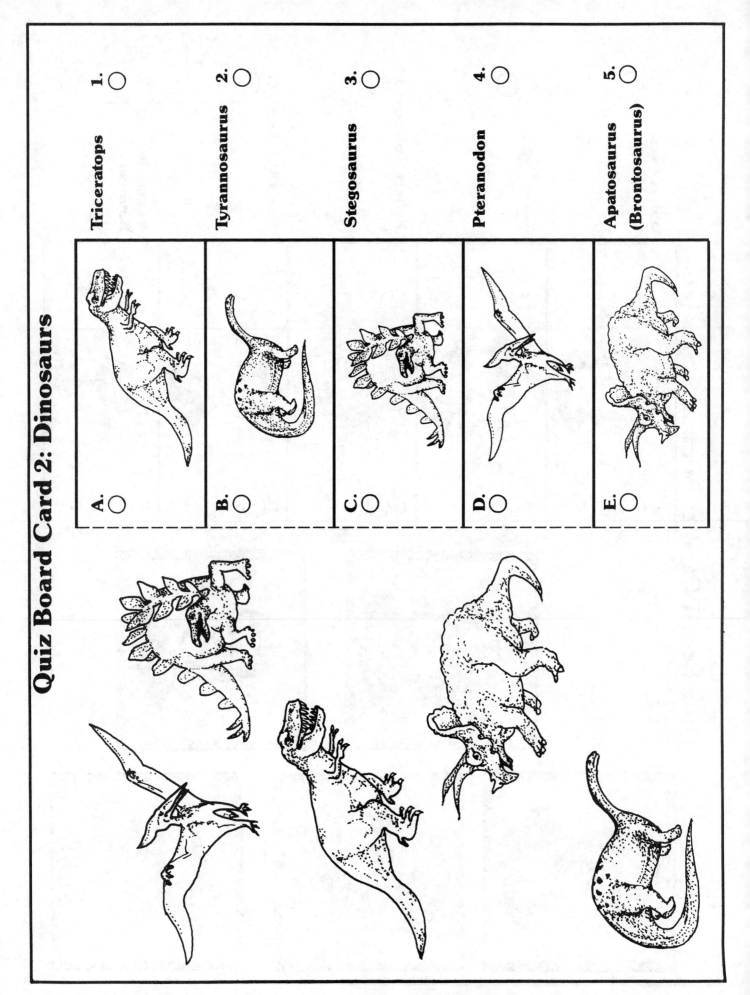

300

GA1150

Quiz Board Card 3: Tracks

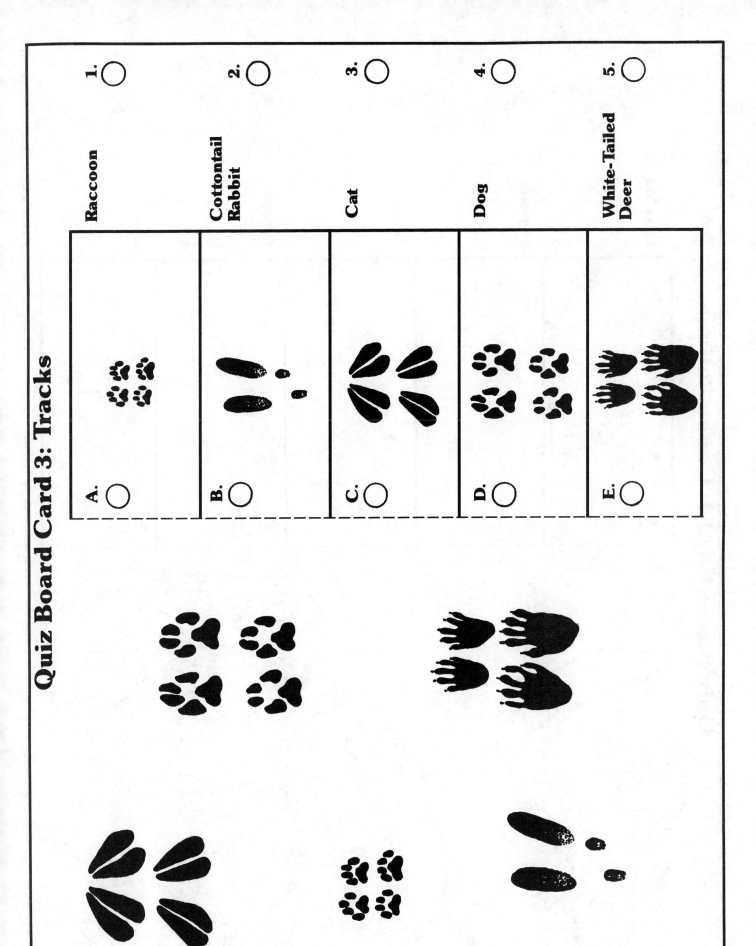

1. ○ Raccoon

2. ○ Cottontail Rabbit

3. ○ Cat

4. ○ Dog

5. ○ White-Tailed Deer

A. ○

B. ○

C. ○

D. ○

E. ○

301

GA1150

Quiz Board Card 4: Constellations

1. ○   2. ○   3. ○   4. ○   5. ○

Ursa Major

Pegasus

Orion

Cygnus

Leo

A. ○

B. ○

C. ○

D. ○

E. ○

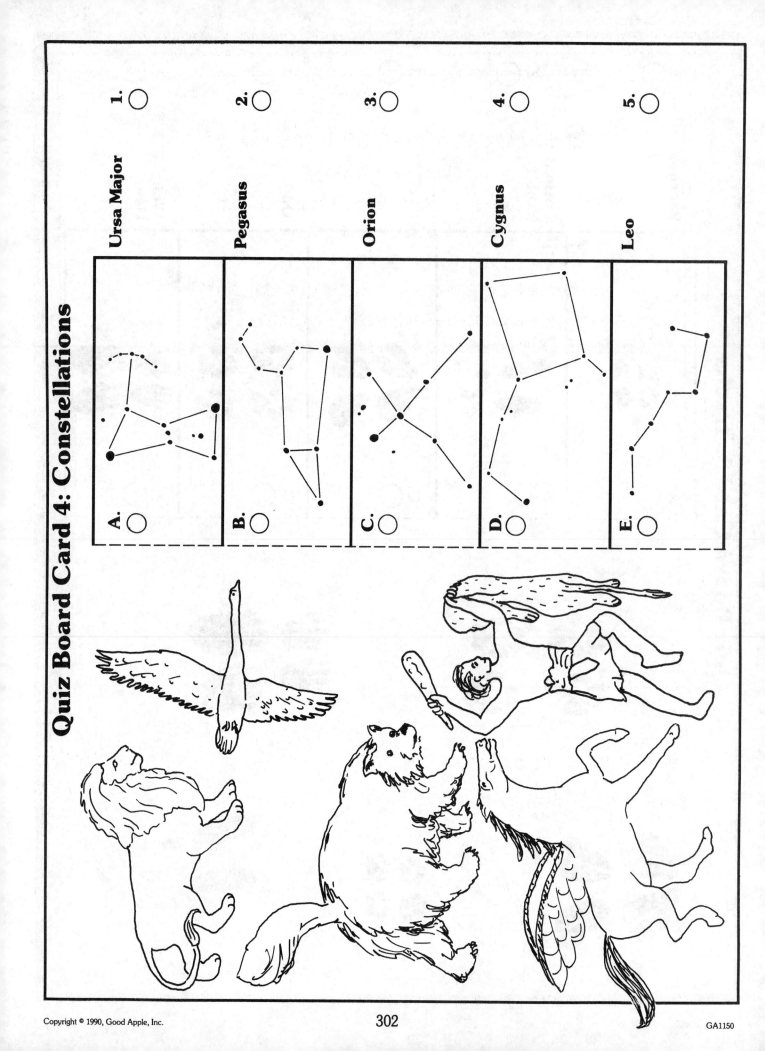

GA1150

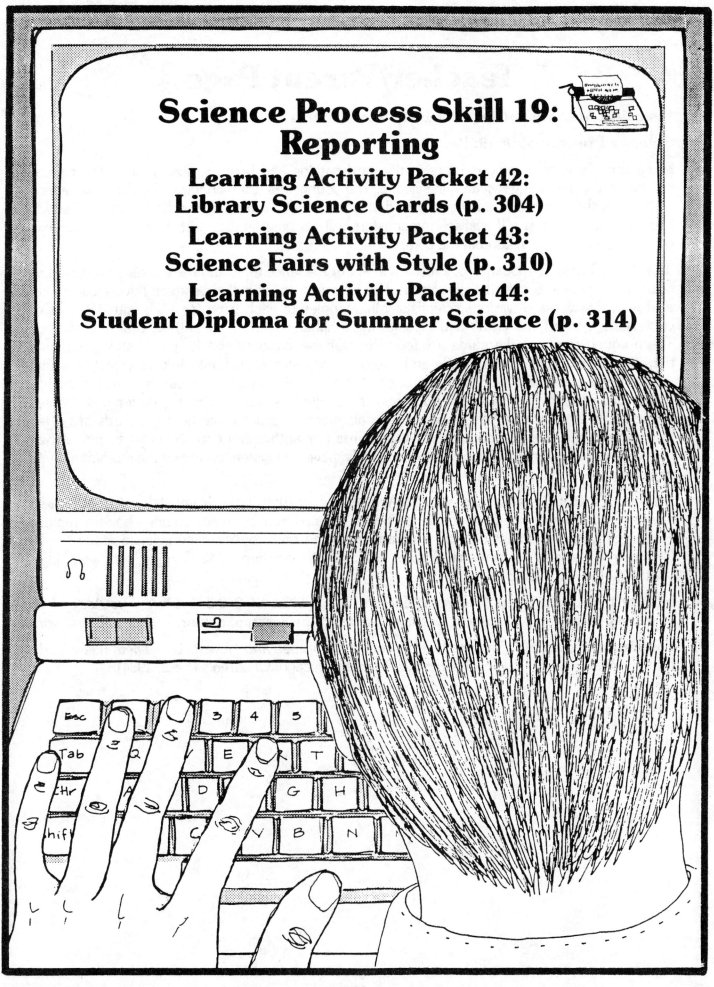

Science Process Skill 19: Reporting

GA1150

Teacher/Parent Page

Learning Activity Packet 42: Library Science Cards

Science Process Skill 19: Reporting

Purpose: To introduce youngsters to the card catalog and how the library and card catalog can be used when doing research in science. The youngsters will recognize that the card catalog features author, title and subject cards that contain information about books and where to find them in the library. If available, youngsters will become familiar with how a computer can be used to locate information in the library.

Teaching Tips: The location of information about a science topic and the subsequent reporting of science findings is basic to all science. The following pages include sixteen library cards that deal with the works of various scientists. Make copies of each page for each youngster. Have youngsters cut out the cards and arrange in alphabetical order by author, title and subject. Teach youngsters that the cards are found in alphabetical order in the card catalog and that there are three cards—author, title and subject cards—for each book. Inform youngsters that the author card is filed in alphabetical order by the author's last name, the title card in alphabetical order according to the title of the book and the subject card according to the topic addressed in the book. Have youngsters place cards in alphabetical order (note how the cards are often located with the use of a computer), three cards per author (four for Asimov) to make their own card catalog system. Using the sixteen cards, have youngsters complete the student activity page on page 309.

Special Tip(s): Correlate with Learning Activity Packet 20: Adopt a Scientist. Involve youngsters also in the reading of up-to-date science books for children because science changes rapidly. For a yearly listing complete with annotations of the most outstanding science trade books for children, write to the National Science Teachers Association, 1742 Connecticut Ave., N.W., Washington, D.C. 20009.

Student Activity Page Answers: Exercise I: 1. $\frac{j}{A}$ 523.6, 2. 248 3. 1984, 4. *The Act of Life*, 5. spiders. Exercise II: 1. author., 2. subject, 3. title, 4. subject, 5. author. Exercise III: will vary

Extending Source(s): Jeanne B. Hardendorff, *Libraries and How to Use Them* (New York: Franklin Watts, 1979). Patricia Fujimoto, *Libraries* (Chicago: Children's Press, 1984).

GA1150

Card 3

Meteors

j523.6 Asimov, Isaac
A   Comets and meteors. Illus. by Paul Mina Mora.
    Follett © 1972
    29p illus. (part col) (Follett beginning science bk)

    Surveys scientific research and findings on the nature and behavior of comets and meteors.

    1 Comets   2 Meteors   I Illus.   II T

09285   531541

5182

Card 4

Comets

j523.6 Asimov, Isaac
A   Comets and meteors. Illus. by Paul Mina Mora.
    Follett © 1972
    29p illus. (part col) (Follett beginning science bk)

    Surveys scientific research and findings on the nature and behavior of comets and meteors.

    1 Comets   2 Meteors   I Illus.   II T

09285   531541

5182

Card 1

j523.6 Asimov, Isaac
A   Comets and meteors. Illus. by Paul Mina Mora.
    Follett © 1972
    29p illus. (part col) (Follett beginning science bk)

    Surveys scientific research and findings on the nature and behavior of comets and meteors.

    1 Comets   2 Meteors   I Illus.   II T

09285   531541

5182

Card 2

Comets and Meteors

j523.6 Asimov, Isaac
A   Comets and meteors. Illus. by Paul Mina Mora.
    Follett © 1972
    29p illus. (part col) (Follett beginning science bk)

    Surveys scientific research and findings on the nature and behavior of comets and meteors.

    1 Comets   2 Meteors   I Illus.   II T

09285   531541

5182

GA1150

7

Outer Space—Exploration

574.999 Branley, Franklyn M.
BRA   Is there life in outer space? Illus. by Don Madden.
          Crowell [© 1984]
          32p illus. (part col) (Let's-read-and-find-out science bk)

          The possibilities for discovering life on other planets in the far reaches of the universe are explored.

          1 Life on other planets 2 Outer space—Exploration I Illus. II T

ISBN 0-690-04374-0
ISBN 0-690-04375-9 lib. bdg.

06598 60211 660083   Grades 2-3
                                                  8331

8

591.1   Cousteau, Jacques
Cou   The act of life by Jacques Cousteau.
          The Danbury Press, USA, 1975.
          144p col illus. (Series: The Ocean World of Jacques Cousteau—Vol. 2)

          I Title
          II Reproduction
          III Marine Fauna

5

574.999 Branley, Franklyn M.
BRA   Is there life in outer space? Illus. by Don Madden.
          Crowell [© 1984]
          32p illus. (part col) (Let's-read-and-find-out science bk)

          The possibilities for discovering life on other planets in the far reaches of the universe are explored.

          1 Life on other planets 2 Outer space—Exploration I illus. II T

ISBN 0-690-04374-0
ISBN 0-690-04375-9 lib. bdg.

06598 60211 660083   Grades 2-3
                                       83-45057
                                          8331

6

Life on Other Planets

574.999 Branley, Franklyn M.
BRA   Is there life in outer space? illus. by Don Madden.
          Crowell [© 1984]
          32p illus. (part col) (Let's-read-and-find-out science bk)

          The possibilities for discovering life on other planets in the far reaches of the universe are explored.

          1 Life on other planets 2 Outer space—Exploration I Illus. II T

ISBN 0-690-04374-0
ISBN 0-690-04375-9 lib. bdg.

06598 60211 660083   Grades 2-3
                                                  8331

306

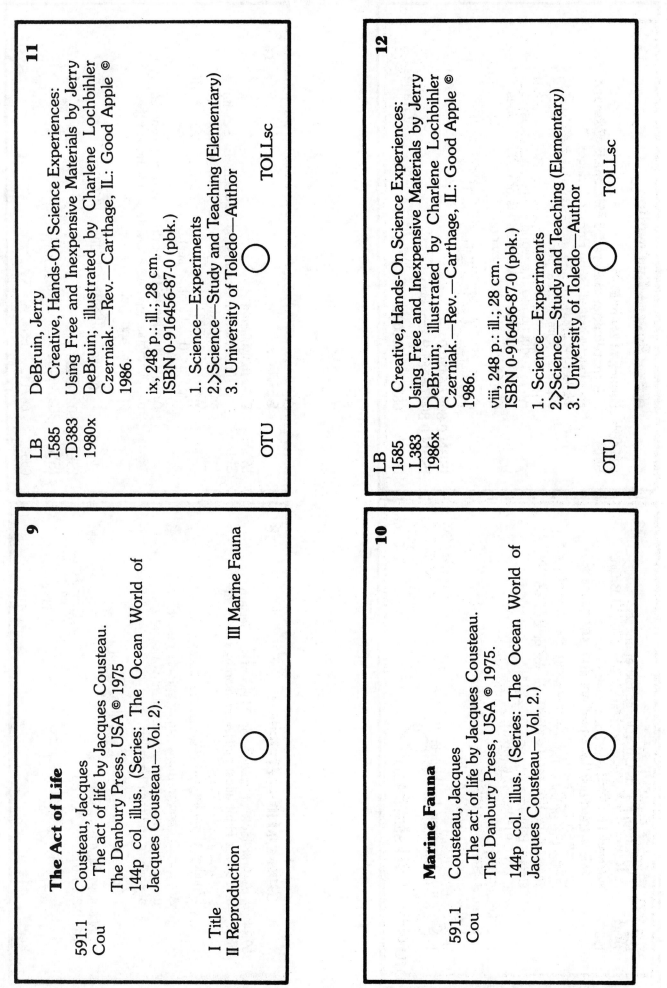

11

LB
1585
.D383
1980x

DeBruin, Jerry
   Creative, Hands-On Science Experiences:
Using Free and Inexpensive Materials by Jerry
DeBruin; illustrated by Charlene Lochbihler
Czerniak.—Rev.—Carthage, IL: Good Apple ©
1986.

ix, 248 p.: ill.; 28 cm.
ISBN 0-916456-87-0 (pbk.)

1. Science—Experiments
2>Science—Study and Teaching (Elementary)
3. University of Toledo—Author

OTU   TOLLsc

12

LB
1585
.L383
1986x

   Creative, Hands-On Science Experiences:
Using Free and Inexpensive Materials by Jerry
DeBruin; illustrated by Charlene Lochbihler
Czerniak.—Rev.—Carthage, IL: Good Apple ©
1986.

viii, 248 p.: ill.; 28 cm.
ISBN 0-916456-87-0 (pbk.)

1. Science—Experiments
2>Science—Study and Teaching (Elementary)
3. University of Toledo—Author

OTU   TOLLsc

9

The Act of Life

591.1
Cou

Cousteau, Jacques
   The act of life by Jacques Cousteau.
The Danbury Press, USA © 1975
144p col illus. (Series: The Ocean World of
Jacques Cousteau—Vol. 2).

                    III Marine Fauna

I Title
II Reproduction

10

Marine Fauna

591.1
Cou

Cousteau, Jacques
   The act of life by Jacques Cousteau.
The Danbury Press, USA © 1975.

144p col. illus. (Series: The Ocean World of
Jacques Cousteau—Vol. 2.)

15

A first look at spiders

595.4
SEL

Selsam, Millicent E.
    A first look at spiders by Millicent E. Selsam and Joyce Hunt. Illus. by Harriet Springer. Walker [© 1983]
32p illus. (First look at ser)

An introduction to the world of spiders discusses the distinguishing characteristics of various types of spiders and their behavior.

1 Spiders I Jt auth. II illus. III T

ISBN 0-8027-6480-0
ISBN 0-8027-6481-9 Lib. bdg.

06607 68714 660083

Grades 3-4
8331

16

Spiders

595.4
SEL

Selsam, Millicent E.
    A first look at spiders by Millicent E. Selsam and Joyce Hunt. Illus. by Harriet Springer. Walker [© 1983]
32p illus. (First look at ser)

An introduction to the world of spiders discusses the distinguishing characteristics of various types of spiders and their behavior.

1 Spiders I Jt auth. II illus. III T

ISBN 0-8027-6480-0
ISBN 0-8027-6481-9 Lib. bdg.

06607 68714 660083

Grades 3-4
8331

13

Science Experiments

1585
.L383
1986x

    Creative, Hands-On Science Experiences: Using Free and Inexpensive Materials/by Jerry DeBruin; illustrated by Charlene Lochbihler Czerniak. —Rev.—Carthage, IL: Good Apple © 1986.
viii, 248 p.: ill.; 28 cm.
University of Toledo author.
"A Good Apple science idea book for grades k-6."—Cover. Bibliography: pp. 217-221.
ISBN 0-916456-87-0 (pbk.)

1. Science—Experiments
2. Science—Study and Teaching (Elementary)
3. University of Toledo—Author
I. Czerniak, Charlene Lochbihler. II. Title

OTU 02 SEP 88 MEG

ToLLnt

14

Selsam, Millicent E.

595.4
SEL

    A first look at spiders by Millicent E. Selsam and Joyce Hunt. Illus. by Harriet Springer. Walker [© 1983]
32p illus. (First look at ser.)

An introduction to the world of spiders discusses the distinguishing characteristics of various types of spiders and their behavior.

1 Spiders I Jt auth. II illus. III T

ISBN 0-8027-6480-0
ISBN 0-8027-6481-9 Lib. bdg.

06607 68714 660083

Grades 3-4
82-42530
8331

GA1150

Student Activity Page: Library Science Cards

Exercise I

Use your sixteen cards to answer the questions below.

1. What is the call number of the book written by Isaac Asimov? _____

2. How many pages are in the book written by Jerry DeBruin? _____

3. In what year was the book by Franklyn Branley written? _____

4. What is the title of the book written by Jacques Cousteau? _____

5. What is the subject of the book written by Millicent Selsam? _____

Exercise II

On the lines below, write whether the information is found on an author, title or subject card.

Information	Card on Which Information Is Found
1. Jerry DeBruin	1. _____
2. Spiders	2. _____
3. *The Act of Life*	3. _____
4. Outer Space Exploration	4. _____
5. Isaac Asimov	5. _____

Exercise III

On the blank library card below, design your own personal author library card. Be sure to include all information found on an author card.

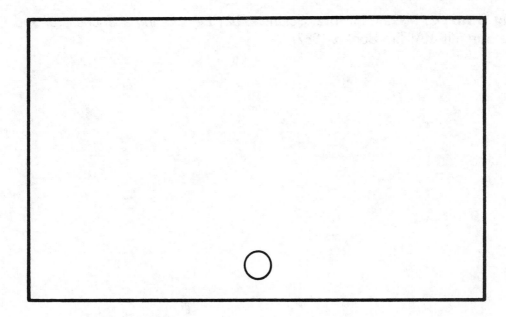

GA1150

Teacher/Parent Page

Learning Activity Packet 43: Science Fairs with Style

Science Process Skill 19: Reporting

Purpose: To provide youngsters with an opportunity to conduct a scientific research investigation and in the process, develop science research skills that are valuable in later schooling and life

Teaching Tips: This activity involves youngsters in the steps followed when conducting and subsequent reporting of results while doing a science research study. Make copies of the sixteen cards for each youngster or enlarge each card for a classroom set. Have youngsters place cards in order. If one set of cards is used, have sixteen children, with one card per person, line up in the correct order of steps followed when doing a research study. Use as a preliminary activity before involving youngsters in actual science fair projects. Make copies of the student activity page on page 313. Have youngsters write the letter of the card in the correct space on the page. Then involve youngsters in doing research on science fair projects. Hold a science fair as a culminating activity to this exercise.

Special Tip: 1. Emphasize the idea that a science fair project is a research study whereby a solution to a particular problem is attempted to be found. 2. Make copies of pages 14 and 15 "Special Tips for Parents. . ." in the book *School Yard-Backyard Cycles of Science* (Good Apple, 1989). Send copy of tips home with youngsters to give to their parents. These tips are an asset to parents who want to help their youngsters with science fair projects.

Student Activity Page Answers: Column A: A, C, E, G, H, F, D, B, P, I, N, K, L, M, J, O. Column B: title page, table of contents, abstract, background research: a review of the literature, background bibliography, statement of the problem, statement of the hypothesis, procedures and methods, materials, variables and controls, results, conclusions, discussion, acknowledgements, references, appendices

Extending Source: Maxine H. Iritz, *Science Fair: Developing a Successful and Fun Project* (Blue Ridge Summit, PA: Tab Books, 1987).

GA1150

Science Fairs with Style Cards

A

Includes your name, school and title of research topic.

B

Features a list of the major sections in the paper. Will probably be done last when you have all the pages numbered and organized.

C

A shortened version, usually 150-200 words, of your research paper.

D

A statement about what others have found out about the problem you are investigating.

E

A list of books, periodicals and other reference materials used in your background research to find out what others have done related to your topic.

F

Precisely state the problem or question you are attempting to answer. "The problem of this research study is . . . ."

G

State what you expected to happen or what is to be proved by your work.

H

State how the project was done. Include the steps you followed when you did your experimentation.

GA1150

Science Fairs with Style Cards

I

List all materials that you used in your research. These may include things that you built, used or borrowed. Include any audiovisual materials such as photographs, too.

J

Describe the things that you changed and those that you tried to control. Identify both the control and experimental groups.

K

Include all data that you collected using charts, models, diagrams, computer programs, videotapes, photographs and tables that you created when you did the experiment.

L

State what you found out as a result of doing the project. Tell how the research data either supported or denied your hypothesis or guess.

M

State the practical value of your research. Also state how your research findings could be used in future research. Tell about new questions that came about as a result of your research.

N

List full names and titles of all people who helped you in your research and what they contributed to your research study.

O

A final list of books, periodicals and other materials used in your study.

P

Include any extra related information and materials directly related to the topic and research study. Include copies of any required forms here.

GA1150

Student Activity Page: Science Fairs with Style

In the blank next to each statement in Column A, write the letter found on the Science Fair Card that best matches that statement. The first one is done for you. Then in Column B, write the steps in the correct order. The first one is done for you.

Column A

_A_	Title Page
____	Abstract
____	Background Bibliography
____	Statement of Hypothesis
____	Procedures and Methods
____	Statement of the Problem
____	Background Research
____	Table of Contents
____	Appendices
____	Materials
____	Acknowledgements
____	Results
____	Conclusions
____	Discussion
____	Variables and Controls
____	References

Column B

1. _____Title Page_____
2. _____
3. _____
4. _____
5. _____
6. _____
7. _____
8. _____
9. _____
10. _____
11. _____
12. _____
13. _____
14. _____
15. _____
16. _____

Teacher/Parent Page

Learning Activity Packet 44: Student Diploma for Summer Science

Science Process Skill 19: Reporting

Purpose: To show youngsters an appreciation for participation in science card activities during the school year and extend their involvement in science into the summer months

Teaching Tips: The following pages feature ninety calendar cards or six one-half month calendars of science activities that can be done by youngsters during the summer months, one activity per day from June 1st to August 31st. When taped together end to end, Tab A to Tab B, etc., and rolled up and secured with a gold string, the cards become a diploma given by the teacher to each youngster before summer vacation begins. Review the diploma of activities with the youngsters. Inform youngsters that the diploma could be posted in the home for all to see and become involved in during the summer months. Or, a card deck of summer science activities can be made with a new card posted in the home each day. Stress that the activities are short and should be done daily, as many activities focus upon events that occurred on the same date in history. Encourage youngsters to make copies of, and use, the student activity page such as the one on page 265 often during the summer vacation.

Special Tip(s): 1. In addition to giving the diploma for summer activity, give a completed student report card found on pages 321 and 322 to each youngster. Provide ample praise for each science process skill mastered and learning activity packet completed. 2. Correlate this activity with "Summer Hike Through Our Universe" on pages 254-259.

Answers: Ample amount of praise for past accomplishments and encouragement for participation in Summer Science Calendar and/or card activities and "Summer Hike Through Our Universe."

Extending Source: Jerry DeBruin, *Creative, Hands-On Science Experiences* (Carthage, IL: Good Apple, Inc., rev. 1986).

GA1150

June 1-15

June 1
Look up the word *seismograph.* The first seismograph was installed at Link Observatory, Mt. Hamilton, California, in 1888 on this day.

June 2
National Rose Month. Make a list of roses present in the thorns of life instead of giving attention to the thorns among the roses.

June 3
Charles Richard Drew was born on this day in 1904. Read about this famous surgeon's work in blood plasma. Count the number of times your heart beats in one minute today.

June 4
W.C. Swan made the first rocket glider flight in 1931 on this day. Find out the pounds of thrust for a Saturn V launch vehicle.

June 5
Celebrate World Environment Day. Pick up litter both inside and outside your home today. Then write the Sierra Club, 530 Bush St., San Francisco, CA 94102 and ask for their Environmental Education Packet. Be sure to design a recycle logo.

June 6
The electric flat iron was patented on this day in 1882. Press a leaf to celebrate this event.

June 7
The first color network telecast was made on this day in 1953. Relax and watch a science TV program like *Nova* today.

June 8
I.W. McGaffey patented the first vacuum cleaner in 1869 on this day. Celebrate by vacuuming your room or a room in your home today.

June 9
Look up the word *horticulturist.* Peter Henderson, an American horticulturist, was born in 1822 on this day. Celebrate his birthday by planting a seed, hugging a plant or by saying something nice to a plant.

June 10
Plan ahead for Father's Day. Make a scrapbook with cartoons or a photo album with pictures that tell why your dad is the best dad in the world.

June 11
Jacques Cousteau, French oceanographer, was born on this day in 1910. Look up some of Cousteau's accomplishments which include the first underwater diving station, observation vehicle and aqualung. Celebrate by taking a swim underwater.

June 12
American ornithologist Frank Michier was born on this day in 1864. He was one of the first people to study birds with a camera. Photograph and identify at least one bird today that you hadn't known before. Study its habits.

June 13
On the periodic table of the elements, locate the chemical symbol for sodium. Sodium vapor lights were first installed on this date in 1933. Find out if you have sodium, incandescent or fluorescent lights in your home. Which requires more energy to operate?

June 14
Flag Day. Draw a U.S. flag. Color the stars' area orange and the white stripes green. Stare at the flag for 45 seconds. Shift your eyes to a white wall. What do you see? Then say "The Pledge of Allegiance" with your family members today.

June 15
Benjamin Franklin proved lightning was electricity when he flew his kite in a thunderstorm in 1752. Find out how many volts of electricity it takes to operate most appliances in your home. Then name the appliance.

GA1150

Tab C

June 16-30

June 20
The first American steamship crossed the Atlantic on this day in 1819. Draw a picture of what happens when warm air hits a cold surface on a glass of lemonade. Then have a drink while you study how a steam engine works.

June 25
People in North America may see an eclipse today. Make a drawing of the position of the sun, moon and earth in a moon (lunar) and sun (solar) eclipse.

June 30
There are thirty days in June. Therefore, take time to list thirty of your favorite science creatures.

June 19
Blaise Pascal, a French physicist, was born on this day in 1625. Physicists study little things like atoms. Do a little good deed for a person today.

June 24
Radar was first used to detect airplanes on this day in 1930. How many words can you detect by rearranging the letters RADAR?

June 29
George Washington Boethals, engineer on the Panama Canal, was born on this day in 1858. On a world map, locate the Panama Canal. Describe its value to nations of the world.

June 18
George Eastman in 1888 introduced the first box camera. Take a photo of a special science happening today.

June 23
Ed Warren made the first balloon flight on this day in 1784. Study how a hot air balloon works.

June 28
Biologist Alexis Carrel was born on this day in 1858. He is known for his work in organ transplants. Read the story of the first human heart transplant today.

June 17
Develop in someone a love for something in nature today.

June 22
Make a fan today. Feel the cool breeze from the fan. Compare this breeze to love, as a breeze like love can be felt but not seen.

June 27
Helen Keller, who conquered the handicaps of blindness and deafness, was born on this day in 1880. Learn at least one letter in the Braille alphabet today.

June 16
First significant helicopter flight of 7 feet (2 m) today. Build and fly a paper helicopter. Time how long it takes to return to earth.

June 21
First day of summer. Look up the words *summer solstice* and *Stonehenge* and tell your friends about each of these important science happenings. Then find out over what tropic the sun is directly overhead on this day.

June 26
Lord Kelvin, a British physicist, was born in 1824 on this day. He used a gas thermometer to tell the temperature. Make a Kelvin Temperature Scale. Then find out what the letters *OK* mean in science. OK is related to Kelvin.

July 1-15

July 1
Look to the sky for fireworks early this month. Identify a constellation of stars tonight as one of your beginning "fireworks."

July 2
The first X ray of the human body was made on this day in 1934. Draw a picture of what the X ray may have looked like.

July 3
To prepare for tomorrow's celebration of the birth of our country, interview your mother and father on what the day was like for them when you were born.

July 4
Give thanks today for independence and for freedom to choose and worship. Then celebrate with a bang. Find out what the word *decibel* means.

July 5
Harry Crosby flew the first rocket airplane on this day in 1944. Find out why Mr. Crosby had to lie flat in order to fly this airplane.

July 6
The Declaration of Independence was published on this day in 1776. It's old. Share your favorite creature or object in nature with an elderly person today.

July 7
Spot the planet Venus low in the western sky at dusk tonight. Make a sketch of the planets found in our solar system today. Remember that Neptune, not Pluto, is our farthest away planet until the year 1999.

July 8
Ferdinand von Zeppelin, inventor of the dirigible, was born on this day in 1838. Make a hanging dirigible to give a friend.

July 9
Elias Howe, inventor of the sewing machine, was born on this day in 1819. Put your friends in stitches by telling them your favorite joke today.

July 10
The author of this page was born in 1941 on this day. He teaches science to youngsters. Find out how old he is. Then make a list of science gifts that you or members of your family could give each other on their birthdays.

July 11
Enjoy summer's weather today. Clip the weather map from your newspaper. Identify at least three weather symbols found on the map. Then make a weather prediction for tomorrow's weather.

July 12
Henry David Thoreau was born on this day in 1817. Read or have someone read to you a part of Thoreau's book *Walden* which tells about how we can get along with nature.

July 13
The state of Wisconsin recorded its highest ever temperature (114 degrees Fahrenheit, 45 degrees Celsius) on this day in 1936. Using an almanac, find out the date of your state's highest known temperature.

July 14
Robert Goddard, the Father of Rockets, patented liquid rocket fuel on this day in 1914. Find out the type of fuel used to propel space shuttles today.

July 15
U.S. *Apollo 18* and USSR *Soyuz 19* linked up in space on this day in 1975. Establish a new link with an old friend today.

GA1150

July 16–31

July 20

Neil Armstrong and Edwin Aldrin, Jr., walked on the moon on this day in 1969. Make a sketch of the moon's size, shape and position in the sky tonight. Then design a moon plaque to be placed on the ceiling or a wall of your room to celebrate this occasion.

July 25

Thomas Eakins, American artist, was born on this day in 1844. He painted pictures of athletes. Try to excel in some athletic contest today.

July 30

Henry Ford, designer of the Model T Ford was born on this day in 1863. Design a car powered by the sun today.

July 31

On this day in 1967, a devastating earthquake struck the country of Venezuela. Locate information on the Richter Scale.

July 19

The U.S. Census Bureau reported on this day in 1982 that 14 percent of the people in the U.S. were poor. Help a poor science person today by giving a gift of science.

July 24

Amelia Earhart, American pilot, was born on this day in 1898. To her, the sky was the limit. Lie on your back and look at the clouds in the sky. Think about what might have happened to Amelia Earhart, as she has never been found.

July 29

Charles Beebe, well-known for his adventures in the bathysphere, was born on this day in 1877. Develop a secret code or puzzle by using the letters in the word *bathysphere*.

July 18

Robert Hooke, an English scientist, was born on this day in 1635. He said things get bigger when they are heated. Tell one story that gets bigger when the heat is on.

July 23

Austin Bart invented the typewriter on this day in 1829. Type or print a letter to someone you love today. You may use a computer to help you with your task.

July 28

An act to legalize the metric system was approved by Congress in 1866 on this day. Find out your height in centimeters and the temperature in degrees Celsius today.

cm °C

July 17

Arco, Idaho, the first entire town to be illuminated by electric power generated by atomic power, was lit up on this day in 1955. Design a bumper sticker that shows your feelings about nuclear power.

ANOTHER MUTANT FOR NUCLEAR POWER

July 22

Gregor Mendel, a botanist, was born on this day in 1822. His work in genetics and heredity is well-known. Make a chart that shows the eye and hair color of each member of your family.

July 27

A.H. Bledsoe, Jr., set the world aviation record for a speed over a closed circuit on this day in 1976. His speed was 2092.294 miles per hour. Find out how jet, rocket and internal combustion engines work today.

July 16

Dr. Bela Schick, allergist, developed a skin test for diphtheria on this day in 1913. Make a list of the symptoms for diphtheria. Then find out if you have had the correct shots for the coming school year.

July 21

George D. Worthington set the world aviation record for hang gliding of 95.44 miles on this day in 1977. Fly a kite today to celebrate this achievement.

July 26

Apollo 15 astronauts Scott and Irwin landed on the moon in Hadley Rille and explored the surface of the moon in the lunar rover on this day. Astronaut Worden, in the command module, conducted the first deep space walk. Take a mile "earth space" walk today.

GA1150

Tab I

August 1-15

August 5
First electric traffic light was installed in Cleveland, Ohio, on this day in 1914. From memory, draw and color a picture of a traffic light. Were you correct? Study what each color means.

August 10
James Smithson helped Congress establish the Smithsonian Institution on this day in 1846. On a map of the U.S., find the city where the Smithsonian Institution is located. Then plan a trip to the city.

August 15
The Panama Canal opened on this day in 1914. Study how a lock works in a canal.

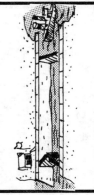

August 4
On this day in 1982, a U.S. federal appeals court ruled that all U.S. cars sold must have air bags or automatic seat belts. Fill a bag or balloon with air today and study how each absorbs a shock force.

August 9
The first electric washing machine was patented by Alva Fisher on this day in 1910. Help Mom and Dad lighten the load of dirty clothes by keeping a special set of clothes clean today. Remember that they can save money on electricity and water by washing only full loads.

August 14
Oliver Shallenberger invented and patented the first electric meter on this day in 1888. With the help of your mom and dad, learn how to read your electric meter today.

August 3
Christopher Columbus sailed from Spain in search of a route to China and the Far East on this day in 1492. Build and sail a boat in the bathtub tonight.

August 8
Matthew Henson, an important American Black who accompanied Admiral Perry to the North Pole in 1909, was born on this day in 1866. Name at least two other prominent black American scientists and their scientific contributions.

August 13
The first English printer, William Caxton, was born on this day in 1422. Print a secret code that describes your true feelings toward a friend today.

August 2
The first street post office letter boxes were placed on streets in Boston on this day in 1858. Send a postcard that describes your favorite summer science activity and mail at the local letter box.

August 7
The International Peace Bridge between Canada and the United States was dedicated on this day in 1927. Study types of bridges. Then make peace with a family member, friend or enemy today.

August 12
Radio and TV waves can be bounced off of a satellite and relayed from one place to another. ECHO 1, the first such communication satellite, was launched on this day in 1960. Develop a nontalking system of communication with a friend or animal.

August 1
August is National Sandwich Month. Be a "ham" today by telling your favorite nature story to a friend.

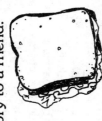

August 6
Gertrude Ederla became the first American woman to swim the English Channel on this day in 1926. Make a list of at least five other records set by women.

August 11
Gifford Pinchot, a well-known conservationist, was born on this day in 1865. Take a picture or sketch a good conservation practice found in the environment today.

GA1150

August 16-31

August 20

Voyager 2, one of the two unmanned interplanetary spacecrafts, was launched on this day in 1977. *Voyager 2* visited Jupiter in 1979, Saturn in 1980, reached Uranus in January of 1986 and Neptune in August 1989. Name the four moons of Jupiter that *Voyager 2* observed while visiting Jupiter and the moons discovered on its trip to Neptune in 1989.

August 25

This day in 1915 ended a hurricane disaster that featured a tropical storm in Texas and Louisiana. Find out the difference between a hurricane watch and a hurricane warning.

August 30

Ernest Rutherford was born on this day in 1871. Find out the meanings of the words *electrons, protons, neutrons, mesons* and *quarks* today.

August 31

Plan to do one special favor for your teacher on your return to school. Have a happy summer!

August 19

Today is Orville Wright's birthday and thus National Aviation Day. Fly a paper airplane today to celebrate this anniversary.

August 24

On this day in the year A.D. 79, a volcano named Vesuvius in Italy erupted. Count to ten before you blow your top today.

August 29

Chop suey was invented by a Chinese chef in New York on this day in 1896. Study the contents of, and calories in, an average sized serving of chop suey. Then develop a recipe for chop suey.

August 18

The first U.S. scientific expedition was authorized by Congress on this day in 1836. Enjoy an expedition to a lake, stream or woods today.

August 23

The first elevator, operating on the principle similar to that of an Archimedes screw, was installed in a hotel in New York on this day in 1859. Using an encyclopedia, read about some of the works of Archimedes. Then provide one uplifting experience for someone today.

August 28

The United States Engraving and Printing Bureau began its work on this day in 1862. Sketch an engraved cartoon of a funny science event today.

August 17

Gold was discovered in the Klondike on this day in 1896. Locate the Klondike. Then on a periodic table of the elements locate gold. Print its symbol on a wanted poster entitled "There Is Gold in Them There Hills."

August 22

South Africa told President Carter on this day in 1977 that they had no intention of conducting nuclear tests now or in the future. Study the difference between nuclear fission and nuclear fusion today.

August 27

Petroleum began to flow from a well in Pennsylvania on this day in 1859. With your mother and father, check the oil level in your family's automobile today. Then learn the kind of oil used in your family's automobile during different seasons of the year.

August 16

Edwin Prescott patented the Loop Centrifugal Railway on this day in 1898. Make a diagram that shows the difference between centrifugal and centripetal forces.

August 21

Astronauts Cooper and Lovell in the *Gemini 5* performed the first extended manned flight into space on this day in 1965. Read the horoscope for Gemini's activity for today in your newspaper.

August 26

Antoine Lavoisier, the Father of Modern Chemistry, was born on this day in 1713. Study the chemistry of a waterdrop today. Then take a run through the sprinkler. Be thankful for this special substance. Turn off a dripping faucet. One drop per second can add up to 650 gallons of wasted water per year.

Tab J

Student Report Card

With help from my teacher, I have completed the following science process cards and activities:

Science Process Skill	LAP #	Activity Cards and Pages	Date Completed
Connecting	1	Send Greeting Cards to Scientists	
Connecting	2	Postcard Science	
Thinking	3	Think Safety	
Thinking	4	Thinking About a Career in Science	
Thinking	5	Deep Thinkers	
Questioning	6	Scientific Trivia	
Reading	7	PSST: The Word Is *Science*	
Observing	8	Overhead Science Recipes	
Observing	9	Comet Halley	
Observing	10	Constellations	
Observing	11	Fall Frolics	
Hypothesizing and Predicting	12	Sink or Float	
Hypothesizing and Predicting	13	Batteries and Bulbs	
Experimenting	14	Pocket Card Science	
Experimenting	15	Film Can Science	
Collecting and Analyzing Data	16	Scientists Around the World	
Collecting and Analyzing Data	17	The Wall of Science	
Collecting and Analyzing Data	18	Black Scientists and Inventors	
Collecting and Analyzing Data	19	Women in Science	
Collecting and Analyzing Data	20	Adopt a Scientist	
Identifying and Controlling Variables	21	If I Could Be a Drop, I Would	
Estimating	22	Joystick	

GA1150

Student Report Card

Science Process Skill	LAP #	Activity Cards and Pages	Date Completed
Comparing	23	Cycles: Beginning to Ending to Beginning	
Comparing	24	Spring's Seedlings	
Measuring	25	Trip Cards of Science Activities	
Graphing	26	Sports Flashback: Olympic Gold Medals	
Classifying	27	Track Them Down	
Using Space/Time Relationships	28	History of Science	
Using Space/Time Relationships	29	Tribute to Science	
Using Space/Time Relationships	30	Tickets to Science Museums	
Using Space/Time Relationships	31	License Plate Science	
Checking and Recording	32	Science Findings	
Checking and Recording	33	Winter Hike Through Our Universe	
Checking and Recording	34	Spring Hike Through Our Universe	
Checking and Recording	35	Summer Hike Through Our Universe	
Checking and Recording	36	Fall Hike Through Our Universe	
Inferring	37	Scientific Relationships	
Inferring	38	Fact or Myth	
Testing and Evaluating	39	Sliders of Science	
Testing and Evaluating	40	Valuing	
Testing and Evaluating	41	Electrical Quiz Boards	
Reporting	42	Library Science Cards	
Reporting	43	Science Fairs with Style	
Reporting	44	Student Diploma for Summer Science	

GA1150

Meet the Author

Jerry is a teacher at The University of Toledo. He is a member of the Department of Elementary and Early Childhood Education, and his specialty is science, although he truly enjoys all facets of education and life.

Jerry was born and raised on a farm in Kaukauna, Wisconsin, and it was there that he nurtured his interest in science, the world around him and life in general. He has taught all grade levels in some capacity or another and currently spends a great deal of his time in schools helping teachers and youngsters.

In addition to being the author of twenty-two books (available in such prestigious places as the Smithsonian Institution in Washington, D.C.: National Air and Space Museum, National Museum of Natural History—National Museum of Man, National Museum of American History) and over 160 educational publications, Jerry is the recipient of many awards. Some of these include the 1984 Outstanding Teacher of the Year Award at The University of Toledo, the 1986 Martha Holden Jennings Outstanding Educator Award and the National Science Teachers Association 1986 Search for Excellence in Science Education Program Award.

Being a local, state, regional, national and international consultant in science education, Jerry's main interest in life is to help people grow in awareness, knowledge and understanding of feelings toward themselves and others. His works nurture this interest.

Meet the Artist

Liz Fox is a free-lance illustrator living on the Oregon coast, whose prior publications include several environmental atlases and reports, as well as work for Good Apple.

Born and raised in Keokuk, Iowa, Liz moved to Oregon in 1978 to attend Oregon State University. There she majored in soil science and received her Bachelor of Science degree in 1980.

Since entering the employment world, Liz has worked as a land-use planner, cartographer, artist, engineering technician, horticulturist and chicken rancher.

Liz believes that learning is a lifelong adventure and encourages others to explore the creative challenges our world offers.

GAI150

Reflecting Backwards
A "Backword"

Twenty-Five Years Ago: A Reflection

I offer an apology to the students who passed through my classroom in West Frankfort, Illinois. It was during those years, the sixties, that nine eager classes of learners experienced a void. You see, I left science class to the last period of the day and hoped there would be an assembly, a track meet, early dismissal, anything. At age twenty-three to "thirtysomething," science still remained a mystery to me.

True, the district furnished textbooks which began . . . "Someday man may walk on the moon." Even I was aware that man had already done this. But I blamed the district, not myself.

Fourteen Years Ago: A Reflection

If I recall correctly, it was in 1976 that I met Dr. Jerry DeBruin. We met in Champaign, Illinois, to discuss the possibility of working together as author and publisher. We attended a University of Illinois basketball game. It was his treat. Being a loyal fan of the Fighting Illini, I was intense about the game. Being a scientist and mathematician, Jerry was intense about his writing.

I don't remember if the Illini won. I do know that I won. An association that has lasted over a decade and continues to grow began. An awareness was awakened. An interest was aroused. Someone who knew something about science was a nice guy, and he made it sound so simple, so easy.

But still not sure about science, I talked Jerry into first publishing some metrics material and even a book about cardboard carpentry. The science book, like the science class, was last on the agenda. Maybe there would be another book in the interim, and I could simply keep shelving the science project.

Ten Years Ago: A Reflection

In 1979 Jerry said, "OK, the science book is next. There will be no more postponements." Reluctantly, I agreed and in 1980 *Creative, Hands-On Science Experiences* was published. Because I was the editor and publisher, I read the manuscript several times. It was interesting. It was fun. I was learning.

I learned that science was not someday; science was today. Science was not black words on a page, but science was "hands-on."

A Final Reflection

It is 1990. Ten years have passed. *Creative, Hands-On Science Experiences* remains a Good Apple best-seller. Over 50,000 copies have been sold. Jerry has written and Good Apple has published over a dozen more science books.

My interest continues to grow. Jerry's desire to share his love of science continues. I have looked forward to each new manuscript by Jerry. I thank him for turning on the light and keeping it glowing.

I wonder if my former students would give me a second chance to present to them my en"light"ened views about science.

As Jerry states in his introduction to this book, *Creative Hands-On Science Cards & Activities*, the number one goal in education is to cause learners to think. Using the wealth of material in this book could result in no less happening.

Just think, someday man may walk on Mars.

Gary D. Grimm

Gary D. Grimm
Former Owner, President
Good Apple, Inc.

GA1150